Net Prospect

The Courting Process of Women's College Basketball Recruiting

Lisa Liberty Becker

2002

Best Wishes –

Lisa Liberty Becker

Wish Publishing
Terre Haute, Indiana
www.wishpublishing.com

LCCN: 2001099363

Proofread by Heather Lowhorn
Editorial Assistance provided by Natalie Chambers
Cover designed by Phil Velikan
Cover photography by Corbis

Printed in the United States of America
10 9 8 7 6 5 4 3 2 1

Published in the United States by
Wish Publishing
P.O. Box 10337
Terre Haute, IN 47801, USA
www.wishpublishing.com

Distributed in the United States by
Cardinal Publishers Group
7301 Georgetown Road, Suite 118
Indianapolis, Indiana 46268
www.cardinalpub.com

To everyone who can't stand the phrase
"play like a girl."

Table of Contents

Acknowledgments

While this book has a single author, many people gave freely of their time and expertise to help transform it from an idea in my head into what is hopefully an interesting read and valuable resource.

Most heartfelt thanks go first off to the 88 women's basketball college coaches, college players, high school coaches, club coaches, parents, camp and recruiting gurus, and other authorities who spent time with me explaining their experiences with and thoughts on recruiting. I truly enjoyed listening to their frank analyses, sage advice, and amusing tales. They deserve much credit for the tremendous growth of women's basketball.

Among this group, several whose willingness to answer questions, open up their address books, and offer suggestions far beyond what was asked of them deserve special mention:

- Joanne Boyle, Duke University assistant coach
- Jill Cook, Christ the King assistant coach and Liberty Belles president
- Kevin Engellant, University of Montana-Western head coach
- Brett Erkenbrack, Cloud County Community College head coach
- Carol Harrison, Humboldt State University assistant coach/interim head coach
- Barbara Stevens, Bentley College head coach
- Tony Pappas, West High head coach

I would also like to thank Beth Bass, current Women's Basketball Coaches Association (WBCA) cheif executive officer, and Betty Jaynes, WBCA co-founder, former chief executive officer and executive director, and current consultant. Not only did they offer their own unique perspectives on recruiting, they, along with WBCA intern Tiffany Fong, enabled me to create a recruiting survey for the participants of the 2001 Phoenix/WBCA High School All-America game. Analysis of that survey resulted in some interesting insights for the players' chapter of the book.

First to open up his large list of contacts early on in the process was Dave Krider, formerly of *USA Today*. Gabrielle Hanna, former editor-in-chief of *Women's Basketball* magazine, offered early comments as well. Thanks also to the *Philadelphia Enquirer*'s Mel Greenberg for his thoughts on the overall topic. Clay Kallam of *Full Court Press* came through with suggestions and interview subjects in addition to feedback on several chapters.

I also had great help making my way through the sticky web of women's basketball recruiting rules and regulations. Jane Jankowski, assistant director of public relations for the NCAA, was an invaluable resource and found answers to my many questions. Steve Mallonee, who serves as the NCAA's director of membership services and Division I governance Liaison, also answered specific inquiries and read the first chapter of the book to ensure factual correctness.

In addition, I am grateful to Bob Clukey, the best of the many coaches that I've had, and to Dick Mullen, the first teacher to really challenge me.

Many family members stood by me with words of encouragement as I completed this project. My grandfather, Tom Shehan, will always be my favorite sportswriter. My aunt, Janice Marston, provided proofreading help. Special thanks to my parents, Judy and Norm Liberty, for their proofreading expertise and more importantly their love and support.

Finally, I am forever endebted to my husband, Rob, who always encourages me to pursue my dreams.

Pregame

OK, I'll admit it. When I first set out to write this book, I really wanted some dirt. I had read *Sole Influence*, after all, strangely fascinated by some of the warped principles and shady characters in men's basketball recruiting. Certainly, I thought, since women's college basketball is becoming as competitive and cutthroat as men's, women's recruiting must have those same unethical dealings and personas — money changing hands under tables, agents getting rich off their prep protégés, sneaker companies in cahoots with college and high school level coaches. I would hunt down those corrupt folks, force them to spill their guts, and divulge their nasty secrets in my tell-all masterpiece. I would be the Ralph Nader of 21st century women's basketball.

However, I soon discovered that my end result would be far from an exposé for several different reasons. First, although many in the space believe that women's basketball is heading down the same evil path as men's in its corruption, and there is evidence to support this theory, it is not yet as soiled because the cash is just not there. Until women's pros haul in seven-figure salaries, recruiting will remain untainted in comparison. Yes, women's basketball recruiting has its shady characters, but they represent a smaller percentage. To write only about them, although exciting, would have been a distortion. It also would probably have driven away many of those I hope will read the book, high school girls' basketball players and their parents.

I had also read some how-to-get-a-college-scholarship books. While I'm sure that some of them help many students, I did not want to write a how-to-book, either. I wanted to focus on my favorite sport, and I wanted to present a more personal, in-depth view of recruiting from every possible angle. Also, although I would represent NCAA Division I, I also wanted to include the other, less publicized levels of women's college hoops. Armed with tape recorder, pen, and steno book, I threw myself into interviewing lots of people involved with women's basketball recruiting. Over the course of eight months, I talked with college coaches at different levels, from NCAA Division I, II, and III to National Association of Intercollegiate Athletics (NAIA) and junior college. I talked with high school and club coaches. I talked with players and parents, camp directors, recruiting report organizers, NCAA officials. Well, I listened, mostly.

Along the way, a story emerged and revealed the book I really wanted to write. I tried to invent a suitable, snappy analogy to women's basketball recruiting, such as buying a house or shopping for a used car, but none of them really worked. Truthfully, the process is really like no other, and it is confusing even for seasoned college coaches. Even those who follow all of the advice given in this book will find no guarantee for recruiting success for any involved party. Recruiting is light years from exact science.

I was somewhat surprised and somehow comforted to learn that recruiting often baffles even the most experienced and successful coaches. "I'm not sure I ever knew exactly why kids chose to come to UCLA," Billie Moore said to me. Moore notched a 436-196 record in 24 years of head coaching at UCLA and Cal-State Fullerton, and she also coached the first-ever Olympic team to a silver medal in 1976. "Somebody like a Jackie Joyner-Kersee (the Olympic track star, who actually played under Moore at UCLA on a basketball scholarship) said from day one, that's where she wanted to come to school," Moore added. "I never knew that until five years after she was out of school. She wasn't going to let me know that. And I'm not sure that you know. Some people come because they think it's a chance to win . . . But you never know what makes that person click." Moore seems as qualified as anyone to demystify the process. When the Women's Basketball Coaches Association (WBCA) operated camps in the mid- and late-1990's, she served as a master counselor and gave recruiting seminars.

Just when I thought that women's basketball recruiting was as pure as freshly fallen snow, however, my interviewees described the head games that every single participant can play. A recruit tells a college coach that his school is number one on her list, when really she is holding out for another college coach to come through with a scholarship. A parent says the same thing to a college coach, using that institution as the backup. A high school coach tells a college coach his player is more talented than she is. A club coach only talks with NCAA Division I coaches. A college coach promises a prospective student-athlete that she'll start, or does not tell her that two other prospects are being recruited ahead of her in her position.

Neither the NCAA, NAIA, nor National Junior College Athletic Association (NJCAA) rules police will arrest any of the above as a result of these conversations. However, their mere existence means that complete and open honesty may be a recruiting rarity. For the most part, coaches and recruits are not out there blatantly breaking major rules, but there are buckets of more minor recruiting violations by NCAA women's basketball coaches. In fact, according to NCAA officials, women's basketball now has roughly the same number of reported recruiting violations as men's basketball. Only football leads the two in that statistic. What's more, coaches at all levels, athletes, and parents admit that they are "as honest as they can be" during the recruiting process — that is, not completely honest. Many say that they wish it did not have to be this way, but that in order to afford themselves the best opportunities, that's the reality.

Unfortunately, partly because of the perceived necessity to hold back information about one's background, personality, or list, both coaches and student-athletes make commitments in recruiting under false assumptions. Combined with the fact that they may not have ample time to get to know each other, this can lead to bad matches in college programs. "Sometimes I wonder, are kids being rushed into decisions that they're not going to be happy with later on?" Nan Elrod said to me. For seven years, Elrod worked on the WBCA's camps and High School All-America game. She is now the Women's Basketball Hall of Fame's director of programs. "It seems like we're seeing a lot of kids now having a change of heart once they've actually gotten on campus, and they're transferring, with some kids dropping basketball altogether," she added. "That's sad, I think." Sometimes coaches or others rush girls in recruiting, and sometimes girls rush themselves, just to get it over with.

Although I consider myself somewhat of a women's basketball expert, when I plunged into educating myself in more detail on the recruiting calendar, terminology, and regulations at all levels, I wondered how anyone could really make sense of the rules. As I surfed web sites, read manuals and talked to officials, I thought, how can parents and students and even coaches, understand the real-world applications of these regulations? Even though every single student-athlete considering playing in college should read the recruiting materials put out by the NCAA, NAIA, NJCAA, and other organizations, this may not be enough. "If you get the [NCAA] *Guide for the College-Bound Student-Athlete*, does it really cover everything?" Elrod pondered. "It gives you some basics and all, but does it really prepare you for dealing with this? It's such a different world, and for so many people it's a one-time experience. How many are actually going to have two or three kids that are any caliber of athlete at all that are going to be recruited? Preparing that [NCAA] Division II or III athlete — that might even be more important. There again, you're dealing with a young person's ego there, that hey, they may have been the best that ever was at their high school, but it's a whole different world out there as far as recruiting." It is, indeed.

Something struck me most heavily in interviewing the people that you will meet in the following pages. For everyone in women's basketball, from coaches at all levels of experience to parents to blue-chip recruits to student-athletes not sure where they will fit in, or if they will fit in at all, the recruiting process is stressful and complex. Although all can take steps to make it easier, it will never be simple. However, I think it helps to get inside the minds of those who have been through the process in some manner, one time or a hundred times. They give some funny and slightly bizarre recruiting anecdotes as well. Happy reading, and consider perusing this book one step in understanding the world of women's basketball recruiting.

I write this during the NCAA's National Letter of Intent early signing period. I can't help but wonder about the futures of the student-athletes who put their names to paper this week and this year. Who will flourish at her selected institution, and who will realize that she made errors in judgment during the recruiting process? Is there really a way to make the process easier?

So who's got next?

1

The Recruiting Process, 101: Bare Bones Rules, Terminology, and Factoids

"Most people don't know anything about recruiting — they really don't," states Vince Cannizzaro. Cannizzaro should know, as he spent 19 years coaching national powerhouse Christ the King High School in New York. He and his staff saw many young women through the college recruiting process, including Chamique Holdsclaw and Sue Bird. "Ninety percent of the kids who are recruited," Cannizzaro continues, "either their coaches are not involved, or they're not aware of the rules, and [so] the kids are not aware of the rules." These days, as an assistant coach at NCAA Division I Stony Brook University, he sees recruiting from the other side.

For parents, student-athletes, and high school-level coaches alike, and even for college coaches, decoding the terminology, calendar, and system of rules guiding the recruiting process can boggle the mind. While NCAA Division I coaches need to pass a written test on recruiting regulations every spring, no one else does. Are parents and girls aware of general recruiting rules? "Unless they've had great guidance by experienced coaches or advisors, absolutely not," insists Tony Pappas, head coach at Waterloo, Iowa's West High and floor director at the Nike Girls All-America Camp. "I've been doing it for 20 years, and I probably know more of the darn rules than about anybody, and I still don't know them all. I wish they'd simplify the

NCAA manual . . . and just make the rules a little simpler. It's written in a lot of legal jargon, and it's very hard to comprehend." Maybe Pappas himself should collaborate with the NCAA, for he has his own recruiting handbook that he uses to inform his players about the process.

As women's basketball slides more into the limelight, and as more girls go through the recruiting process, their peers may be slightly better educated about the basics. Although more colleges do try to inform prospective student-athletes about recruiting rules, college coaches can only do so much. "You would be surprised how many colleges send you their recruiting rules," says Dave Butcher, head coach at Ohio's Pickerington High School, a nationally-recognized program. "There are a lot that send them to the athletes and the coaches. But how many of them actually get read? I post mine, I pass mine out. I think almost any camp . . . they have a clearinghouse talk and they have a guy that actually comes in, talks about grades, blah blah blah. But that's part of their whole gig as a requirement. A lot of the education for parents, I personally think a lot of responsibility is me. That's my responsibility, to tell the kids the rules, to make sure they understand, to make sure the parents understand. I don't know who else's responsibility it would be. I guess you would put it back to the parent and the player, but a lot of them don't understand that."

Back in the days when women's college coaches could do virtually anything in recruiting, it was possible for one to outwork another to get a player. However, aside from players, families, and coaches, no one cared much about watching games or about a program's success. Women's basketball has seen incredible growth and keeps growing, placing more emphasis on coaches' recruiting. In an attempt to keep coaches from gaining unfair advantages over each other, governing organizations have tightened the reins on them. "Everything under the NCAA, usually rules that are passed, it's either because somebody has abused something or because it's for cost-saving purposes," comments Mickie Demoss, associate head coach at NCAA Division I University of Tennessee, who has served on NCAA Division I women's basketball rules committees.

Even though college coaches may send out explanations of recruiting rules, they cannot send mail other than questionnaires directly to athletes who are not high school juniors. "I don't think people know the rules and regulations early on," says Duke University head coach Gail Goestenkors. "We do send out recruiting brochures to kids, and when we write them our one letter that we're allowed to write them or we send them our questionnaire, we always send them the rules in a nutshell so they know. But you still get parents calling you. A couple of times a day you'll get a phone call from a parent saying, my daughter this, that and the other — call me back — which we're not allowed to do. So early on, they don't know the rules, but they learn through the process, really, the recruiting process." Unfortunately, this could be much too late for everyone aside from elite recruits, who represent a small percentage of total prospective student-athletes.

From the parents to athletes to coaches, everyone who will be involved in the recruiting process needs to understand the lingo and rules. While the NCAA, NAIA, and NJCAA all have web sites and publish guidebooks, even the most astute hoopophile can have difficulty digesting their wording. Simple explanations of the most common terms and rules, as well as some important recruiting calendar dates, follow. Details focus mainly on the NCAA but do include the NAIA and NJCAA. Although this chapter may be a good starting point in readers' recruiting education, the best way to grasp the truths of the process is to talk with those who have experienced it.

The Basics of NCAA Recruiting and Terminology

First things first — how many scholarship slots are available at each level? NCAA Division I institutions are allowed to carry 15 athletic scholarships per academic year. Division II institutions are allowed 10, and Division III cannot carry any athletic scholarships.

Prospective student-athlete is a term commonly used in recruiting. A student becomes a *prospective student-athlete, PSA* for short, when she begins her freshman year of high school. She becomes a *recruited prospective student-athlete* when a college coach contacts her directly about the possibility of becoming a member of that collegiate institution's team. Just because a college coach sends a questionnaire to a student-athlete, it does not mean that the coach is recruiting her.

Although recruiting really has no beginning or end, the official recruiting "season" begins each June for Division I and Division II. For these two divisions, a series of contact periods, evaluation periods, quiet periods, and dead periods make up the recruiting calendar. NCAA Division III recruiting is not restricted by these periods.

Contact/Contact Periods

College coaching staffs may make either in-person recruiting contact with a prospective player or evaluations during *contact periods*. A contact is any in-person meeting between a college coach and a prospect or her parents where anybody says more than a greeting. Any on- or off-campus meeting is a contact, regardless of whether any meeting is arranged.

In Division I, contact periods occur during portions of September, March, and April. In Division II, they occur in September-October and March-May with the exception of the late signing period in April.

Evaluation/Evaluation Periods

Evaluation periods are blocks of time established by the NCAA during which evaluations can take place. During an evaluation, a college coaching staff can watch a recruit play and assess her skills. Though coaches can watch and take notes, they cannot speak with the recruit or her family. A visit to the prospect's school during which no contact occurs would also count as an evaluation, for example, if the coach was there to judge her academic qualifications. Coaches can observe practices or games, but they usually choose the real-setting competition of games.

For Division I, there are several stipulations on evaluation periods. In states where basketball competition occurs in the fall or winter, or that have junior colleges, college coaches may make evaluations between October and February. However,

4

each coaching staff has a limit of 40 evaluation days total for all of its recruits. Division I coaches also have an open evaluation period during the last three weeks in July, during junior college championship play, and during tryouts for the USA Basketball Olympic Festival. For states that have spring basketball, Division I staffs may make evaluations during the last three weeks in April (with 40 evaluation days total per staff during this time) and the last three weeks in July. In the state of Hawaii, evaluation periods run from March through May, once again with the 40-evaluation days limit, and the last three weeks in July.

In Division II, the structure is simpler. The open evaluation period for coaches stretches from mid-June to the end of August. Coaches may also evaluate during any of an athlete's high school or junior college contests, in addition to any other sanctioned club-level competition from mid-May to mid-June and any high school all-star game. They are not limited in terms of the number of evaluations allowed.

In both divisions, a college coach can make only one visit per week to a recruit's school during a contact or evaluation period. However, the coach can observe a recruit on consecutive days during a tournament, with the entire experience counting as one evaluation.

Quiet Periods

Quiet periods provide an opportunity for Division I and II recruits to visit college campuses and meet with NCAA coaches and players. These visits must take place on college campuses. Aside from phone calls and letter-writing, no other recruiting activity can occur during quiet periods.

Division I basketball has five quiet periods: August 1 through the first week of September, the end of September through the first week of October, from the second week of October through the end of February on those days not designated as evaluation days, in March on those days not designated as evaluation days, and mid-April to the second week of July.

Division II has five different categories as well, although they differ somewhat: the first two weeks of June; August 2

5

through the first week of September; mid-October through the date of the prospect's first high school or junior college game, with the exception of the early signing period of the National Letter of Intent, which is a dead period; mid-May through mid-June, with the exception of sanctioned club-level competition; and any other dates not specified as a contact, evaluation, or dead period.

Dead Periods

In recruiting terms, dead periods are just what they sound like. During dead periods, no evaluations, contacts, or any other sort of meetings or visits can happen either on the college campus or at the prospective player's school. However, coaches can call or write to student-athletes during these times.

Dead periods coincide with the National Letter of Intent early and late signing periods in NCAA Divisions I and II.

The early signing period for the National Letter of Intent occurs during a full week in November, and the late signing period lasts just over a month from mid-April to mid-May. Monday through Thursday of both the early and late signing periods is a dead period, with the remainder a quiet period.

National Letter of Intent (NLI)

The basic premise of the *National Letter of Intent (NLI)* program is to provide certainty in the recruiting process. Most colleges that offer NCAA Division I and II athletic scholarships use the NLI. Ivy League institutions and the service academies (Army, Navy, etc.) participate in Division I athletics but offer no athletic scholarships. No Division III schools, NAIA schools, junior colleges or preparatory schools are members of the NLI Program. However, many NAIA institutions and junior colleges do use a Letter of Intent to formalize a commitment between recruit and institution, implemented either by the national association, their individual conferences, or even individual schools.

In actuality, the Collegiate Commissioners Association (CCA), not the NCAA, administers the National Letter of Intent Program. Since its birth in 1964, when its members included seven conferences and eight institutions, the NLI Program has grown to include over 50 conferences and 500 institutions.

Signing the National Letter of Intent, in effect, ends the recruiting process. Member schools agree to not pursue a student-athlete once she signs an NLI with another institution; however, in actuality, not all college coaches abide by this part of the agreement. After signing an NLI, the prospect is also ensured an athletic scholarship for one academic year. An institutional financial aid agreement accompanies the NLI. If the student-athlete does not enroll at that school for a complete academic year, she could be penalized, with the possibility of losing up to two seasons of eligibility.

During each academic year, the *early signing period* is the first of two designated time periods during which a recruit can sign a National Letter of Intent. It lasts for one week in November. Although a college can offer a scholarship before November, the recruit cannot sign that official letter until the early signing period. Without a doubt, colleges want their top recruits to sign on the dotted line during the early signing period.

Each year, more women's basketball athletes commit during the early signing period. They then have one of the most stressful decisions of their lives out of the way, and they can relax and enjoy the rest of their senior years. Some feel pressured that if they do not sign early, their scholarships will be offered to others, especially if they do not have stellar senior seasons. They may also worry about injuries. However, they have the chance of increasing their scholarship opportunities by waiting. Opponents of the early signing period argue that girls do not have enough time to get to know coaches and programs by November.

The *late signing period* is the other only time on the recruiting calendar during which a recruit can sign a National Letter of Intent for an NCAA institution for the following academic year. The late period runs from mid-April to mid-May.

Monday through Thursday of the early and late signing periods, as well as the time surrounding the NCAA Women's

Final Four, are dead periods. With the exception of telephone calls, email, and postal correspondence, no recruiting activity may take place during these times.

The NLI agreement is null if a student-athlete signs it on a day outside of the early or late signing period. A student-athlete signs a National Letter of Intent with an institution and not with a specific team or coach. If the coach who recruited her leaves, the NLI is still valid and she is still bound to the school for one year.

If a high school prospect signs a National Letter of Intent and then changes her mind, it's not as easy as just signing another piece of paper. If she does not attend the school with which she first signed, or if she does not satisfy the terms of the NLI Program, she loses two years of eligibility at the next NLI institution. Although she can receive athletics aid and/or practice at another NLI school, she must sit two years "in residence" at that college. However, if the school that she left agrees to enter into a Qualified Release Agreement, the penalty is reduced from two years to one. The original school is not required to provide the student with the Qualified Release Agreement. However, many coaches will grant a release if a player wishes to leave.

There is a big difference between the National Letter of Intent and other Letters of Intent, such as those used by NAIA schools or junior colleges. If a recruit signs an NLI and later decides to instead enroll at an NAIA institution or junior college, there are no penalties. The reverse is also true — if she signs a Letter of Intent at an NAIA school or junior college, she can change her mind and later sign a National Letter of Intent without having to sit out for a year. Only after signing an NLI and then changing from one NCAA Division I or II institution to another would she lose a season or seasons of eligibility.

When a prospect signs a National Letter of Intent, she is guaranteed athletic financial aid for one academic year at that institution and nothing more. She does not automatically get quality playing time. In fact, she is not even assured a spot on the team roster. By attending the college with which she signed for at least one academic year, and not just by completing one playing season at that school, she satisfies the NLI. Unlike institutional athletic scholarships, which do need to be offered and renewed every year, an athlete only signs a National Letter of Intent once.

Although recruits do not have to sign a National Letter of Intent, most do. Once they do, the program that they have signed with must give them a scholarship the next year, and other NLI schools can technically no longer recruit them.

Recruiting rules state that after a prospect signs a National Letter of Intent, the school with which she signed can have an unlimited number of contacts with her.

Official Visits

When a college pays for a recruit to visit its campus, that college provides the student-athlete with an official visit. At all three NCAA divisions, official visits cannot take place before a recruit's senior year of high school. Divisions I and II allow the athlete one official visit to a particular campus, and she cannot receive more than five official visits total, even if she is being recruited in more than one sport. At the Division III level, while a recruit can only make one official visit to a particular campus, she can receive an unlimited number of official visits from different schools. The official visit can last no longer than 48 hours from start to finish, and the recruit often stays overnight with a current player on the college's team. However, the college can pay for her to stay in a hotel.

The college extending the official visit can pay only for a recruit's transportation, lodging, and food during her visit. It can also give her and her parents complimentary general admission to games during the visit. If a current member of the team hosts the student, that host is allowed $30 per day to entertain the prospect and her parents in Division I and II and $20 per day in Division III. Whereas Division I basketball coaches are limited to offering 12 total official visits per year, Division II and III coaches are not limited at all. Nevertheless, at any of the three NCAA divisions, as well as other levels, the invitation of an official visit means that the college has a serious interest in the prospective student-athlete.

Unofficial Visits

Unofficial visits are non-expenses paid visits to college campuses. A recruit and her family must pay for transportation, lodging, meals, and other expenses. A prospective student-athlete can make as many unofficial visits to as many campuses as she likes, and she can make them before her senior year of high school. Other than up to three complimentary game admissions, she must cover all costs for her visit.

For many student-athletes, official and unofficial visits can prove a deciding factor during the recruiting process. Recruits get to chat more informally with coaches, spend extended time with team members, perhaps see the squad practice or compete in a game, attend classes, and get an overall sense for the campus. Hopefully, by the time the visit ends, they have gotten a small slice of life, so that they can imagine what it would be like to attend that institution and be part of that program.

Home Visits

The other part of the recruiting process that can close the deal is the home visit. Division I coaches may make home visits to high school seniors during the last three weeks in September, during March except for the end of the month, and during part of April. Division II coaches may make them to high school seniors in September or the beginning of October, during March except for the end of the month, and during part of April. Considered a contact, home visits provide an opportunity for college staffs to talk with a recruit, her family, and anyone else she wants to be there. Sometimes she invites her current high school and/or club coach. These visits, which often take place in the evening, usually last anywhere from under an hour to several hours. Not only do they provide an in-home setting for college coaches to make a formal sales pitch, they also afford an opportunity for students and parents to ask questions that may not have already been answered. Some coaches begin by talking about academics and social aspects of their schools, while others focus mostly on basketball. With athletes they consider tops on their lists, Division I coaches almost always make home visits, and Division II coaches often make home visits. At the Division III level, home visits occur more rarely, only when the coach's recruiting budget allows and when a top prospect is wavering between several schools.

Recruiting Opportunities

Contacts and evaluations fall under the larger umbrella of recruiting opportunities. Division I coaches have five recruiting opportunities to use on any one prospect during any year; no more than three of these opportunities may be contacts, and the remainder must be evaluations. Division II coaches, on the other hand, are allowed three contacts per recruit but an unlimited number of evaluations. For Division III, there are no limits on the number of recruiting opportunities. In Divisions I and II, one of the three contacts is sometimes the home visit. Prior to a prospective student-athlete's senior year of high school, all recruiting opportunities are evaluations.

Verbal Commitment

If a student-athlete "verbals" to a college, it means that she has said that she will accept an athletic scholarship to play at that institution, but she has not signed anything. In other words, she's made a verbal commitment. Athletes who make verbal commitments do so before the early signing period of their senior years of high school. A few have been even known to do so well before senior year. California's Sade Wiley-Gatewood, for example, verbaled to the University of Tennessee just after her freshman year of high school. Though both coaches and recruits think long and hard before extending or accepting verbal offers, neither a verbal offer nor a verbal commitment is officially binding.

Twin sisters Kara and Kim Braxton from Oregon, both nationally-ranked high school players, verbaled to the University of Florida in the fall of 2000. However, the pair later retracted their verbal commitments, instead opting to sign early with Georgia. Since the girls did not sign anything until November, it was completely within the rules for them to change their minds. Conversely, a college coach could make a verbal scholarship offer to a recruit and later retract the offer. Once again, nothing binding has been signed. We do not read about this as much in the papers, but it does happen.

Redshirt

Although used as both a noun and a verb, and as two separate words in everyday life, the official college athletics definition of redshirt is a student-athlete who does not participate in NCAA competition in a sport for an entire academic year. The NCAA allows each athlete four seasons of competition per sport. If a player injures herself between seasons, before regular season games begin, or before she has played in many regular season games, and she will likely not be ready to play again during that season, her college program might declare her a "medical redshirt." That way, she would not use up a year of her eligibility.

Although every recruit, like every athlete, worries about injury, redshirting pertains more specifically to prospective student-athletes in another manner. Some college coaches at the NCAA and NAIA levels will declare a first-year player a redshirt. The athlete would practice with her college team but would not compete in any games. Since a redshirt does not use up a season of competition, she would still have four seasons left to play. If a college coach thinks that a student-athlete has the potential to impact the program but that she needs a year to improve her skills, gain maturity, or concentrate on academics, that coach might redshirt the player. Some college coaches bring up the topic of redshirting with families during the recruiting process, while others do not. If they do not, prospective student-athletes and their families can ask coaches during the recruiting process about their use of redshirts, before picking a school.

NCAA Initial Eligibility Clearinghouse

Everyone who intends to participate in NCAA Division I or II athletics as a college freshman must register with and be certified by the NCAA Initial Eligibility Clearinghouse before embarking on her college career. By registering, student-athletes show that they have met or will meet certain academic or *initial eligibility* requirements. Recruits should register with the Clearinghouse after the completion of their junior years of high school. To do so, they need to fill out a copy of the Student Release Form found in the *NCAA's Guide for the College-Bound Student-Athlete.*

The prospective student-athlete sends the top copy of her completed Student Release Form to the NCAA Initial Eligibility Clearinghouse, along with a fee. Her guidance counselor sends the second copy with her transcript from her freshman through junior years. After she graduates, her counselor will send the final copy of the Student Release Form along with her complete high school transcript. An NCAA Division I or II institution that is actively recruiting a player can request a report on her status from the Clearinghouse.

Among other criteria, initial eligibility includes the successful completion of 13 *core courses* in high school. When developing its student reports, the NCAA calculates a grade point average (GPA) from those 13 core courses. For Division I, these courses include four years of English, two of math (at the level of Algebra I or higher), two of science, one additional of any of the preceding three, two of social science, and two years of additional academic courses. For Division II, the only differences are that three years of English are required instead of four, and two additional courses instead of one in English, math, or science. Both Division I and II also require a minimum 2.0 GPA and require the athlete to graduate from high school. In its database, the Clearinghouse has a listing of every single high school in the country, along with each school's qualifying core courses.

NCAA Division I initial eligibility also includes the "sliding scale." In addition to passing core courses and graduating, a student must achieve a certain combination of grade-point average and ACT or SAT score in order to qualify academically to play. The higher the grade-point average is, the lower the ACT and SAT scores may be. For example, if an athlete has a GPA of 2.5 on a 4.0 scale, she needs a 68 or above on her combined ACT or an 820 or above on her combined SAT score. However, if she has a 2.0, she must score at least 86 on the ACT or a minimum of 1010 on the SAT.

If a prospective student-athlete does not meet the numerical requirements on this scale, she may be a *partial qualifier*. In this case, she could practice with the team during her first year of college and could receive an athletic scholarship that year. There is a separate sliding scale for partial qualifiers. In order to be a partial qualifier, a girl must achieve a minimum of 2.525 GPA. With that average, student would need at least a 67 ACT or 810 SAT score. If her GPA was 2.75 or above, however, she could be a partial qualifier with a minimum ACT of 59 or SAT of 720. A partial qualifier begins her collegiate career with three seasons of eligibility instead of four. However, if she receives her bachelor's degree in four years and decides to stay for a fifth at the institution, she could earn this year back.

If a student-athlete does not meet any of the above academic requirements, she would be deemed a *nonqualifier*. A nonqualifier cannot practice or compete with her team during her first year at the school, nor can she receive an athletic scholarship. Her seasons of eligibility are subject to the same rules as those of a partial qualifier in that she may earn a year back.

NCAA Division II initial eligibility, on the other hand, does not use sliding scales. Student-athletes must graduate, have a minimum 2.0 GPA in their 13 core courses, and must score at least an 820 on the SAT or 68 on the ACT. A Division II prospect could also be a partial qualifier by either attaining the minimum GPA or test score.

An NCAA academic committee can grant an initial-eligibility waiver to students who do not meet the initial eligibility standards, if the committee members find that a student's overall academic record warrants it.

Phone Calls

Although nothing can really substitute for face time, much of the recruiting relationship between a college coach and a prospect develops over the phone. The starting date for phone calls is different for NCAA Divisions I and II. In Division I, a college coach can call a prospect's home once in June, on or after June 21st after her junior year in high school. In July, the coach can call no more than three times, not more than once per week, and not more than once each week from that point on. In Division II, a coach can call on or after June 15th after her junior year of high school and cannot call more than once per week from then on. In both divisions, there are no restrictions on the lengths of the individual calls or the time of day in which they can occur.

However, a student-athlete can make as many calls as she likes to college coaches, whenever she wants to. What's more, she may call coaches as early in her high school career as she likes. After July 1 following her junior year of high school, she can even call collect or call a toll-free (1-800) number to speak with a coach, if one is available. Her parents and high school or club coaches have these same freedoms. In addition, college coaches may also call high school or club coaches whenever and as often as they choose.

Exceptions to coaches' phone limits exist around the National Letter of Intent signing and other events. College coaches can make unlimited phone calls to a recruit on the NLI signing date and two days following the signing, as well as for the five days preceding a recruit's official visit and on the day of an off-campus contact.

NCAA Division III coaches may phone recruits as much as they like, with absolutely no restrictions whatsoever. However, many who coach at this level say that they somewhat adhere to the rules placed on Divisions I and II, calling no more than once a week.

Mail, Fax, and Instant Messaging

According to current NCAA regulations, no rules govern content of communication via regular mail, email or fax. Following September 1 of prospective student-athletes' junior years of high school, NCAA coaches can send as many letters, email messages and faxes as they'd like. Prior to that date, they may send out camp brochures, NCAA educational information, and fill-in questionnaires, but no letters. Many coaches do a mass mailing to juniors each September, where they enclose an introductory letter about their programs as well as other information. While receiving these pieces of mail is exciting for players and families, many college coaches send out hundreds of recruiting packets each fall.

Although college coaches cannot send mail directly to high school athletes until their junior years, nothing stops them from sending letters to athletes' coaches at any time. However, if the letters concern specific prospective student-athletes, according to the rules, the coaches cannot pass these letters along to the athletes until they are high school juniors.

As things currently stand, the NCAA considers email the same as regular mail — correspondence. However, in August 2000 the NCAA implemented a bylaw regulating the use of instant messaging (IM). As it is instantaneous and has become quite popular, IM now falls under the same rule system as phone contact.

Allowed Materials

NCAA Division I recruiting regulations extend even to the types of materials college coaches can send or give to prospects, in addition to when they can do so.

Division I coaches can send letters, faxes, email, blank postcards and institutional note cards to prospects. Anything attached to the above must be printed on plain white paper with black ink. While coaches can hand out game programs or student-athlete handbooks during official or unofficial visits, they cannot mail them. However, they can mail one media guide or one athletics recruiting guide (a college is only allowed to produce one of these two guides), provided that it has one color of printing inside the cover. Other than that, they can mail official school admissions and academic publications and videos that are available to all students, educational information published by the NCAA, one wallet-sized game schedule, and business cards.

In addition, Division I and II college coaches cannot produce "recruiting videos" per se. They can only produce highlight films, videotapes, or audiotapes that contain information related to a particular event or season. Any narration on the tape must concern only that event or season. College coaches can show the film or tape during on-campus or off-campus visits, as long as they do not leave them with a recruit or her current coach. No restrictions apply to films or videotapes available to all students, such as admissions videos.

Division III schools can provide any official publications on academics, admissions, and athletics as well as other general materials that are available to all students.

Tryouts

Interestingly enough, one of the three NCAA divisions does allow a college to host tryouts for prospective student-athletes who have not yet enrolled at the institution — Division II. This tryout must take place at a time other than the basketball season or after the prospect's high school eligibility is completed, such as in the spring. It can include evaluations of the player's skill, speed, and strength. Division I and III institutions cannot host tryouts for recruits. Some but not all Division II programs do have tryouts.

A Special Note on Division III

In descriptions of recruiting regulations, mentions of NCAA Division III are rare. As it cannot offer athletic scholarships, Division III does not use the National Letter of Intent, and few recruiting restrictions exist. Division III coaches cannot make in-person, off-campus contact with prospective student-athletes prior to the completion of their junior years of high school. They also have regulations on official and unofficial visits, materials, and tryouts, but not much more. There are no contact periods, evaluation periods, quiet periods, or dead periods on a recruiting calendar. No limits exist regarding phone contact. Division III recruits do not need to register with the Initial Eligibility Clearinghouse.

However, a recruiting process still takes place at the Division III level. What's more, top Division III schools pursue Division II and even Division I recruits. A prospect may be recruited by two or three different levels herself. Depending on the situation, some girls may need to learn recruiting rules for all three.

NAIA Recruiting

The National Association of Intercollegiate Athletics (NAIA) was the first association to offer women's college athletics, beginning in 1980. The NAIA offers an alternative for athletes to earn a scholarship and compete in college but on perhaps a smaller scale than the NCAA. It offers two divisions of women's basketball, Divisions I and II, and almost 300 total teams compete between the two divisions. NAIA Division I teams can carry a maximum of 11 full athletic scholarships and Division II teams six. However, many are further limited in scholarships either by the conferences that they play in or by their institutional budgets.

In order to qualify academically to play in the NAIA, prospects must meet two of the following three requirements: achieve at least an 18 on the ACT or 860 on the SAT, post a minimum GPA of 2.0, graduate in the top half of their high school classes.

NAIA members are four-year institutions, and student-athletes have four seasons of eligibility in any one sport. As with other intercollegiate play, participating in one contest counts as a season of competition. Hardship requests can be granted in case of injury or illness, when an athlete has not participated in more contests than allowed by the NAIA. That athlete would not use up one of her seasons of eligibility in that case.

NAIA coaches have very few limitations in their recruiting. Other than giving gifts to recruits and taking their own players with them on recruiting visits, the coaches can do what they would like. They are restricted more by their budgets, personnel, and time than anything else. However, an NAIA coach cannot offer a paid visit to a prospective student-athlete unless his or her institution would do so for any student interested in attending the school.

The NAIA as a national organization does not use a Letter of Intent. However, many individual conferences do choose to implement one, as a formal indication that a recruit has committed to play for an institution in that conference. For those in the NAIA who do use a Letter of Intent, there is no official signing date.

Junior College Recruiting

In existence since 1938, the National Junior College Athletic Association (NJCAA) consists of over 500 accredited two-year institutions, almost 400 of which have women's basketball teams. Like the NCAA, the NJCAA has three divisions — Division I, Division II, and Division III.

Division I and II schools can carry 16 athletic scholarships. In NJCAA Division I, scholarships can cover tuition and fees, room and board, books, and transportation costs for one trip per year from home to the college. However, Division II scholarships can cover only the cost of tuition, fees, and books, not room and board. Like its NCAA counterpart, NJCAA's Division III cannot offer any athletic scholarships of any kind. For all three divisions, no more than four members of the team may be foreign players.

In order to play NJCAA basketball, entering student-athletes must have a high school diploma or the equivalent.

Junior colleges can offer one official or expenses-paid visit to a prospect, which can take place prior to her senior year of high school. Regulations for the actual visit match those concerning NCAA official visits.

While the NJCAA does use a National Letter of Intent, it is completely separate from the program used by in the NCAA. A recruit cannot sign an NJCAA National Letter of Intent prior to April 8 of her senior year of high school, and she must sign it within 14 days of receiving it. As with the NCAA National Letter of Intent, a student-athlete cannot sign with two different NJCAA institutions without forfeiting eligibility.

Junior college coaches may hold tryouts for high school students, provided that they get permission from the State High School Activities Association in the student's home state.

NJCAA student-athletes have two seasons of participation in any sport. Once again, participation in any part of any regularly scheduled matchup counts as one season of participation in that sport. If a player is injured or becomes ill and is unable to complete a season, the NJCAA can grant a hardship waiver, if she has not participated in a large percentage of the regular season schedule.

Not every junior college belongs to the NJCAA. Other governing bodies include the California Community College Commission on Athletics (CCCCA), which has just over 100 member schools. The CCCCA does not permit its members to give athletic scholarship aid.

Junior college recruiting rules cover official visits, academic requirements, and National Letter of Intent signing. Aside from these three areas, coaches and prospective student-athletes can do mostly as they see fit in recruiting, restricted only by their own staffing, money, and time.

For more recruiting information, contact:

NCAA
- 1-800-638-3731 — automated information line
- 317-917-6222 to speak to a real person in the NCAA's Membership Services Department
- www.ncaa.org — click on Rules & Eligibility

National Letter of Intent for NCAA institutions
- 205-458-3000
- www.national-letter.org
- questions@national-letter.org

NCAA Initial Eligibility Clearinghouse
- www.act.org/ncaa
- 319-339-3003 — automated information
- 319-337-1492 — to speak to a real person

NAIA
- 913-791-0044
- www.naia.org, www.naiascholarships.org

NJCAA
- 719-590-9788
- www.njcaa.org

2

Recruiting, Intensified:
NCAA Division I Coaches

Far removed from the days of one-dribble women's basketball played in bloomers, NCAA Division I women's hoops has become a hypercompetitive, fiery battleground. Coaches have more on the line, with potential for greater payoff. Accordingly, their recruiting efforts are more concentrated, extreme, and passionate.

Sometimes things work out for the best in recruiting, despite college coaches' errant assessments. Case in point is Tennessee associate head coach Mickie DeMoss' tale of recruiting WNBA superstar Ruthie Bolton-Holifield when DeMoss was an assistant at Auburn University. "Basically, we tried to talk her out of coming to Auburn," DeMoss chuckles. DeMoss and current Florida coach Carol Ross, then also assisting at Auburn, had signed Ruthie's older sister Mayola, who DeMoss says was the better player in high school. As an Auburn freshman, Mayola kept indicating that her sister wanted to come to Auburn, and Ross and DeMoss wanted to keep Mayola happy. "So we put her off from signing early, and we waited and waited." The duo even tried to pawn Ruthie off on Jerry Blair at Stephen F. Austin, but he decided to pass. After Ruthie made her campus visit at Auburn, DeMoss was almost resigned to the fact that if Ruthie wanted to come to Auburn, she was coming to Auburn.

However, she and Ross had one more ploy in mind. "Carol

and I drove Ruthie back home," DeMoss continues, "and in the car we were like, 'Ruthie, we're going to be really honest with you. You may not even make the traveling squad next year. We're going to Hawaii. How are you going to feel when everybody's packing their bags and you're sitting in your dorm room and everybody's getting ready to go to Hawaii? How are you going to feel?' She goes, 'Not too good.' So I thought, OK, we're making progress. Carol would chime in and she'd say, 'Ruthie, how are you going to feel when you walk across campus and everybody's going to go, hey, there's Mayola's little sister? Oh, yeah, that must be Mayola's sister. They're not even going to know your name, Ruthie. You're just going to be known as Mayola's little sister. How are you going to feel about that?' She goes, 'Not too good.' Then we'd do another scenario, like, 'How are you going to feel when Joe [Ciampi, Auburn head coach] is just all over you about something and he says, you're not as good as your sister, I wish you could play like Mayola, blah blah blah. He's just all over you, and you get kicked out of practice, dah dah dah. How are you going to feel?' 'Not too good.'" Then Ruthie curled up and took a nap for the remainder of the drive, further angering DeMoss and Ross, who had cooked up more badgering scenarios for her.

Finally, the car came to a stop in the Boltons' driveway in McLean, Mississippi. "I said, 'Ruthie, now have you thought about all of the things that we've talked about?'" says DeMoss. "She goes, 'Yes, ma'am.' I said, 'OK, well, what have you decided?' The only other school recruiting her was William Carey, a little small school down in Mississippi. We said, 'Now you could go to William Carey and you could be the show. You could run the show — you'd be the star at William Carey. You come to Auburn, people aren't going to even know who you are, and so on.' And so we go, 'OK Ruthie, have you thought about what we said?' 'Yes ma'am.' 'OK, what have you decided?' 'I want to come to Auburn.' I said, 'Well, if you want to come after all this, then Auburn is the place you need to be, Ruthie.'" DeMoss then left for Tennessee, and she was shocked when Ross told her that Ruthie was Auburn's best player as a freshman. "We just challenged her and didn't even know we were challenging her," she remarks. "Then she went on to be a two-time Olympian."

•••

Accountability grows with each season for NCAA Division I women's basketball coaches. While mounting resources and publicity have promoted women's college basketball, coaches also now feel more pressure, externally and internally, to win. Providing an enjoyable experience for players and amassing decent graduation rates, while still important, will not ensure them job stability. They must have successful records and advance to postseason competition. Since they feel more strain to excel in the victories column, and since women's basketball has become more competitive overall, they apply more pressure to student-athletes during the recruiting process. Assistant coaches and recruiting coordinators have also assumed a crucial role. In many ways, coaches' livelihoods depend on decisions made by teenagers, a somewhat frightening reality.

In the basketball world, the increasingly popular term 'recruiter' has taken on a negative connotation. "I think that when people think about recruiters, they think that they're some slick-talking, fast-talking salespeople," states DeMoss. "I'm sure there are recruiters out there that are like that, but I don't think that you're going to have long-range success if you rely just on some type of a quick fix, slick-talking, let-me-just-tell-you-what-you-want-to-hear type of thing. I think eventually it catches up with you."

How much of recruiting concerns selling a program, and how much is about finding a good match? At top schools, the selling takes care of itself through history, success, and exposure, and recruiting lists are smaller. At Connecticut, associate head coach Chris Dailey says the staff never recruited high numbers, "even when we were bad." Those trying to build up poorer programs find themselves in a quandary. Few top recruits want to sign with an unsuccessful program, but how can a squad rebuild without convincing talent to jump on board?

For Eastern Illinois head coach Linda Wunder, whose squad finished 7-20 in 2000-01, the challenge becomes getting the finest possible players to help her program improve. "For our level, the most difficult part is finding the right fit and the right level of player that we have an opportunity to get," she explains. "It's easy to identify top-level players, but I think from a realistic standpoint, your chances of landing them are sometimes not extremely high. Then you've got to find the next level of player that you will have an opportunity to be able to recruit and also be able to get." Wunder's yearly recruiting list features a few elite players, a slew of athletes on a secondary list, and a third level, so that she always has second and third choices.

Sub-.500 teams might find it best to address their histories right away when recruiting. Zareth Gray, who spent two years assisting at Eastern Illinois, wastes no time skirting the subject. "When I first talk to a kid, I'll usually tell her that the entire coaching staff came here in 1999. I'll explain to them our first year and how it was a transformational year for the kids," she says. "I know it's probably burning in their heads, and they just don't know how to ask it. A lot of kids have questions, but they don't know how to ask them or are scared to."

In 1999, New York's Stony Brook University made the transition from NCAA Division II to Division I. Head coach Trish Roberts, whose résumé includes stints at Maine, Michigan, and the ABL's Atlanta Glory, insists that she pursues the best. "We don't want Division II players, even though we've only been Division I for a few years," she stresses. "We're not going to get better unless we recruit top athletes. With Vinny's background, and I feel with my background, we are able to attract some of those kids."

The celebrity cast that took over coaching duties could not deny the fact that Stony Brook had not won 10 games in a season since 1995. However, Cannizzaro focuses on the present with recruits. "The first thing I say to a player is, look, we're one of the top 50 academic schools in the country," he says. "We're a new program. The opportunity to play here is right now. You have a great opportunity. You've got to look at the situation, which I think a lot of kids don't do. They do not look at what happens after four years."

Nonetheless, Roberts knows that sales plays a role. "It's just like being a used-car salesman," she comments. "You've got to know how to sell your program, and you've got to win. A lot of times kids don't want to go to a losing program, and that's why the rich keep getting richer. That's why the Tennessees and the UConns are always going to get those top athletes. Every now and then one will slip through the cracks and bring a school to the next level, like a Jackie Stiles. You just hope that you're that lucky school, that you can get one of those kids." Sometimes, it only takes one significant signing, and other top recruits follow. Convince a prep standout that she can be instrumental in a team's rebound, and a coach can quickly be on the road to success. The recruiting dogma of these staffs? Always recruit up.

Programs on the verge of making it big have an easier time of this. According to New Mexico head coach Don Flanagan, his staff always tries to recruit against top 25 teams and sometimes the top 10. That was not the case, however, at the beginning of his tenure. "We used to recruit against really poor programs and now we're recruiting against top 10 programs from time to time," he explains. "Even though we lose to those guys most of the time, you want to be competing against those teams for athletes." He might emphasize that though recruits might be tempted by higher-ranked teams, they may be happier at New Mexico, with a higher probability of being impact rather than role players. The fact that the Lobos were fifth nationally in attendance in 2000-01 also helps the cause.

While mid-major and lower-level Division I schools struggle to gain a national reputation, the upper echelon fights against the stereotype that recruiting comes easily. Although DeMoss admits that her recruit-to-signee ratio is low, she insists that recruiting still requires hard work. "People look at us and say, you all just go out and say, OK, we'll take you, you, you, and you," she remarks. "I wish it was that easy. My stress level would be a lot lower." The Lady Vols' low numbers adds to DeMoss' anxiety level. While the country's top programs would also like dibs on Tennessee's five recruits, head coach Pat Summitt does not want higher recruiting numbers.

"If people are saying that they're not like Tennessee or Connecticut and they can't just go get who they want, that's insulting," Dailey retorts. "It's a compliment in some ways, but I find it to be insulting in others. It's like they don't think we do any work to get the kids that we want. The hardest part, and the biggest part, of recruiting is identifying the kids that are going to fit in your program. I think because we've been successful that it says we work pretty hard at identifying the right kids." Even when she and head coach Geno Auriemma arrived in 1984, that was their focus. Now, the emphasis has switched from building to remaining at the top.

Recruiting Defined

Many events occur during the recruiting process. Coaches watch and evaluate prospects. College coaches, prospects, prep coaches, and parents interact in a number of different ways. If Division I coaches had to pare all of this down to a brief definition of what recruiting is really about, they would have distinct and diverse explanations.

Dailey sums it up in once sentence. "I look at recruiting as the process that matches a university to an individual," she states. For clarification, she adds, "It's the process of us identifying what our needs are, and going out and finding kids who want what we have. You might start out on one end, and they're on the other, and as you learn and share information, you learn more about each other. You gradually move toward the middle until it becomes a match." According to Dailey, building relationships proves more important than salesmanship. She prefers not to use the word sales for fear that it conjures up unfavorable impressions.

Duke assistant Valley agrees with Dailey's assessment and the matching concept. "I think it's all about finding those great matches and making people feel important," she explains. "It gets back to developing relationships, making somebody feel that she is important and is needed on the team, where she can make a difference."

"Recruiting is sales," decrees Ed Wyant, assistant coach at the University of New Mexico. "We have a product. Do they want to buy into the product?"

While he does not like to think of recruiting as sales, Flanagan acknowledges the similarities. "I always look at recruiting from a coaches' standpoint, not from a salesman's standpoint but from a coaches' standpoint," he says. However, he does admit, "You have to sell yourself and your program. I don't consider myself a salesman, but I do believe in our program. They say that the number one thing for sales is that you've got to believe in your product."

"From my perspective," DeMoss begins, "recruiting is offering and presenting an opportunity to a young lady or a high school student to attend your particular university, get an education, play a sport that they obviously excel in, and hopefully to grow as a person. I think as a recruiter, you're the messenger. You deliver the message. Within delivering that message, your particular style I'm sure will come across. Hopefully, it will be delivered very honestly and accurately with what you can offer."

The term recruiting as it pertains to women's basketball may be difficult to define. Is it going out and finding players? Selling them on your school? Building a relationship that recruit and recruiter think will be beneficial? Making a match? No wonder student-athletes and parents are confused during a process that those in charge have trouble putting into words. Accordingly, the diverse descriptions often match different colleges' overall philosophies.

The Never Ending Evolution, Evaluation, and Execution of The List

Recruiting is all about lists. Student-athletes have them, scouting services have them, and college coaches most certainly have them. Usually, college coaches separate their lists by class. In NCAA Division I, this means seniors, juniors, and sophomores, and sometimes freshmen. What's more, club basketball[1]

---

1. The term *club basketball* encompasses any non-scholastic competition, including Amateur Athletic Union (AAU) play. Many people use AAU to mean the more general term, as a fallback to the days when AAU provided the only major opportunity for female athletes to play basketball outside of the regular school season.

now begins at the 11-and-under age group. Coaches compile their lists largely by attending games, camps, and tournaments, as well as through personal contacts. While the elite recruit barely more than they actually need, others may go four- or five-deep in each position with an upcoming opening.

Although many Division I institutions designate one road coach as the recruiting coordinator, not all do. Duke assistants Valley and Joanne Boyle, both seasoned in the recruiting realm, each take charge of and follow a class through. Valley takes underclass players one year, and she stays with them as they become seniors. At the same time, Boyle will begin with seniors and then start once again with underclass athletes. Taking charge of a class means that the coach serves as the primary contact for letter and email writing, phone conversations, and evaluations. At some other schools that do designate recruiting coordinators, that coach keeps the master list of events and players, decides who travels where in the summer, coordinates mailings, and so on.

The recruiting coordinator may sometimes be but is not always a junior member of the coaching staff. DeMoss, who has served as a Division I head coach and has had had many other head coaching opportunities in Division I and the WNBA ranks, continues to be Tennessee's recruiting coordinator, although her title is associate head coach. Connecticut does not distinguish a recruiting coordinator, but that is one of Dailey's main tasks. "Recruiting is something you have to do every day, but I would say that I am the coordinator," Dailey states. "It's the primary responsibility of any really good program, I would think, because it is so important to the success of the program." In recruiting, assistant and associate coaches now assume greater influence, and their personalities are often a main reason for a prospect's commitment.

"We're all doing about the same thing," Flanagan says of the steps colleges take in recruiting. Immediately following their own seasons, coaches are often out watching weekend tournaments. Depending on how the early signing period progressed, they might still be working on their next season's incoming freshman class. Otherwise, they send letters and email to recruits and work the phones with high school and club coaches.

If recruiting has a down time, the end of April and May might qualify. During this period, coaches cannot evaluate players in person. "But you're still recruiting during that time," explains Bernadette Mattox, University of Kentucky head coach. "You're still writing, you're still doing those types of things, you're still calling coaches. It never stops." This often provides a good window to get background information from recruits' current coaches before college coaches head out for July recruiting.

According to NCAA regulations, prospective student-athletes may call college coaches at any time. However, this rarely happens. June 21st following students' junior year is the college coaches' first opportunity to call them directly. "We try to have the kids call us before June of their junior year," says Dailey. "Email has actually helped with that. We try to get kids to call us, but if you're 16, are you going to call someone like, yeah, I want you to call Coach Auriemma tomorrow. Oh, sure. I've seen him on TV. I don't want to call him. I'm scared." Talking to coaches can be nerve-wracking enough for teens when the coaches contact them. So coaches get that one June phone call, and they can make three calls in July, no more than one per week.

On July 8, the madness begins. From then until the end of the month, college coaches can evaluate players as many times as they'd like. "The month of July is the dreaded month for many coaches because you never know where you're going to wake up," says Roberts. "You're in a hotel, you're in Atlanta . . . Then the next two or three days you may be somewhere in Texas. So you pack a suitcase, and you're gone the month of July." Many players road-trip it in July as well, which can make those three phone calls difficult. Coaches try to catch athletes in their rooms, hoping that their underclass roommates do not answer, which would be an NCAA violation. They can, however, send faxes to players' hotels, which many do for the most wanted.

It's back to the office in August to revise lists, make calls, and send letters. Each staff has its own method for ranking players. Duke uses the categories elite, elite plus, and elite minus. Others rank order by position or rate on a scale of 1-5. A few do not rank or rate at all. Other than working with lists, coaches also talk with recruits on campus for unofficial visits before the school year. "That's when I start to get more influential in the process, in August," says Flanagan. "We're putting them in position, and we're basically looking for our needs. Everybody that we're recruiting at this point right now can help us." Hopefully for coaches, verbal commitments start rolling in come July and August, if not earlier. In 2000, Flanagan received three August commitments, from athletes who all took unofficials at the same time.

Three essential components of recruiting — the first direct mailing to juniors aside from the questionnaire, the home visit, and the official visit — occur in the fall. As of September 1 of athletes' junior years, college coaches can send them mail directly. Mail goes out en masse, often in the high hundreds, from most programs. In addition, coaches can do home visits during the last three weeks in September, which could be the first time they sit down for an extended period with a prospective student-athlete, her family, and others — high school coaches, club coaches, family friends. It provides an opportunity for college coaches to try to wow their audiences, show a film about the school, answer questions, and perhaps share a meal.

Cannizzaro has seen home visits from two different angles, first high school coach and now recruiter. "The worst sales pitches are not so much what they actually say as how they present it," he asserts. "You've got to be enthusiastic because you're actually selling something. It's like going to a lecture. The lecturer could be presenting all the information in the world to you, but if it is done in such a way that it's dull and unexciting, you can doze off." Roberts adds, "At the home visits, you do a big-time presentation. For us, we have a recruiting film, because sometimes a visual of your campus and your athletic program can help sway the kid your way."

Although coaches are allowed unlimited home visits during that September window, programs vary greatly on the number that they do. Wunder does not do as many as she used to, perhaps 10 or 12 if she needs to sign four. "I'd rather spend a little bit more time on the kids that we really want as opposed to going out and seeing a large number of kids in the home," she says. The Tennessee, Connecticut, and Kentucky crews will do few home visits as well, perhaps one for each player that they really want as well as one or two more. On the other hand, New Mexico did around 12 in 2000 and twice that many the year before. Then there's Duke, who does multiple visits for the same person. "With a kid that we really, really want," relates Boyle, "we'll go back in and do either two or three home visits with them. Usually it's not a home visit . . . We'll do two home visits with them or a home visit and a school visit." Duke head coach Gail Goestenkors remembers doing 17 home visits her first year at the school.

Usually, on-campus official or paid visits follow in October and early November. There, Division I hopefuls are treated to up to 48 hours of meetings with everyone from coaches to academic department deans to athletic directors, meals and hanging out with current players. There could be special goodies as well, depending on the school, the recruiting competition, and the recruit. When a prospect arrives in the gym, she might see her name up in lights. She may hear a sports announcer detailing the end of a game, with her scoring that college's winning basket as the crowd erupts. She could see a locker made up especially for her with uniform and sneakers inside. If she stays in a hotel, she might find her room decorated with school swag. Though she cannot take any of it home, it still has an effect. She may even see her picture in the school's fictitious next day's paper with a writeup about her great game.

"We don't do the locker room with their uniform," states Dailey. "We treat them like they would be treated if they were a player here. We don't put them in a hotel. They stay in a dorm with the kids. Because you know what? It loses its effectiveness. You do it with everybody. We have not done that for anyone that we have ever gotten. What happens if you only do it for one kid — what do the kids who are already at school think?"

If coaches take care of recruiting business during the early signing period, they can then immediately concentrate on the next recruiting class. However, even before early signing, head coaches must turn the bulk of their attention to their current teams. Many assistants miss their own practices and games due to recruiting obligations. DeMoss used to be absent more than she is now. "I do miss practices, not a lot because fortunately, we don't recruit a lot of kids," she comments. "I don't miss games, but I know of assistants who do miss games. But you know, that's why you recruit, to watch these kids play. To reap the benefits of your work is to be able to enjoy watching them play." The demands of road recruiting are a factor in the high turnover among women's basketball assistants.

Recruiting really has no beginning and no end. "Recruiting is probably as important as coaching, but it certainly isn't my favorite job," says Flanagan. "It's just because it's a 24-7 job. It's almost like you can never do enough to win a recruiting battle."

At struggling programs as well as national powerhouses, college coaches constantly create, revise, and revisit their recruiting lists throughout the year. At its largest, the list provides a base for mass mailings that go out to juniors in the fall, letters that do not even mean the school is recruiting the addressees. At its smallest, the list contains commitments to play at the college, contributions to the program's future. For many coaches, list items get the most attention during a pressure-packed summer and fall.

No Vacation Rentals for DI Coaches

College coaches, club coaches, and prep players hoping to compete at the next level do anything but dog it during the summer. Camps, tournaments, and shootouts abound, and college coaches have that three-week open evaluation window in July. They sport their largest logos and sit in bleachers from morning till night, and they line up to talk with non-scholastic coaches about players. Exhausted athletes play game after game, sometimes in search of a national title.

Fatigue from the frantic schedule affects coaches' perspectives as well as athletes' play. "I do enjoy the summer recruiting period," remarks Dailey. "You know what's funny — I try to do our key evaluations at the beginning because by the end of it, I'm miserable, and they look bad, they're miserable. So by the end of it, I'm just like, 'She stinks.' I might have at the beginning said, 'Well, you know, she's not bad.' I don't have a good attitude by the end." The summer period used to be a few weeks longer, and college coaches much prefer the current setup.

Some tourneys differentiate age categories, ranging from 18-and-under to 11-and-under. The 17-, 16-, and 15-and-under matchups attract the most college coaches. Boyle and Gale Valley did attend some 11- and 12-and-under games some years ago when a six-week summer evaluation window existed. "We promised we'd never do it again," Boyle remembers. "I was like, what am I doing here? Parents were looking at me. I don't know why we went, I really don't. I guess we could back then so we did." Now with three weeks and more summer events to choose from, coaches must pick venues wisely. Assessing players proves monumental, as they can evaluate three or four years out at one location.

Since much of recruiting occurs during the summer, club or non-scholastic coaches now often play a major role. In July, college coaches may not speak with players in person at their games. However, a club coach could easily spend an hour working a line of college coaches after the game buzzer sounds. Many college coaches wait for their few minutes of face time, some finding the scene degrading. "We line up, 20-30 of us Division I coaches," explains Wyant, "just to shake a club coach's hand and say, 'Wow, she is so good, and can I fax her tonight at the hotel?' We shouldn't have to do that."

Valley has a different perspective. "I don't like waiting around for coaches to get through," she admits, "but I appreciate them taking the time in giving you information about the kids. To me, that's just all part of the job, and it's part of doing your research in doing the background checks on the kids. If you see someone face-to-face, I think they're going to give you more, and you can develop a relationship with them. On the phone is just so clinical. They don't know what you look like, and I know what they look like but they have no idea who I am, so it is easy for them to maybe not be as forthright with their comments." Before 1996, college coaches could also write notes to players, which club coaches would then hand-deliver. There is some talk at the NCAA about disallowing in-person contact between college and club coaches during the summer, or even eliminating the summer evaluation period altogether, both of which would definitely change recruiting. Some feel that their main purpose in the summer is evaluating talent. However, others rely on summer coaches as a primary source of information, assessment, and communication.

Many know of the recruiting evils that exist in men's college hoops, of some club coaches acting as agents, wheeling and dealing with shoe companies, taking money, and influencing players' college decisions. Does this atmosphere exist in women's basketball? Some feel that it is heading down that same road, that non-scholastic coaches wield too much power in recruiting.

The NCAA does not currently regulate club coaches in recruiting. "No one is coming down on club coaches," Valley states. "It is hard to prove the rules that are broken, and so it just goes on and on. There's really nothing in it for them to maintain the rules. Some will say, 'Oh, I don't care. I am just trying to help my kid get a scholarship. I think this rule is stupid so I'm not going to adhere to it.' There are a lot of coaches like that, and the justification that they use is 'Hey, I'm just trying to help my kids and these rules are stupid.' So I'm going to let you talk to them behind the bleachers, or whatever else goes on. I think they need to have somebody that they report to in some form or fashion." In general, girls' summer basketball coaches do not accept cash or break major rules. However, a growing number are closely involved with their players' recruiting, much more so than high school coaches, often creating a strained relationship between the two parties. In addition, those with ties to college coaches could easily steer players toward certain universities.

Girls participate in club ball for different reasons, whether to be with their friends, just to keep playing, or to get exposure. Whatever the motivation, the desire to be recruited often plays a role. Kentucky assistant coach Leslie Nichols sees the merits. "Just because you're the best in your city or your state doesn't mean that you're going to be recruited," Nichols comments. "Any time you get a chance to go out there and compete against the top players in the country and do well, that's just going to make your opportunities better." At the same time, she sees pitfalls in the system and some of the egos involved. Although not sure how to solve these issues, she thinks that girls' summer basketball deserves closer scrutiny and could use an overhaul.

Babysitting

Many teenagers do it in their spare time for extra cash, and many college coaches also babysit. Some spend hours watching recruits who they have already decided would fit into their programs and who have already expressed interest. As they have already evaluated a player's skills, they are there only to be seen by her. While coaches have varying opinions on its effectiveness, quite a few do babysit. They fear losing the edge to other schools that do follow their recruits around.

Babysitting can alter an entire staff's schedule. "The way we plan where we're going is based on the information on the forms of the kids who send them back, and the kids you really want to follow, the kids you want to babysit," Nichols explains. "It's all basically babysitting for kids that you've talked to on the phone. They're interested in you, you're interested in them. You want to let them know how interested you are by being everywhere they are during the summer. They can keep you pretty busy." In the meantime, up-close-and-personal attention might be taken away from other recruits, some of whom may still need to be assessed by coaches.

The popularity of babysitting could be another by-product of the highly competitive women's basketball recruiting arena. "We hadn't really done that until the last few years," says Valley, who joined the Blue Devils' staff in 1989. "But now we're doing that more and more, where we will make sure they see us at all of the events. We do make an effort to try to be seen by our top kids. I think it's important." In order for coaches to commit to babysitting, they must really want the player, and

35

they must think that she wants them, too. Deciding whether a player's interest level merits a sitter seems similar to other aspects of recruiting. Coaches do as much research as possible, trust their instincts, and hope that these feelings ring true.

Coaches try to read recruits when deciding how much attention to give. "If she likes to have the attention, that's fine with us," says Flanagan. "We want to show that we're committed to that recruit. If they say, 'Oh Coach, I saw you at such-and-such,' you say, 'that's great. Where are you going to be next tournament, next week?' Of course we already know where they're going to be. Somebody will go there and make sure they sit right up front, make sure that they're supporting that player." This illustrates one way in which coaches personally cater to their prospects' desires.

Once coaches have established that a student-athlete's got game, most do try to show her how much she is wanted. Balancing that effort with keeping on top of other recruits can exhaust a coach's recruiting time. "I try not to babysit," says Dailey, "and I don't know if the kids appreciate it or if they expect it. At some point it is certainly verbalized — 'Hey Coach, you came to all of my games.' But I also tell them, look, if I don't come to your games, it doesn't mean I don't like you. It means I had to go somewhere else." For lower-level teams, babysitting may be more crucial. If coaches do not show up at recruits' games, that can be one more notch against the school.

However, is there now so much babysitting that players have become desensitized to college coaches' presence? "Being in the high school situation for all those years, I think the players after a while, they become jaded to it," Cannizzaro explains. "If they see the coach sitting there every game, they know they're being recruited by the school. I don't think that they have to see the coach there every game. Some coaches feel that they've got to be there because the other schools are there. But I think the college coaches put more into it than is really there. I think if the kid is interested in the school and you're not there that day, that's not going to mean anything." Nonetheless, until prospective student-athletes tell college coaches flat-out that babysitting does not mean anything to them, the trend will likely continue.

Reflections on What Recruits Go Through

College coaches know that they are a primary source of stress for prospective student-athletes. They acknowledge the difficulty that prospects have with the process, realizing that many high schoolers and their families do not know the rules or how to brave the process successfully. If a coach breaks a rule, intentionally or unintentionally, students and parents may not know because they rely on college coaches to educate them. Most trust that if a coach does something, it is allowed.

"I think there's more pressure now than ever on coaches to recruit, and because of that, there's more pressure on the recruits," states Goestenkors. "We all feel like those one or two players can help us win a national championship. I'm sure they feel the pressure from the college coaches, from their parents to a degree, from their friends, from all aspects. I think it's probably very difficult. But I think players are getting a little smarter because they've seen other people go through the process and end up transferring and making poor decisions." Players now venture out earlier to look at colleges, many visiting schools unofficially as sophomores or juniors, so that their senior years will not be so crazy. The financial investment can be huge, with the hope of a return on the investment — a scholarship.

With women's basketball coaches putting more time and money into recruiting, and with more competitive programs, prep players have more choices. While a positive in general, this can make the process more nerve-racking, especially for those who do not begin thinking about it early. "Some kids have been recognized since they were in eighth grade, so you feel like you've known them forever," quips Dailey, "and they have other teammates who have gone through the process. They have a better idea of what to expect. Some are better prepared. But some don't ask any questions. I think that it just depends. Many more kids are being recruited. Because more people are out there recruiting, I think it's sometimes harder for kids to narrow their lists." Those who wait to see who shows interest can be even more overwhelmed.

Increased basketball opportunities for women have placed more weight on the college decision. "Now it's not only do I have to get a scholarship, I have to get a scholarship at a major university or I'll become a failure," says New Mexico assistant Yvonne Sanchez. "I think there's a ton of pressure on kids these days from club coaches, high school coaches, maybe from parents. It's becoming a job for them." To succeed at this job, girls must dedicate themselves to the sport at younger ages. Basketball is the most popular high school sport for girls, both in number of teams and number of individuals. In 2000-2001, according to National Federation of High Schools (NFHS) statistics, 452,728 girls played on 16,756 high school basketball teams. Even with the rising popularity of girls' soccer, there were half as many high school girls' soccer squads. Furthermore, the multi-sport athlete, especially where basketball is concerned, has become a rarity in recent years.

"What we've come up against," Boyle explains, "is that you have some kids who know the system and have a lot of people working in their corner that have gotten them to narrow down their schools in July and August. They know the five schools that they're interested in. You have other kids who still have 20-30 schools. When you talk to a kid in August and she still has 20 schools, you're like forget it." Students may take only five official visits in the fall, and if they have no idea in August which schools are their finalists, college coaches may decide that their time is better spent elsewhere. "I think the kids go back and forth because they're getting pulled in one direction from club coaches, they're getting pulled in another direction from their parents, they're getting pulled in another direction from their high school coaches," Boyle adds. "I think they're trying to deal with a lot at 17 and 18 that maybe they aren't capable of really handling." Coaches know that prospects will be perplexed by the process, as teenagers faced with a monumental choice, probably the first major decision of their lives.

Everybody enjoys attention, and when getting lots of it from influential adults, some recruits exploit the situation. "I've dealt with kids where they're running a whole big game," says

Nichols. So you just have to basically hope that you're dealing with someone who is taking it seriously and not playing any games. I've had a kid who said that she's got a second line in her house so that she can just talk to recruiters." Sometimes coaches cannot tell when the voice on the other end of the line truly holds interest in the institution or just enjoys swimming in a sea of compliments.

Whether high school athletes and their families know the rules ahead of time depends heavily on the player's high school and club coaches as well as which camps or tourneys she attends. High school coaches who have experienced recruiting hopefully know at least the basics of what to expect. These days, many high school and club coaches take time out with their squads to talk specifically about recruiting. If the athlete attends an NCAA-sanctioned shootout or camp, she will listen to a recruiting seminar.

Despite these opportunities, many college coaches feel that female hoopsters and their families are generally not aware of recruiting's rules. Most high school students do not play on top high school or club teams, and they may not pay attention during those recruiting talks. While many college coaches may try to educate them, they cannot speak directly with athletes until June after their junior years. Although the NCAA's web site and literature explain recruiting in detail, families need to take a proactive stand in seeking out that information.

"If [prospective student-athletes are] in a situation where they're not getting any guidance, they could at least — if they're informed about it — contact the NCAA," states Cannizzaro. "But most kids are not going to do that, and they're going to assume that the colleges are abiding by the rules. They're going to assume that if you call me three times in a day, that's OK, not realizing that you can only call me once a week. If they don't know the rules, how would they possibly know that that's not the right thing to do?"

College coaches believe that high school-level coaches and counselors should keep themselves informed about recruiting. However, Flanagan admits that he never read NCAA manuals during his tenure as a high school coach. "I think that as college coaches, we want to educate student-athletes to the process," Flanagan says. "I think everybody's responsible, though, from the high school coach to the counselor, to give input and be as informed as possible to help the recruit make the decision. We try and inform players all the time about rules, regulations. That's the first thing we're doing when we're talking on the phone in that first phone call. We're telling them right away, we can only make one call per week. Is there a good time for us to call you?" College coaches informing recruits of the rules operates twofold: it helps athletes learn the process, and it also serves as a sort of self-policing. If someone else calls more than once a week, girls and/or parents might recognize the violation.

Even for families who take the initiative to contact the NCAA, reading the materials may not provide a real-life understanding. "It's hard for them to get the proper information because a lot of it is a rule, but then you have interpretations of the rule, actual practical application, how does it apply," Valley comments. High school and club coaches, unless they have extensive experience with recruiting, face the same dilemma. While all of the above parties may know general rules, specifics are often lacking. "We get parents coming in here, and they say, 'This is the first time we've gone through it, and we don't know even what questions to ask'," Valley continues. If a player has an informed high school and/or summer coach, and if colleges take the time to educate her, fantastic. However, the onus always falls back on the parents and the prospect, who may not always be so lucky as to have this much-needed help.

Games People Play

Of course high school prospects want to play for top programs, and of course colleges want to land the best possible players. Although they do not identify them as such to their faces, both sides have backups. Recruits and coaches often try to be as up front as they can, but they may not always reveal every detail. No one likes being told she is not number one, and if number one does not commit, the setup changes.

Savvy student-athletes know to ask college coaches how many others stand ahead of them on a recruiting list. If a player falls fifth or below on the list and poses the question, how do coaches respond? "We're not dishonest when it gets to that point," says Wyant, "but to let a kid know that they're way down the list, sometimes that's the kid you end up getting. Sometimes kids will ask. They're a little bit more bold with their questions these days." Early in the process, a coach might respond that he or she is recruiting three forwards, for example, and that the player falls in that group.

Although the revelation may later hurt them, some coaches let recruits know their ranks right away. They emphasize that factors other than rank count as well. "I would probably say, right now we're looking at three people ahead of you or whatever the number is," states Wunder. "But I also would tell a kid that it means a lot to me that she wants to come here. I have taken a kid where maybe she wasn't my top choice, but I know that she really wants to come to my school. A lot of times those kids pan out better because they want to be there and they're going to work hard for you. They may actually end up being better players than the kids you're wining and dining."

The difference between not telling the truth and not telling the complete story can be minute. While coaches say that they do not flat-out lie, many are nonetheless wary of completely revealing their lists. "You always want them to believe that they are basically the top choice," says Nichols. "It's not that you're being dishonest or anything, but you know, it's like you explain to someone, you've got a top five, so if you want to come, we're offering you a scholarship. We'll take you today and everybody else will drop off. But until we get an answer, this is why we have to have a pool and we have to have a couple kids to draw from. They pretty much understand that." As women's college basketball becomes more of a profitable business, this issue will likely continue to escalate.

Even for coaches who give direct answers to where players stand, responses depend on the stage of the recruiting process. "If someone asked that question in the spring," comments Goestenkors, "I would say, 'There are three people ahead of you right now. However, you may have really improved over the season and you may have passed them by, so I don't want you to drop us because we're very interested. We need to see how all four of you play this summer. So you're fourth based on last year, and so much happens over the course of the year.' We want to stay on their list because that is so true." Goestenkors adds that in her experience, this conversation rarely takes place. "We don't get asked very often," she says, "and I don't think they're afraid — I think they don't know to ask it."

Some programs devote much of their recruiting effort to determining a good overall fit. While they have recruiting lists, they also have separate rankings for basketball ability, academics, personality, and so on. "I think we've spent a lot of time finding the right matches," remarks Valley. "We have cut kids off the list because when we get them on campus we don't like them. That has happened, not very often, but it has." For programs subscribing to this theory, assessing whether players will buy into the team's philosophy is significant. At Duke, players who dream of huge stats will not be happy. "We may rate them 1,2,3, but we don't say hey, you're number three on our list. You do that, and you're going to lose the kid," Valley adds. "And we really do want to know what the kid's like. If she wants to come in and shoot the ball 30 times, that's not going to work in our program." Considering those qualities becomes the real challenge for coaches.

On the other list, the recruit's list of colleges, coaches want to know where they stand with players. Unlike the teenagers, they are not afraid to ask. According to coaches, many prepsters are reluctant to answer because they do not want to hurt coaches' feelings. Just as they like to feel wanted during the process, they assume that the college staffs have that same need. In reality, the coaches, adults who are rejected by prospects every year, want to know point-blank and early on. That way, they can focus their time, effort, and budgets elsewhere.

However, some recruits have other motives. "I tell kids all the time, if you're not interested in us, please tell us right away so we can move on because we're wasting our time and our money," Roberts insists. "Some kids do, and some kids will string you along. They may want to go someplace really badly, and that school may have shown a little bit of interest. They still have their hopes up high that there is a chance that they can go to that school, and yet they don't want to tell this other school no. So they're playing the game, just like some college coaches play the game — they string kids along. If they don't get who they want, they go to that second person on the list. If they don't get that second person, they go to that third person. Yet they're telling that second and third person, you're the first on my list, you know. It's a game, that's what it is." Nonetheless, coaches have the advantages of experience with the process, knowing what questions to ask, and the gumption to ask the tough ones.

In addition to posing probing questions, coaches listen and observe carefully for clues. "Once you get to know a kid, I think it's easier to figure out where they are coming from, if they are acting differently or if there is something that is bothering them," says Dailey. "One of the biggest mistakes in recruiting is that coaches tend to always want to talk instead of listen. If coaches did more listening, I think they would better use their time because they would know when they're going to get a kid. When you listen, I think you can hear either verbally or nonverbally what they're trying to tell you . . . If I'm always talking I can't listen to anything they say." Developing a relationship through letters, phone conversations, and in-person contact also proves crucial.

Although they may hone their listening skills getting to know recruits, coaches do need to do some talking. They can only wait so long, and their methods of offering scholarships vary. Some focus on one person at a time, giving her a certain deadline, or giving her an open-ended window if her recruiting stock is high. "If I clearly like one kid more than another, sometimes I will give her a deadline," Wunder says. "Then after that deadline I will say OK, I'm going to open it up, and then I will go ahead and make it to several people." Others focus on a small group at a time. Still others offer to a group at the same time: whoever says yes first will get the scholarship(s). Tactics depend on the coach's outlook as well as the level of the program.

"It's not fair for them to want to know where they stand with us and them not tell us where we stand," Dailey declares.

The waiting game exists on both sides, student-athletes waiting for an offer from their number one choices and colleges waiting for their top choices to make up their minds. However, it seems that only the college coaches give deadlines.

Negative Recruiting

College coaches spend hours communicating with teenagers and their parents about the merits of their programs. They try to impress with their personalities, team records and histories, personnel, and philosophies. Unfortunately, in this increasingly competitive space, some also use negative recruiting to try to gain an edge. Once some coaches find out the other schools on a recruit's list, they say negative things about programs, coaches, players — why a recruit would not want to play for a certain coach, how the athletes on that team are unhappy, how the recruit would never get any playing time there, and so on. Coaches can be surprised to hear from prospective student-athletes what their peers say about them.

Perhaps coaches turn to negative recruiting when they run out of things to say about themselves. Perhaps they use it when up against higher-ranked colleges. Countering those comments proves tough, especially with teenagers, who tend to be less skeptical than adults. "Probably the most difficult thing for us in recruiting is handling a lot of the negative recruiting that we get from other schools," DeMoss explains. "Other coaches, they'll take shots at us and our program, so we have to constantly defend ourselves. The main thing is playing time. We need to convince athletes that they are good enough to play at Tennessee, that they are good enough to be successful here, and that they can handle Pat's style. Some coaches will try to use that against us and say, you're not going to be able to play for Pat, and so on. We go right in and say, look, Pat's tough. If you don't want that, then you don't need to come to Tennessee. We use that as a positive, so it's really to our benefit when other coaches talk about that because it usually backfires on them." The Tennessee staff sometimes hears what others say about them when asking recruits what their concerns are about the school. By now, DeMoss says, she has pretty much heard them all

If a college coach and a prospect have a good rapport, the student may even indicate which other coach made which comment. Other times, coaches can tell when colleagues have said negative things about their programs by questions athletes ask. "Negative recruiting attacks you at the core of your being, just because it's wrong," insists Valley. "They are trying to manipulate a young person to come to their school for maybe the wrong reasons. Especially now, there's a lot of money in the sport for coaches. People feel a lot of pressure, and so sometimes I think that they make bad decisions on how they handle themselves." What most worries coaches is the negative recruiting that they do not hear about. If they do not know what is said about them, they have no way of dispelling rumors. If they do not establish comfortable relationships with student-athletes, they may never hear any of the disparaging remarks being made about them.

Sizing Up the Rules

Many current women's college basketball coaches have been around long enough to have also experienced recruiting under a system of few regulations. They could talk to and watch athletes as early and as often as they wanted to — personnel, time, and budget were the only limitations. Aside from giving money or gifts to prospects, they could do virtually anything.

The recruiting process is now much more tightly regulated. While coaches acknowledge the need for more rules, most would change at least some of them if they had the power. Two trains of thought exist regarding the current labyrinth of regulations. Some believe that the specific rules are necessary because people are out doing things they should not and gaining an unfair advantage; indeed, women's basketball and men's basketball now have roughly the same number of reported NCAA recruiting violations, although many are minor infractions. Others think that less regulation would actually result in a smoother process. Some simply feel that the existing system places too many limits on what they can do.

Many of coaches' suggestions on improving the current process revolve around summer recruiting. Some would like to

45

be able to call athletes at the beginning of June, or once a week during the month of June, or once sometime during the junior year. "Coaches could be chasing this one kid who has no interest in them, but because they haven't been able to talk to her, they don't know so they don't want to take that chance of not recruiting her," DeMoss remarks. If contact began a few weeks earlier, coach and player can have at least talked before the official process bombards them in late June. It might make things easier on both parties.

"In July, other than being able to talk to the club coaches, I would like to see phone calls and faxes to the kids, those kinds of things, stopped," Wunder explains. "Let the kids play and let us evaluate and not worry about who we're going to call. I'm in the gym on the cell phone watching somebody else play, talking to a different kid. That way, they can focus on what they need to do for their teams, and the coaches can concentrate on evaluating them." While flattering to players, July calls and faxes often concern complimenting athletes' summer play, not at all on decision-making.

Although already cut back from six weeks to three, the summer period remains under fire from coaches. Some would like to see it eliminated altogether. "I would get rid of the July recruiting," Roberts states. "You've got kids who are playing 25-30 days straight in the summer, and by the end of the summer, they look horrible. We have followed kids from the beginning of the summer, and then we end up at a camp that they're at toward the end of the summer. They look horrible. They're so tired, they're not sharp, they're dragging. They're trying to impress the college coaches because they're trying to get a scholarship, when in actuality they're hurting themselves." Instead, the NCAA could give its institutions a certain number of days throughout the entire year to go out and recruit. Those who disagree with this general notion rely heavily on July for evaluation. They need that period to focus solely on recruiting without the added pressure of their own practices or games.

"I don't think coaches have enough time to talk or communicate with prospective student-athletes," states Mattox. "We start, and after a couple of months it's time to stop. I'd like a little bit more time to recruit them." At the same time, Mattox regards NCAA regulations as necessary to govern a process that becomes more intense each year. Indeed, her appreciation for the recruiting rulebook stems from her own high school recruiting experience. She divided her collegiate career between Roane State Community College and Georgia and went on to become Georgia's first All-American. However, getting there was hard. "The coaches were really tough in that they weren't very nice about other coaches and other schools," Mattox remembers. "Some of them just tortured me. I don't want to ever have a young person have to go through what I had to go through."

While coaches see the reasoning behind many recruiting rules, a few regulations seem to defy logic. For example, when out evaluating players, coaches cannot talk to them, other than a hello if they literally run into each other. The well-informed prospect understands this scenario, but the naïve might not understand the coach's behavior. However, one can only imagine the scene without the rule. Some athletes would have the same post-game lines as club coaches do. How would they handle them? Many are nervous enough simply knowing that coaches are there to watch them play, without the added pressure of personal contact.

Although coaches agree that recruiting needs renovation, they have trouble defining the specifics. "I would like to take the club coach out of the mix, not completely, but take the unscrupulous people out of it," says Wyant. "How you do that — who's a good person and who's bad — that would be tough. But the goal would be to get the influence of the club coach out of summer recruiting." Though some non-scholastic basketball organizations have governing bodies charged in part with making sure coaches stay in line, they are not connected in any way with the NCAA.

While coaches understand why a system of recruiting regulations must exist, many say that the rules make it difficult to get to know a student-athlete. Also, the allowed opportunities to evaluate her skills and potential may not be enough to determine if she would be a good fit. If coaches were allowed to contact them earlier, what would some high school juniors' academic years be like? After all, most do not ask individual college coaches to recruit them.

A Different Scene

Since the inception of women's college basketball, a tremendous amount of change has occurred in recruiting. While no one argues against the improvement of opportunities or game competition, whether recruiting has improved remains up for debate. For NCAA Division I veterans, recruiting is now entirely different. From coaches helping each other to the summer window, it has definitely evolved with the game.

Increased parity in women's basketball means that the best high school players no longer choose the same one or two schools. "It used to be very clear-cut who would get the best kids," states Valley. "But a lot of programs have come up and become better, and more money has been put into it. I think that kids nowadays are starting to branch out a little bit more. We're getting some good kids, as are all of the top programs. There's more talent, but they are also spreading out a little bit instead of always just going to the same places." This means more competition among the top colleges, all vying for top players and less likely to help each other.

A diminished sense of collegiality is one of the changes that have surfaced among college coaches as a group. "Years ago," remembers Dailey, "everyone would go to the same camps, and everyone would go out at night. I don't think you see as much of that anymore because the competitiveness is greater. There are more camps that people go to. There are more players. There's more money being put into women's basketball, and there's more pressure. I think that's a big change. It's affected people's relationships. It's affected people's willingness to be friendly, more so. If you're feeling pressure or you've got a lot going on, as everyone does, you're not as likely to go out at night and then get up early the next day. It just seems very different than when I started."

Just like the high school girls they are there to see, college coaches now separate into their small cliques. Certain coaches will sit next to each other at games, will talk to each other on the road, but not everyone. Previously, in the interest of growing a sport, women's college coaches would be more forthcoming in chumming it up with any colleagues. Nowadays, aside from their circles of cohorts, they do not give their commentary so freely. However, this is not to say that all women's college basketball coaches are nothing but cutthroat in recruiting. After all, not only are they in more fierce competition with each other, there are simply many more of them now, and there are also many more girls' high school tournaments and contests to watch.

Recruiting has also modified itself because of the alterations in the girls' basketball "off-season." In particular, the summer has brought huge changes. When summertime offerings were fewer, coaches out evaluating would all see each other at the same three or four events. They would be able to see most of the country's elite at those events, too. Now, it can be difficult for coaching staffs to prioritize from among the myriad of camps and tournaments held from coast to coast and even abroad. "You have to sit down and really be organized," says DeMoss. "Sometimes you just roll the dice and say OK, I hope that these are the best events for us to go to." Coaches also try to attend events featuring players they have been actively recruiting as well as those they might think about recruiting several years out.

Some coaches believe that with the larger number of summer opportunities for girls, the summer talent pool has become watered-down. "There were one or two camps that kind of monopolized everything. They only invited or had the top kids in the country at those camps, and all the college coaches would be there," says Roberts. "Now, it's become a money thing where they let anybody in. You have to stay at a camp a lot longer just to wean the bad ones from the good ones. Sometimes the good ones don't look as good when you're playing with somebody so bad. We talk about that all the time, how it used to be where certain camps only had the best kids there. Anybody can go to these camps now." By promoting their camps as exposure events, the organizers have the opportunity for profitable business. On one hand, this abundant summer circuit provides an arena for more girls to be noticed; on the other, coaches find it more difficult to separate potential talent from those not suited for their levels.

Outworking the competition and finding quality prospects that others have overlooked are both much more difficult now. "With the advent of and the popularity of women's basketball, and having the WNBA, there are just more pressures on you to be successful in recruiting," states Myra Fishback, former Stony Brook assistant coach. "You used to be able to get out and work schools and get that kid. The other thing is that there are no secrets. If a kid is good, everybody knows about her." Stricter regulations that allow coaches out for a maximum of 40 days at specific periods during the academic year make it tougher for colleges to win recruiting wars just with effort. Landing a sleeper has also become more rare in part due to increased media coverage and technology. More events, the Internet, increased amounts of mass snail mail and email, and more paperwork have made it more difficult for a talented player to slip through high school unnoticed.

Division I coaches know that the recruiting process is also different for the student-athletes themselves. For nationally-known players especially, the onslaught of attention can be overpowering. "I think recruiting has really intensified," says Goestenkors. "The first day that we're allowed to write kids, you'll talk to them and find out they're getting two hundred letters in the mail. Their heads are spinning. It's very difficult for them to make a really good choice."

Some coaches have seen a definite adjustment in athletes' attitudes as well. "A major change I've seen is an ego boost from the current student-athlete," Wyant comments. "It used to be, hey, little Johnny's got the strokes from second grade on, and he thinks he's All-World. Now, little Suzy's starting to think that she's better than she really is. Sometimes that's a negative, that they've been told . . . It's been in the boys' and the men's forever, and now it's just starting to surface in the women's." Girls who grow up receiving compliment upon compliment could very well forget the difference between confidence and arrogance as they enter the recruiting process.

The rules have changed, the atmosphere has changed, and coaches' and athletes' mindsets have changed in recruiting. However, the goal in recruiting remains finding a good match. In many cases, that goal must now be accomplished in less time.

The Earlier, the Better

Each year in women's college basketball, more recruits make official commitments to universities during November's early signing period. Among early signees, many have already made a prior verbal commitment. An increasing number commit verbally as high school juniors and sophomores, and now even freshmen. When will we see the first eighth grader verbal to an elite college program?

Fewer female hoopsters, in any case, wait until the late signing period to make their college choices. This is a good thing for college coaches, who can then start on the next year's recruiting. Why the early signing trend? Are coaches turning up the pressure that much more to do so, or do prep athletes fear that they must sign early in order to get their top choices?

Perhaps the student-athletes just want to get the process over with. "They're doing their weekend visits, they're doing their schoolwork, they're doing everything else, and the third week into it, they're just like, enough," Boyle explains. "All of the attention is great for a couple of weeks, and then it just gets old. They have to tell 30 coaches who are calling their house, no, that they're only interested in these five. Parents are overwhelmed. It's really become the family crisis." While some families can handle this longer than others, by November most everybody has had enough.

In addition, many women's basketball recruits these days are convinced, or convince themselves, that quality players sign early. "Most times, if the kids are that good, there's not usually a lot left in late signing," says Fishback. "The good ones that are left in late signing, that's because they can't decide." Middle- and lower-level colleges especially sometimes wait for certain players until the late period, so that they can pick through the leftovers of the higher levels. College coaches realize that students wait until the late period for one of several reasons. If indecision is not the reason, they hope that their recruiting stock will rise as a result of a stellar senior outing and that a better offer will present itself. In any case, those who wait run the risk of losing an opportunity altogether.

If a student has taken the time prior to her senior year to research colleges and meet teams, she may be sure about which school she wants to attend. In this case, signing early is probably the way to go. However, if she has not learned everything she can about the realities of the program, signing early can backfire. "I think the early signing period is good because it allows girls to focus then, after they sign, on the rest of their senior year," Goestenkors ponders. "However, I also think a lot of kids are making mistakes. They don't get a chance, many times, to go see a coach and a team play. We're all wonderful talking on the phone. We sound like really good people. Then all of a sudden when they get yelled at for the first time, they're shocked. If they had been able to come to a practice or a game, they would have had an opportunity to see, OK, this is how this person coaches. Can I handle this type of coaching? I think because of the early signing, sometimes they really don't get a chance to see the big picture and make a logical choice. They make emotional choices instead of sometimes logical choices."

Perhaps, then, the large amount of transferring in women's college basketball relates to the large number or recruits signing early. Not only may prospects not have adequate time to evaluate schools and coaches, coaches may not have enough time to evaluate high school players. "The colleges are getting out there as fast as they can and trying to sign up a player as quickly as they can because they don't want to wait," states Cannizzaro. "They say well, we have five kids, and this kid says she really likes us, and let's get her. They took the kid who maybe wasn't really the kind of kid who actually fits into their system or is at that level. Then they wind up having to go out and try to recruit a player the year after to replace the player they got."

As Cannizzaro also notes, "But it's like everything else — does everyone always make the right decision? No, of course not." Both prospective student-athletes and college coaches can do as much homework as possible, but neither can tell whether the decision was right until the athlete arrives on campus.

Advice to Prospects and Parents

Unlike students, NCAA Division I coaches have the benefit of experiencing the recruiting process year after year. While no two situations are the same, many college coaches see high school prospects making the same mistakes over and over again. They offer some advice to those just starting the college search.

Just as college coaches start their recruiting research early in players' careers, student-athletes need to begin researching college choices well ahead of time. "If they're serious about basketball, then this recruiting process should start their freshman year in high school, so that they can prepare academically," Roberts says. "Once it comes upon them, they will be organized, and it's not going to be as stressful. If they're seriously interested in a school, they need to be proactive, and if that school shows an interest, then follow that school."

The monstrous homework assignment includes evaluating one's own skills. Determining which college division will fit a player, and within that division, which level of school, is difficult. "I would be realistic about how good I am, or how good my daughter is if I'm a parent," DeMoss advises. "That's tough when you're a parent — I don't know how you do it." A trusted high school, club, youth, or even college coach could be a beneficial source. As things currently stand, many prefer to let the recruiting process itself indicate the level. However, if the goal is to take charge from the beginning, unbiased evaluation may be a better route. "I think there's a place for any kid who wants to play basketball in college," Dailey comments, "provided they are able to be realistic about their abilities and that they are able to match their ability level to a school that they would like to go to."

Another harsh reality of recruiting is the amount of snail mail sent out by college coaches. "I think one of the big things that a lot of parents and students don't understand is the difference between a letter and a scholarship offer," says Nichols.

"They say, 'Oh, we got a letter from Kentucky, Kentucky!' The parents take the letter all over town, saying, 'My kid's going to go to Kentucky!'" Division I programs send out hundreds, even upwards of a thousand, letters and questionnaires out to high school students each year. Of those hundreds, most programs will actively recruit 30 or 40 at most, more likely less than 20.

College coaches often develop relationships with young players who attend summer clinics on their campuses. Even if athletes do not end up considering the college, they can learn about college ball and perhaps about recruiting as well. "We have campers who come here who are not going to play in the ACC [Atlantic Coast Conference]," says Valley. "Maybe they will play Division I, or maybe they'll play Division II or Division III, but they ask us advice on things. We can help educate them and get them going in the right direction." Since college players often serve as counselors at the camps, prospective student-athletes can get to know some potential future teammates. No rules restrict contact between athletes and coaches at camps, so campers may talk to counselors and coaches freely. Not only can they get to know the personalities of the staff, they can also ask questions about recruiting, questions they may be afraid to ask once the process actually gets underway.

According to Cannizzaro, who has counseled many prep players on their roads to college ball and beyond, it is essential for girls to make a list of qualifications that schools must meet in order to be considered. Too often, players wait and see who recruits them, without first considering their own personal requirements. "The first thing with student-athletes is to establish criteria of what they want," Cannizzaro insists. "What kind of a school are you looking for? Is it a big school, small school? How far are you willing to go away? Academically, what are you looking for? Is there anything specific?" Once the student puts that list to paper, her high school coach, club coach, parents, and whoever else can help use it as a benchmark to evaluate universities. For the blue-chipper, having that list in hand could also make it easier to say no right away to colleges who do not meet her criteria.

College coaches stress the need for prepsters to be brutally honest, as difficult as it may be for them. If they have no interest whatsoever in a school, they should tell that coach right away, even during the first phone call. "I wish girls would just be honest and up front," Wunder comments. "I think they worry more about hurting your feelings. A lot of times coaches will take it a whole lot better if recruits tell them from the get-go that they aren't interested in the school." Instead, they might stay on the phone for hours when they know they will never sign with that college.

Until a prospect tells the coach she is not interested, that coach will keep spending his or her recruiting budget on phone calls, visits, and mail to that person. "I think that for a lot of kids, it's just that they don't know how to handle themselves," adds Valley, "and so a lot of them are just trying to be nice. They're afraid to say no, and so they say yeah, you're in my top three. Really, you're not, but they just don't want to tell you. We'd rather know what's going on, and then we can either bump up the recruiting or cut our loss and go."

Once recruit and coach establish mutual interest, the player and her family should try to really get to know the players and coaches in that program. "Make sure that when you go on a visit that you talk to the players when you're with them, and you ask them, how is Coach X?" says Cannizzaro. "What kind of a coach is the coach? Do they scream, are they yellers, are they disciplinarians? Are they one way on the court, one way off the court? Is the person I'm talking to in the office and in my home the same person who's going to coach me on the court? Ask as much as you can, and ask every player. Don't just talk to one or two players, or the stars, or the players who play. Find out from the kids who don't play that much how they feel. If a kid's not playing but says, 'Coach is great,' that says a lot." Attending practices and games could help give a truer picture about what life is like for women's hoopsters at the school, how they get along with each other and the coaching staff, and other dynamics. "See the style of the coach," Goestenkors insists. "See the style of the team, what style they play. Asking questions is important. Don't be afraid to ask questions." Division I athletes spend a majority of their collegiate years with teammates and coaches, and finding out their personalities and quirks is easier done while watching them in action.

Although basketball is a large part of the decision, coaches admonish recruits to think carefully about other areas of college life. Attending classes, meeting with professors, and talking with students not on the team will help give a well-rounded view of the school's atmosphere. "If you're there a year and there's a career-ending injury, then all of that other stuff doesn't matter," Mattox says. "But are people there the people you want to spend the rest of your three or four years with? I think that's important, that the people you're going to be around are people who care about you and who want what's best for you." Coaches encourage prospective student-athletes to delve deep into the school's characters and offerings. That way, there is a much better chance for a lasting match.

However, some coaches steadfastly believe that searching for a school is not at all like searching for your soul mate — there is not necessarily only one perfect school for a student-athlete. "I think it's crazy when coaches say, this is the school for you, if you don't come here you're nuts, et cetera," Dailey remarks. "It's just a process, and recruiting is like anything else. Kids are going to find things they like about each place and things they don't like about each place, just like coaches do. There are kids that you like, and there are some things that you wish they could do better. You just have to decide what the most important factors are and what you're willing to live with, and then you make your decision based on that. What you have to have in a player, what you have to have in a school, those are most important."

As much advice as coaches give recruits, as much advice as they themselves take, and as much homework as anyone does along the way, coaches are the first to admit that recruiting has no tried-and-true formulas. Accordingly, there doesn't seem to be much logic in a statement made by many girls after selecting their college programs: when I was there, it just felt right.

Whatever their ultimate goal, coaches work to identify the athletes who can best help their programs win. Some try to recruit the best athletes possible, some the most skilled in basketball, some the hardest workers, hoping that they can accurately predict a player's college potential. Even without questionnaires, they can find out a player's stats, grades, and interests. But how do they learn the intangibles — work ethic, desire to work as a team, ability to mesh with current players, personality, willingness to adopt the program's philosophy? While phone conversations, home visits, and campus visits hopefully provide insight, coaches do not have crystal balls. Until they can read the future, they will keep spending countless hours on the phone, on the road, at the computer, and hosting recruits, in their endless pursuit of that perfect match.

3

The 'Tweeners:
NCAA Division II Coaches

From lambs to monkeys to parents without a clue, recruiting for NCAA Division II schools can be quite a different experience than the one enjoyed by Mickie DeMoss when she visits the nation's elite. For instance, the quest for players sometimes takes North Dakota State head coach Amy Ruley into rural areas. During one home visit in particular, she had gone to see a recruit in a farm community. "This family had a young lamb that they brought in," she remembers. "We're sitting in the kitchen, and I'm looking at this girl's mother across the kitchen table from me, and behind her in their living room, this little lamb that was initially in the kitchen has hopped on into the living room. I see it right in the middle of their living room, squat, and you're kind of caught — should I tell her the lamb's peeing in the living room, or should I not worry about it? I was kind of like, 'Oh oh, the lamb, the lamb!'" Even after close to a quarter century coaching at North Dakota State, Ruley is still not quite sure how to react to misbehaving livestock.

"We've had some really bizarre parents' behavior," says Pam Martin, head coach at Humboldt State University, which gave no athletic scholarships whatsoever until several years ago. "It's the 7'1" dad who probably played maybe high school ball, and he's going on and on about — this is when we were nonscholarship — so what are you going to give me? And he just kept going on and on, and it was like, how many times do I have to tell you? I told him, we're nonscholarship. We have nothing to give your daughter. He goes, well, no, but you know what I mean, like an apartment or something. Then he'd go on and on about, well when this was happening in the CBA [Continental Basketball Association], and blah, blah, blah . . . and this was one of those out-of-control parents. Meanwhile, the immature daughter is just sitting there and hasn't answered any questions because by the time she gets her mouth open to answer the question with what she thought that she wanted to say, her dad is piping in about, what else are you going to give me?" Needless to say, that student-athlete did not sign with the 'Jacks.

Shortly after he was hired to take over the program at Southern New Hampshire University, Dennis Masi had quite a strange visit with a signee. At the time, he was still living in New Haven, Connecticut, and a player that the former coach had signed lived in nearby Orange. He decided to see if he could stop by and meet the family. "I'm doing the professional thing, and I'm just going to go over to the house, and I called to ask if I could come over and introduce myself," Masi recalls. "A family with a lot of money. So I walk in and I'm sitting on the couch, and I hear a screeching, screeching, screeching. I'm like, the dog is running around, the cat's up under the stairs. I said, 'Can I ask you one question', and she goes 'What.' I said, 'What's that noise?' She goes, 'It's my pet.' I said, 'Your pet?' She said, 'Yeah, I have a pet monkey.' I look at her and say, 'No you don't.' She goes 'Yeah, I keep a monkey in the room, and she comes to the games and everything.' I said, 'Can I see the monkey?' 'Absolutely.' I walk in and there's a freakin' monkey in her room. It's got diapers on, and she's walking around the house with the monkey on her. The monkey comes over and stands by my feet and kind of just touches my legs, and I've never been around a monkey. I'm backing away, like is the monkey going to bite me?"

And there's more. "So I go watch her play summer league — never seen her play," Masi continues. "Here comes the mother, with the monkey. The monkey's on her shoulders with a diaper on. It just summed up that whole first year. It was just unbelievable."

■ ■ ■

While NCAA Division II overall gets little press, it does feature some top-notch squads and competition. The not-as-successful Division II programs, however, struggle year in and year out to sign players. Even the best teams' coaching staffs often feature only one or two full-timers instead of three or four. While Division II coaches have fewer recruiting rules and regulations to contend with, their schools also have smaller recruiting budgets and lower profiles. What's more, they have five fewer scholarships to offer — 10 as opposed to Division I's 15 — and many programs cannot afford to carry the 10. The upper echelon recruits mostly against the more prestigious and often better-funded Division I. However, many would not prefer to be involved in the more hectic Division I recruiting scene.

Division II coaches' biggest hurdle in recruiting is battling the Division II stigma. Many constantly grapple with a community that still believes Division I is the only way to go. With the rise of the WNBA, it seems that this attitude will only become more prevalent.

Full Scholarship, Partial Scholarship, and Nonscholarship Offerings

In Division I, the phrase "We'd like to offer you a scholarship" often means "We'd like to offer you a full ride." However, in Division II, the equivalency rule designates no more than the equivalent of 10 full scholarships. Coaches may divvy that up however they choose, with 10 full, five full and 10 half, eight full and eight quarter, and so on. They could, though, be further restricted by conference regulations or their own budgets.

In addition, coaches may be additionally limited by their own schools' administrations, both in the amount of scholarship money at their disposal and in how they divide up the money. What's more, coaches might find themselves recruiting athletes for whom they have no scholarship money. Still, some find a way to keep signing top players with these limitations.

For those who go the full scholarship-only route, competition proves a factor. "We typically recruit against Division I colleges, and we talk to kids who are being offered full scholarships by Division I schools," states Barbara Stevens, head coach at Massachusetts' Bentley College. "We just don't feel like we can walk into a home after a Division I coach has been there and offered a full scholarship and say, 'Well, we'd like you to consider a half scholarship.'" Nonetheless, Stevens often rounds out her roster with several students not on any athletic scholarship. "Some of the kids who are not on scholarship are kids we actively recruited," she adds, "and then a couple are pure walk-ons. They literally walked into our office and said, 'Can I try out?'"

Other quality Division II teams feature a balance of full, partial, and nonscholarship athletes. Almost 80% of Ruley's players have entertained Division I scholarship offers. However, North Dakota State, which has won five national championships, still offers many partials, reserving the fulls for top recruits. "The kids that are being recruited by legitimate Division I schools and being offered full rides," she says, "we offer full rides to those kinds of kids." North Dakota State also has walk-ons most every year.

"I don't get into cutting scholarships up like that," states Masi, who takes a different approach. He often offers individuals full scholarships for two or three years, continuing with the strategy of his predecessor. "This was the best way, we thought, to get the building blocks that we wanted to, and then to move on," he says. In 1998-99, the season before Masi arrived on campus, the squad did not win a single game. His method seems a different way of offering a partial scholarship. Perhaps the term full scholarship, even though it does not continue throughout the collegiate career, sounds more enticing.

Some prefer to split up offerings such that almost everyone on the roster has a partial but no one has a full ride. "None of the players are on full scholarship," says Steve Kirkham, head coach at Colorado's Mesa State College. "We don't have that kind of money." At Humboldt State, which also has no full scholarships, about half of the team has partial scholarships and the other half has no athletic aid. "We're almost like a nonscholarship in some ways," comments Martin. Aside from recruiting against conference rivals, Humboldt competes with some NAIA and NCAA Division III institutions for players.

Can schools that do not give full scholarships compete with Division I and II schools that have them? Some do so quite nicely, and efficiently, by combining athletic money with academic scholarships and need-based aid. "There's some kind of creative financing when you start putting our scholarship opportunities together," explains Ruley. "Kids that are being recruited Division I but that maybe aren't the top choice recruit for those schools. Those kids, we might be able to put together a package for them, especially if they've got some academic money." Academic scholarship money does not count toward the equivalency rule. "Kids who have that opportunity or high financial aid need who know they can get additional free money, we can package those other scholarship opportunities that they have with athletic scholarship opportunities to give them the best financial situation possible, and also make our money go as far as we can," adds Ruley. From the athlete's standpoint, it does not make a difference, as long as they can attend college at little or no expense.

Many Division II institutions employ this scholarship packaging method. "Most of our kids have some academic money, too," says Kirkham. Since decisions on financial need and academic scholarships often come later in the process; it can be a waiting game. Coaches wait to hear how much money the prospect will receive academically or because of need; then they add athletic money to that sum in order to equal a full ride, or close enough to a full ride that it is very affordable for the family. "What we find within our system," explains North Dakota State assistant coach Kelli Layman, "is that we might bring an athlete in that might need totally athletic money, if the money is high on the recruiting list, and then they get into the academic and all of a sudden now she's eligible for academic money. So that backs off the athletic money as they get academic money." The early signing period can complicate this situation, however. Some recruits may feel pressure to decide before knowing the academic or need-based side of their packages.

For coaches who prefer to dole out scholarships as full rides, filling out the roster can be difficult. "To make a squad that lasts throughout the entire basketball season, you need to supplement your 10 fulls with walk-ons," Stevens asserts. "For example, in the spring of 2001 we were still trying to bring a young woman into our program as a nonscholarship but recruited player. Sometimes it works out for you and sometimes it doesn't."

After a nonscholarship recruit decides to attend, actually being on the team can be tough as well. "To try to get someone to walk on or to come into a program and not give them any scholarship money when they know that there are players getting scholarship money is another touchy issue," Stevens continues. "It's hard. Some kids can deal with it and have no problem with it, and other kids really feel like they're being slighted." This could be one reason why Division II programs lose players to Division I institutions. The tradeoff of playing even for a nationally-ranked Division II team if it means paying one's own way might pale in comparison to a Division I scholarship.

A Regional Affair

Even at the most successful Division II institutions, which may have two full-time coaches on staff and an adequate budget, recruiting is primarily regional. "There are a number of very good players in the region, and we feel like for us, local recruiting is an advantage," explains Ruley. North Dakota State attracts athletes by its history alone, including those from far away. However, Ruley, whose recruiting targets primarily the Dakotas and Minnesota, has seen the effects of Division I recruiting becoming more national. The Dakotas have many Division II institutions but none in Division I. As she often competes for so-called Division I athletes, she finds herself recruiting against Division I schools that previously have not ventured to that area of the country.

At Bentley, recruiting travels rarely stray out of the Northeast. Stevens does not even attend national summer tournaments on the East Coast. She doesn't need to. "Our recruiting allows us to see all those regional and in-state tournaments in the spring and summer," says Stevens. "We know the state champions that are going to go on to the nationals because we've seen them already. Not that we don't recruit nationally, I mean we do, but it's not like we're going to go watch Colorado play Nebraska." That strategy has worked well thus far for the Falcons.

Geography is a main recruiting obstacle at Mesa State. In order to watch a prospect, Kirkham must go over two mountain passes, no matter the direction. Fortunately, Kirkham is well-connected in the surrounding region and knows many high school coaches who help him drum up recruits. What's more, Kirkham's basketball camps at Mesa draw upward of 3500 participants each summer. "We do a ton of our recruiting in our camps, of course," Kirkham says, "and then we do a lot on videotape. In general, we don't get too far out." For him, driving to see a "local" player in action can mean a six- to eight-hour trip.

Women's basketball at Southern New Hampshire University has not had such a winning history. Masi has begun with recruiting lists of around 400 since he arrived on campus. He targets the East Coast from Canada to the nation's capital. Though Southern New Hampshire's recruiting is still regionally-focused, the region covered is larger than that of many other programs. Masi hopes that the increased area of concentration gives him an edge recruiting-wise over opponents who may not venture beyond the Northeast.

Division II's Northern California Athletic Conference, to which Humboldt State formerly belonged, used to be the only nonscholarship conference in the country. Humboldt switched conferences and started offering scholarship money in 1998, and the program is still making the slow transition from a nonscholarship to a scholarship program. As they always have, Martin and assistant coach/interim head coach Carol Harrison still recruit regionally; most recruits hail from California, Oregon, and Washington. Even in-state prospects, however, often live quite far from Humboldt's hometown of Arcata. Also, since changing conferences, Humboldt has few in-state opponents. "The closest kids can come to watch us play is at

Humboldt, and that is many times 6-14 hours away from their home," explains Martin. Add the team's struggle to break .500 and its lack of full scholarships, and it's not hard to see why Martin and Harrison have a tough time attracting talent.

The Competition

Even for the winningest programs, recruiting in Division II can be difficult. The top Division I teams have only themselves to compete with for players. However, Division II still carries the reputation of being second best, the middleman. In recruiting, Division II institutions constantly fight to disspel that label.

"More and more, we recruit against the Division I schools," states Ruley. "The mid- to lower-major Division I schools recruit this area pretty heavily, so those are the schools, as well as our own conference schools. We feel like we kind of have an upper hand in the conference, but the Division I's are our biggest challenge." She believes that North Dakota State features the competition, reputation, following, and overall atmosphere of a Division I team, with the added bonus of vying for a national title — all of which she stresses in conversations with recruits.

Because they compete against two levels for talent, some Division II coaching staffs must almost do twice the recruiting work. Their lists are certainly larger. Stevens, for example, describes having around 50 names initially for four available slots. "After the first phone call you're probably down to a quarter of those," she explains. "There are a number of reasons why our list gets cut down very quickly. We're Division II, we're a business school, we're a small school."

Some approach their large lists systematically. "Our senior list can be over 100 at the beginning," comments Layman. "We basically do a tier grouping. Out of a 100, ideally we'd like to have the first 20 on our list. Any combination of that 20 would be great. Then you have a second tier, and so forth and so on. Because we're Division II, you not only do that top 20, you do the next twenty because those are the Division I kids that you're going after." Division II staffs drum their fingers while a prospect visits a Division I school, hoping that she chooses the better overall opportunity rather than the higher division. During that waiting period, if the coaches feel confident about their chances, they may put other recruiting efforts on hold.

Such was the case in 2000-2001 with Bentley, who had already signed three and needed one more. With the fourth, it came down to Bentley and a Division I school. After much debate, the prospect chose the Division I route. "That was a person that we had focused on, and we really thought we could get her. Then we had to start over again," says Stevens. "She wanted to take her game to another level — that's how she put it to me. I have a feeling she had her script written when she called me . . . I know it was very difficult for her, but she had people telling her that she was a Division I player. We fight that a lot. We fight the image of Division II a lot, that you're lesser."

Aside from the level of play, Division II colleges use other arguments to counter the Division I-is-best stereotype. "For kids who think they have to be Division I, we ask them, what are you looking for? What is that you feel that you will experience at the Division I level?" comments Naomi Stohlman, former North Dakota State recruiting coordinator. "They find out that we have some of those things that they think are just Division I. ... If they want to go Division I and play on a team that's like 4-20 but say they played Division I, maybe that's something that they like." Although the program always attracts athletes who initiate contact with them, the coaches still find themselves trying to convince a recruit to take away the I or II and choose the best situation for her personally.

If a program is not so winning, it may recruit against NCAA Division III or NAIA institutions. While Division II has the upper hand, it is not the ideal recruiting situation. Even though players may choose Division II over III, so-called Division III athletes may not help a program improve. "When I first got here, we were recruiting kids, and there were some Division III's involved," states Masi. "Now we're starting to recruit against some of the better schools here in the league. So we're starting to get in there with the Division II teams that we should. Division III, we're away from. For us to get to where we have

66

to go, we have to recruit kids who are Division I players. Some schools in our league get definitive Division I players. Others get the low Division I players who would rather play Division II and compete for the NCAA's than play low Division I and really have no shot."

At Humboldt State, Martin and Harrison must constantly replenish their roster, often needing to sign eight or nine for a single season. Ever since the school switched conferences, many signees play there for one year and transfer. For two years straight, the conference Freshman of the Year was a Humboldt athlete, and both of those players since transferred to full scholarship opportunities. "We don't seem to compete with our conference opponents because they're giving full rides and we're not going to even be in the same ballpark with those kids," says Martin. "We get their reject kids. We compete with some Division III and NAIA schools as well — more NAIA schools because they can give money out, whereas with Division III it's the academic end of things."

When recruiting girls who draw attention from different levels, Division II coaches have advantages and disadvantages. Perhaps the biggest advantage is that the NCAA allows Division II institutions unlimited evaluation of prospective student-athletes. On the other hand, they may not have as much scholarship money to offer as their recruiting opponents. More significantly, the division as a whole still is branded the "in between" division. This may change as more eminent high schoolers choose Division II over other opportunities.

Recruiting on a Budget

Since Division II recruiting concentrates more on the regional scene, coaches do not spend as much on recruiting travel as their DI counterparts. As with any level, the recruiting budget affects the success of the team, and vice versa. Some coaches see their budgets as quite adequate, while most others wish they could do more than their budget allows.

However, many also think that colleagues have much more money to spend on recruiting than they do. "They have an unlimited budget in a lot of those bigger schools, and they can run down to Kinko's and make up postcards and stuff with the kid's photo on it and say, 'Here's what you're going to look like in a team uniform,'" says former Southern New Hampshire assistant coach Chris Wood. "We can't even come close to that. Ours is much more of a personal approach, where we're selling people and the philosophy as opposed to the big bucks, here's where your locker is going to be and it's a solid oak locker and each locker has its own stereo and all that stuff." Masi adds, however, that while the recruiting budget at Southern New Hampshire is "not even close," the support from athletic administration pertaining to specific requests has been "fantastic."

"By far, our recruiting budget doesn't allow us to do what we need to do," asserts Martin. "It doesn't even scratch the surface of what we need to do, especially because of our location and because it's difficult to get people interested in coming here. This isn't the place people are going to think of to come. If we had to rely on kids who just were interested in Humboldt and happened to play basketball, our team wouldn't be very good. We're not very good right now, and we recruit kids to come here." Martin and Harrison only attend a few high school exposure tournaments in Oregon and California. Furthermore, recruiting budget increases require commitment from school administrators, who might be reluctant to pour money into an unsuccessful program.

Many thriving Division II teams, however, also see recruiting budget shortfalls. "My recruiting budget is not even close to adequate," says Kirkham, whose crew has captured several conference titles. "There are schools in our conference that have 10 times as much." Kirkham recruits out of his car, not a plane, and he and his staff do not go to nationally-known team and individual camps and tournaments. "Those kinds of kids we get after they find out they're not going big-time anyway," he continues. "The club coach will call me and say, this kid thought she was going to Santa Clara, and she was third on their list. They got their top two, and now she's looking for a place to play."

For the Division II upper echelon, community and athletic department support are usually strong, both in funding and spirit.

"North Dakota State is really good about making sure that we get the money that we need to recruit," states Layman. "As everybody knows, that's your bloodline. I think we're good in that respect — but we could always use more." North Dakota State has led the nation in Division II attendance for many years, and athletics get lots of media coverage. Stevens also has no complaints about her recruiting purse or team finances.

The money aspect of recruiting can be a vicious circle in all levels of women's college basketball, with Division II no exception. Winning squads are more likely to have higher recruiting budgets, so that they can maintain or increase their talent level. Although teams below .500 need funds to find the talent they need to improve their status, their coaches must first convince the higher-ups that recruiting is a worthy investment.

Involvement of High School and Club Coaches

In the Division II space, coaches do not always pursue relationships with both high school and club coaches in recruiting. Their recruiting has a more regional base, and club ball is more popular in certain states. While some talk to both high school and club coaches, others ask the student who she feels comfortable with, and still others sometimes deal only with the athlete. Although they do not attend as many summer games, Division II coaches have some of the same concerns about club hoops as their Division I counterparts.

Overall, Division II coaches see the high school coach as the primary contact in recruiting. Because coaches recruit student-athletes from surrounding regions, they see high school coaches more during the year, and the two develop more extensive relationships. They may also view high school coaches' roles as integral since many work full-time at the school. "If we have the opportunity, we will also try to talk to the club team coach, but we try to stay involved with the high school coach, number one," asserts Ruley. "High school coaches, in most cases, are part of the faculty. They know what these kids are like beyond their club experience."

Depending on a prospect's home state, Wood dealt with both high school and club coaches frequently. "In New Hampshire, the club circuit is not particularly strong, and it's almost always the high school coach who spends the majority of time with the student," he explains. "But in Maine and Massachusetts, it's almost all club coaches that we deal with. The high school coaches are very reluctant to take the time to talk in a lot of cases. The club coaches seem to have an unlimited phone bill."

The level of the player can also affect which coaches are involved. Many Division II coaches recognize that non-scholastic coaches now wield much influence. "I think you have to talk to the club coaches now because they are such a big part," says Layman. "I think your blue-chippers or your kids who are really good, who all of us are recruiting, the club coaches are really involved now. So if you don't go through them, you're probably not going to get that athlete."

Timing of the recruiting process and when an athlete makes her final decision also affect who takes part. Coaches may sign athletes whose high school coaches they never dealt with, or even sign athletes after talking only to the students themselves. "Some high school coaches of kids that are currently on our team, I've never met," says Stevens. "It's a situation in which we may have identified an individual from a club team, followed the club team, and spoken to the club coach frequently throughout the course of a spring and summer. We've then called the individual, had her on the campus unofficially in August, and then set up an official visit to have her. Really the kid has made her decision in early October, let's say."

Relationships also depend on the level of the college team. Programs that sign most recruits early do not need to talk as much to the high school coach, while those who depend on the late period do. One of the main reasons why college coaches contact high school and club coaches is to get their opinions of prospects' ability. However, they may not always trust that assessment, depending on the source. "It's harder and harder to find coaches who give you an honest evaluation," states Harrison. "There are exceptions to everything, but I find that high school coaches tend to be more honest about the kids than club coaches do."

Whether or not they consistently deal with club coaches,

most Division II coaches agree that the girls' basketball "off-season" deserves scrutiny. While important to the process in most cases in Division II, club basketball does not always work in the best interest of the player. "There are some excellent, excellent summer coaches," says Masi. "Then there are people who are out to say, 'I have four kids in Division I.' Some coaches will say, 'You know what, Coach, I'd like to see her go Division II...' Then there are some, I have been told by club coaches, 'Coach, don't even think about it. She's too good for you.'"

Once again, the clash between high school and club coaches sometimes surfaces. "We've had student-athletes that we've recruited tell us that their club coach told them basically to direct everything to them and not their high school coach," explains Ruley. One of the first questions some coaches ask athletes during that first phone call is not only her relationship with her high school and club coaches, but also the relationship between the two. "It's tough now because unfortunately a lot of the club coaches don't get along with a lot of the high school coaches," Masi explains. "I'm finding that a lot. What I do is when I introduce myself, I ask that question to the father or mother, whoever I'm talking to, plus the player."

Harrison had a taste of the sour side of the club scene in the late 1980s, when she was an assistant coach at an NCAA Division I school. A non-scholastic coach of an athlete who had had a great career at that college called her. "He wanted to see what we were going to chip in for the summer traveling program for his team," Harrison recounts. "I said, 'What are you talking about?' I was younger and dumber, and it wasn't that, it hadn't gotten that out of hand yet in women's sports. That was my first real look at, this is how it's going to go now. It's going to be not only the competition for them and what we can get but what we have to do on the side." These feelings, in part, led to Harrison's departure from Division I basketball.

The best approach in deciding who to deal with seems to be assessing the personality of the individual coach. "To be honest with you, there are a lot of good [club coaches]," Kirkham comments. "In the state of Colorado, I think we've got about five different teams. Four of them are great, and one of them's an

71

absolute user and abuser of young females. At the club level, sometimes it's about their ego and making some extra money, and I placed this kid over here and I placed this kid over here."

Even if they do not interact much with summer coaches, Division II coaches admit that they can exert much influence over an athlete. "You're traveling all over the country, and you're getting great exposure," says Layman. "Summer coaches are telling kids, 'I know this coach, this coach, this coach. I can help you get in.' Well, for an athlete who again doesn't know the rules, is uncomfortable with the situation, in fact it's all new for them, they're going to rely on somebody who can say, I can help you do this." But what is the true motivation for helping?

Many have seen summer girls' basketball evolving into more club coaches trying to serve as the primary recruiting contact. While this atmosphere is old news to boys' high school ball, it is still in its infancy on the girls' side. "There are some club coaches who are excellent, and then there are others who are using it for personal gain, for personal recognition," says Ruley. "That's what has caused probably some of the disappointment on the part of the recruiters, and probably with some of the kids. I think their job should be to help develop the skills and prepare the kids, but certainly not to serve as an agent for them." Truth be told, just about anyone can start a club team. While many summer coaches are skilled and knowledgeable, they may not need to go through a hiring process to start their own squads.

Most Division II coaches rely at least somewhat on the summer to recruit. Nonetheless, some believe that club ball and summer recruiting hurt the game. "Summer should be a time when kids get better on an individual basis — ballhandling, shooting," says Kirkham. "They don't need to be playing games. A lot of summer coaches do a great job, but they're not the majority. With a lot of them, those kids show up and they just play games. I watched some of these kids play in the summer, and they play fullcourt man-to-man, run-and-gun, all the time . . . Our system takes some different skills than you learn from just going up and down the floor and jacking shots. I watch a lot of them, and it's like, my God, these kids are not getting any better. They're not learning anything."

72

From college coaches' perspective, high school and club coaches should serve similar purposes in an athlete's recruiting process. Though a high school coach might know a recruit better as a complete person, both should be another source to provide college coaches information on a prospect. "If [the recruit] feels comfortable with the club coach, then maybe that's someone you need to communicate with more," states Stohlman. "Ideally, communicating with both people is important." If the rapport is not a close one, or if the college staff does not have full-time assistants, this could be difficult.

Challenges of Division II Recruiting

Aside from fighting the current image of Division II, coaches name several other issues as their biggest recruiting frustrations. Competing against Division I for talent, finding the time when they're part-timers, and losing a prospect when they know she will excel in their program also rank high on their lists of challenges. Nonetheless, most prefer the toned-down atmosphere of recruiting at their level to Division I.

Masi has found that other than the time commitment, recruiting has not been an insurmountable task. Prospective student-athletes and families do frequently ask about the program's record. The coaching staff responds that the team fell into a downturn, and now it's on its way back up. They move on as quickly as possible when asked that question, emphasizing the opportunity to be part of the rebuilding. "I stay away from the record," Masi says. "We're going to take care of you off the court. You're going to graduate. You're going to grow as a young woman. My first year, we had all these maybes, and I was sweating. One young lady just started the ball. She said, 'Coach, I want to play at New Hampshire College [the school changed its name to Southern New Hampshire University in 2001]. I want to be one of the players to get you back to where you're going.'" Once that first athlete committed, others followed. However, the coaches clearly have their recruiting work cut out for them for seasons to come.

"I think the hardest part of recruiting is dealing with kids who have a false hope fueled by a lot of attention from DI schools that really aren't interested in them," states Harrison.

"That's frustrating because they don't really want to give you the time of day and yet you know that this is where they're going to end up." Harrison has seen high schoolers faced with the DI-DII dilemma choose Division I and end up unhappy, complaining about their disappointing Division I experiences. In particular, she warns, Division I colleges that sign athletes late are looking simply for warm bodies to fill roster slots for a year, until somebody better comes along.

For schools like Humboldt, recruiting difficulties transcend the debate between Divisions I and II. "I think the toughest thing is that we're really honest about who we are and what we are, and yet the kids can't decide anything," says Martin. "They're 17- and 18-year-olds who have no idea what they're doing, and they can't set priorities. Sometimes you feel like even though you don't want to sell to them like a used car, you are because they can't make any decisions. Some of them can't even decide what pair of shoes they're going to wear today because they have too many choices."

More fundamentally, the most difficult part of recruiting can be its very nature as an imprecise process. Getting a handle on a player's potential, determining who will be a good fit with the program more than a year out, and examining an athlete's intangible qualities cannot necessarily be put to numbers on a list. "The thing that's stayed the same over the course of my career is just, given the limited opportunities, trying to evaluate the potential of a kid — not only her athletic potential but academically, and socially, how she's going to fit in," says Ruley.

"For me personally, the hardest part of recruiting is picking up the telephone and making that initial phone call to an individual that I've seen play," admits Stevens. "I can pretty much talk to anybody, but trying to just have a conversation with a 16-year-old at times can be very difficult. I mean I can do it and I do it, but I don't like it." While Stevens sees recruiting as a necessary part of her job, she would rather be planning or running practices. "I'd probably say that recruiting is my least favorite part of the job, period — all parts of it," she adds. Even after signees arrive on campus, coaches must still work to assess whether they really fit the program and the school.

Though some of the most trying challenges faced by Division II coaches in recruiting are the same for all collegiate levels, some specific difficulties exist as well. With the increased publicity and media attention of some Division II colleges, the stereotype may change over time. In all likelihood, the recruits themselves will alter the stigma. Hopefully for Division II coaches, as more so-called Division I prospects with the opportunity to play Division I basketball at a fairly high level opt instead for Division II, players and families alike will realize the merits of the in-between division.

A Changing Scene

While Division II colleges as a group have a way to go before convincing the general public that they are a legitimate competitive collegiate option, some media and many athletes and coaches have already caught on. Some successful Division II coaches have had opportunities to make the switch to Division I but have chosen to stay where they are. "Everyone says, 'Would you want to be a Division I coach?'" ponders Stevens, who actually does have experience at the DI level. "I never say never, but I don't know that I could get into that rat race of recruiting that they have to get into."

For North Dakota State, increased publicity has definitely had an impact on recruiting. "Probably the visibility of the athletes is what's changed the most," says Ruley. "Having the opportunity to play in a full house with local media attention, with television. All three major affiliates are in town, so they're covering our kids all week long, and they're at practices and the local newspapers and things are covering them." Young female athletes who grow up following local college hoops have seen the Bison on the tube many times before they reach recruiting age. When they begin thinking about colleges, they cannot help but consider the program they have followed on television and in the paper.

More choices for prospective student-athletes means more intense searching and consideration as well as increased chances for other parties to benefit. "I think that women have gotten much more intelligent in the fact that they know there's a ton of opportunities for them, so they shop a little bit more," Layman muses. "They're a little bit more cautious and want to look at everything first. I think it's becoming more market-oriented as well. What I mean is, the kids have a lot more opportunities, but yet there are other people who are getting their hands into it who are trying to market those athletes. I don't know if that's necessarily a good thing. I don't think it is."

Whether this tendency mirrors society as a whole, it does seem to mirror that of men's college basketball. Division II coaches can see women's college recruiting heading in the same direction of the men, though the two are not nearly on the same level. "It's never been good for the men, and I don't really think it's good for the women, and I think we're heading that way," says Layman. "It's nothing bad about summer coaches or anything like that, but now you add them into the mix along with the high school coach and the parents, and you now have a lot of different factors that go into effect. Sometimes I think that muddies the water for the athlete."

Some see the negative aspects of the women's recruiting environment as a likely and inevitable unfortunate progression of events. "It's no different than the men's. It's just that the women's programs aren't looked at as much, I think," Martin states. "All the problems that the men have had, the women are now having, no matter whether it's recruiting or violations. It's around the corner — it's happening now. There's no way of preventing that from happening. It's too competitive."

Martin, who also coached in NCAA Division I, adds that girls themselves have picked up on attitudes and behaviors they have seen elsewhere. "You look at the athletes, and the athletes are doing the same thing," she continues. "It's what are you going to give me, what are you going to give me, you owe me. If you are looking at 15-20 years ago, that attitude wasn't there, and it is certainly here now. It starts out at an early age for the men, and it's starting to get earlier for the women. Everyone's competing for them, and it sets up naturally. The kids think, you really need me, and what are you going to do to convince me to do this? It's just the path you go down when you treat students like they're God." Especially when the recruiting situation is extremely competitive, coaches feel that they must also constantly compliment prospects in order to keep up with colleagues. As with other levels, Division II recruiting has grown in both positive and negative manners.

Coaches' Advice to Recruits and Families

"Be patient and really research your options" is Stohlman's advice to high schoolers looking to play in college. These words of caution can be difficult for a student-athlete to follow in an atmosphere that may include demands from Division I and Division II coaches, especially when girls feel pressure to make decisions earlier and earlier each year. To do things right, athletes must begin their college searches earlier than junior year.

Although the stress level in Division II recruiting typically falls down a notch from that of Division I, the process is far from easy. Athletes can alleviate some of the anxiety by determining which division suits them. One of the best ways to do this is by watching college games and practices at all different levels, in person and anonymously. "Go to your local JC, go to your local four-year school," advises Harrison. "Then go to the big-time scholarship school. Sit down, walk down there at floor level and look at those people. Go with your high school coach." Prepsters should bring their analytical hats with them when they watch these matchups. High school and/or club coaches can help, provided that they try hard to take an objective viewpoint. "Let's be realistic," continues Harrison. "I think a lot of players, they watch Connecticut or Tennessee on TV. You can't get an appreciation for how athletic and explosive and big those people are because the Tennessee person's against the Connecticut person. Going to camp is great because you get to see them and kind of play pickup with them, but not everybody can afford that." Watching a team in action, especially during practice, also gives a better sense of the coaching staff's personality, which may not always be evident in visits when they wear their best recruiting faces.

"I've had kids in my program who have even said to me, 'Could you yell at me more? I need to be yelled at more.' Or, 'I need a little more positive reinforcement, or I need, I need . . .'

which is fine," says Stevens. "But you've got to know that before you get yourself involved in a situation in which . . . I'm who I am. I have my style. Then all of a sudden you're like, well, I can't really play for this person because this isn't what motivates me, or this is intimidating to me. You shouldn't be in a situation where all of a sudden, you're like, wow, I didn't know she threw chairs, or wow, I didn't know we were going to run until we dropped. You should know as much as you can about what you're getting yourself into, both ways. If you don't, then shame on either side for not doing the work that they needed to do, because it's four years of your life. Yes, you can make a mistake and transfer and go someplace else, but it's not usually a happy process."

Researching people, teams, and colleges early on also proves essential to a smooth-as-possible process. Those who wait until the first day of calling will be at a disadvantage. "Go look during your summer before your junior year, and take a look at campuses," Layman encourages. "Go and kind of surprise the coach and visit with them. Really check it out prior to getting inundated by phone calls. Then students can say, 'No I'm not interested in your program,' or 'Yes, I am.' They can take some of the pressure that's going to be out there, off themselves." Even prior to visiting campuses, though, athletes and families should narrow down their lists to 10 or 15 colleges that they already have boned up on. As sophomores, they can create lists of qualities they want in a college and find some that fit the bill.

Watching college teams practice and compete requires high school athletes to take charge of their own recruiting. They should not be afraid to pick up the phone and call coaches, to self-promote. "If you really want to play, there's a place for you," states Kirkham. "You've got to be able to market yourself. So put together a videotape, put together a one-page résumé. Identify some schools that you're interested in. You might try to find out if any of those coaches would talk to you and not lie to you about where you can play. Don't be afraid to call coaches. You'll know if it's a coach you want to play for in the first conversation." If the coach genuinely seems interested in the recruit's welfare, he or she is worth talking to. Even if it is not a match, the athlete will learn about how the process works. She will be that much closer to identifying her ideal type of college and program.

Talking to those not involved with the team can also be helpful in decision-making. If you ask the custodian who cleans the locker room what the attitude of the coach is after a win or a loss, you're going to find out because they've got no reason not to tell you," says Wood. "If you just sit back and let people tell you what you want to hear, that's not a very good way to base your decision." The benefits of speaking with those behind the scenes do not just apply to finding out a coach's character, but to determining a good overall fit. If a student-athlete and her family spend time examining what type of environment she will thrive in, on and off the court, she is more likely to have a happy, productive, and fulfilling college experience, academically and socially as well as athletically.

These coaches also encourage student-athletes to keep their options open, from the day they begin to think about which level will suit them to the day they make a commitment. "You don't know what's going to happen," says Masi. "You may change your mind. OK, I don't want to sit on the bench in Division I. I want to play. I know a lot of kids who have slammed the door on Division II and later are trying to open those doors." Masi also advises student-athletes to accept help from current coaches but to make their own decisions. Just because a high school or club coach knows basketball does not mean that he or she knows which college program would best suit a particular player. "Be honest, but take more upon yourself," he adds. "Don't rely on club coaches and high school coaches, because I have seen both drop the ball. Sometimes they're more favored — I like you so I'm going to work harder for you than you. It's not the case if you send *me* a tape, and I like you. I'm now going to follow up. You don't need a coach or anybody to do that. Listen to what your club coaches and high school coaches say, but ultimately listen to yourself."

Awareness of what it means to be recruited in the first place also is an issue in Division II, as it is in any division. Coaches see the problem of athletes believing that they are being re-cruited, or recruited for a scholarship, when that is not the case. "A lot of people get roped into thinking they're being recruited, and they're not," comments Martin. "We've heard some stories from some of the kids that we're recruiting about some of the schools in our conference. All of a sudden they're saying they're talking about money, and then when it really comes down to it, they're really not talking about money. But that's the kid's perception of what's going on, too.

"You need to ask the hard questions of the coach," Martin continues. "Then you know if they're stumbling around those answers. You know whether or not it's really an honest an-swer. You're looking at so many guards — well, where am I in your guards, and are you looking at me for money? A lot of kids assume because someone's contacted them and is recruit-ing them that they're talking about money, and it may not be."

While the rules, competition, and atmosphere may be some-what different in Division II recruiting, the basic tenets for navi-gating the process successfully are the same as Division I. Do your research ahead of time, ask tough questions, carefully consider the responses, and decide what is best for you as an individual. In an ideal world, college coaches will be direct about full, partial, and nonscholarship aid opportunities. Still, if the coach does not provide exact information, the impetus comes back to the prospective student-athlete and her family.

4

The Waiters: NCAA Division III Coaches

Though Division III institutions have the reputation of lower-key athletics, the competitive atmosphere of women's basketball has filtered to all levels. Even when no scholarship money is up for grabs, Division III recruiting can be high-octane, as can its coaches. Tammy Metcalf-Filzen, head coach at Minnesota's Carleton College, once heard about an incident concerning a coach in her conference from another in-conference coach. "A coach in our conference brought three successive athletes on campus and promised each of them that they would get 40 percent of the offense if they came to that institution," she relates. ". . . One of them ended up going there, and there's no way she had 40 percent of their offense. In fact, that was a kind of running joke between my assistant and I. We would say, do you think she had 40 percent today? I don't think so."

■ ■ ■

Many NCAA Division I and II colleges have a hard time recruiting student-athletes. Even with scholarships to offer, they still find it tough to fill their slots with quality players who will come together in a cohesive team unit. Consider, then, the realities of NCAA Division III recruiting. Coaches have no athletic scholarship money at their disposal. As a result, their bargaining points to prospects and families are that the financial investments will pay off in a positive and meaningful basketball experience, strong relationships with students and staff at the school, and a sound education that will prepare them for a successful future. They might even have a little bit of a life.

Despite its nonscholarship status, Division III recruiting can still be intense. While coaches have much less restriction from rules, they also have fewer staff, smaller budgets, and often other responsibilities at the school aside from coaching basketball. Some head coaches are not even full-time staff members themselves. Perhaps most significantly, in recruiting, they kneel at the mercy of their admissions and financial aid offices. As a result, the timeline for recruiting in Division III is different. Although coaches still evaluate high school talent during their own seasons and during the summer, their recruits usually make decisions in the spring rather than the fall. However, as there is no Letter of Intent, no official, binding paperwork, coaches never really know for sure who their incoming freshmen are until players arrive on campus for the fall semester.

Julie Goodenough, head coach at Texas' Hardin-Simmons College, estimates that "nationwide probably half of the Division III schools have full-time or part-time assistants, and the other half don't." Goodenough, whose squad advanced to the 2000 Elite Eight and 2001 Sweet Sixteen, has two graduate assistant coaches. Of the 16 teams in her conference, she guesses that 10 have full- or part-time assistants. At George Fox University in Oregon, also nationally-ranked in women's hoops, head coach Scott Rueck has two part-time assistants. Metcalf-Filzen has two part-time assistants and one student assistant at Carleton, a perennial conference champion. Finally, at Washington University of St. Louis, whose squad brought home four national titles in a row from 1997-2001, head coach Nancy Fahey does have a full-time assistant as well as two part-time assistants. Steve Cohran, Fahey's full-timer, handles many of the recruiting duties.

Having a full-time assistant coach is more the exception than the norm. That usually leaves the head coach in charge of recruiting as well as coaching current players, with additional duties at the school such as teaching classes or assisting in an-

82

other sport. For example, basketball is considered 65 percent of the position for Metcalf-Filzen, who also teaches physical education.

"The biggest difference between us and a Division I school is that they get to go out and evaluate their kids in the summertime maybe five, six, seven times. If we're lucky, we get to see them once or twice," says Cochran. Technically, Division III coaches could observe prospects an unlimited number of times throughout the year without breaking any rules. However, few even get on a plane to recruit because of staffing and budgetary issues. "A lot of kids we don't see except on film," Cochran continues. "We do get a lot of films and phone calls about kids. Lately, it has turned out really well that way. The kids who, let's say for example, they are doing their research and looking for a school, and they send us information. That's how we got Alia Fischer, who was our three-time National Player of the Year."[1] And yes, Washington University is one of the rare Division III gems that recruit against Division I for players. For the rest of Division III, recruiting competition typically includes conference opponents, and perhaps some NCAA Division II's, NAIA schools, and junior colleges, depending on location.

Recruiting in the Nonscholarship World

Most coaches in NCAA Division I and II, as well as some in junior colleges and the NAIA, have something tangible to offer prospects. While trying to convince players that their teams are the best fit, they are often offering a free or partially-paid college education in exchange for four or more years of dedication to basketball at the school. The player gives her time and effort, and the program gives targeted money. It is in essence an employer-employee relationship, except that the employees' pay must go toward schooling. Keeping with this train of thought, Division III coaches could be considered employers at volunteer organizations.

---

1. Fischer earned Women's Basketball Coaches Association Division III Player of the Year honors in 1998, 1999, and 2000.

How do Division III coaches recruit athletes with no scholarships to offer? "You have to sell yourself as a coach, and you have to sell your program and your school," states Rueck. "We've gotten a couple kids who have gotten a lot of looks from the DI and DII's." Rueck also emphasizes the big-time atmosphere at George Fox, where women's basketball attendance is third in Oregon, bettered only by NCAA Division I Oregon and Oregon State. "We outdrew Portland State [NCAA Division I], Portland [NCAA Division I], Western Oregon [NCAA Division II], Southern Oregon [NAIA], we outdrew everybody," he continues. "The atmosphere of our games is unbelievable for a DIII school. That is a big advantage, plus the opportunity to play potentially for a national championship."

The academic factor often looms large in the Division III recruiting picture. When up against scholarship programs, coaches focus on an investment in the future and solid preparation for a successful career after basketball. Many recruits have already heard of the colleges for their academic prowess. "Sometimes we do compete against Division II schools," says Metcalf-Filzen. "One of the things that we try to do is give the players a vision of, where do you want to be 10 years from now? Especially if our students are geared toward something that will require graduate school, that really does help. For example, we had a student who had a significant scholarship at a Division II institution, and she wants to be an orthopedist . . . So we really try to sell the academic piece in that sense . . . You can get into medical schools from Carleton with a 3.5 because it is such a regarded institution. You might go somewhere else and come out with a 4.0 and never get in.

"We were recruiting a player," continues Metcalf-Filzen, "and her mom asked me, 'Why should I send my daughter there at $30,000 a year when she doesn't know what she wants to do?' My job was to try to sell that and say, 'That's precisely why she should be here because all of these doors are possibilities for her.'"

The NCAA estimates that 3.1 percent of high school athletes play women's NCAA basketball and .02 percent of high school athletes go on to play professionally. Despite these numbers, with the success and prominence of the WNBA, even Division III prospects talk of playing pro. Fahey, for example, has heard these comments from recruits, that Division III ball will not give them the exposure that they need to make it to the pros. It's her job to bring these young women back down to earth.

Instead of convincing players to spend countless hours on basketball in return for a paid-for college education, Division III coaches must tell athletes what they're going to get for their money. "I think the biggest thing is, when we talk, we talk a lot about what the investment is," comments Fahey. "Is it a four-year investment? We consider ourselves a four-year plus investment. Basketball, eventually, you have to look beyond the next four years and what it's going to do for you. We talk a lot about that. We also talk about their college experience. Division I, I played it, and there's nothing wrong with it, but it can be a different college experience. We try to really talk about the total college experience, not only school and basketball, but there is another aspect that you don't want to miss out on. At the same time . . . we compete at a level that we may not win one again, but we have been competing at that level, the national championship level. There is that opportunity, at least, to do that, versus other situations perhaps. I think the biggest thing we do play on, though, is their futures."

Academics and careers aside, coaches also stress influence on the program when talking to girls and their parents. "It's very hard to recruit against schools that can offer scholarships," admits Goodenough. "Here, even if you get the maximum financial aid package, they still have to pay something to come to school here. And the junior colleges around, if they are recruiting a kid, normally we are not going to get them because they are going to go there on a full ride. The Division II schools that we recruit against, often times we will get those kids because they are just going to get their books paid for or something at a Division II, and they're probably not going to get to play much, whereas they could come here and make an immediate impact." Like Division II coaches recruiting against Division I, Division III coaches can play the trump card of the opportunity to come in right away and get quality minutes. This perspective can make a difference with athletes not used to riding the pine.

Once again the definition of recruiting as finding the right match between player and school comes into play. "We try to talk to the kids about two things," explains Cochran. "One, throw the Division Is, IIs, IIIs out of it and say, what's the best fit for you? Where do you fit in best? What are you looking for in a school? We approach it that way." However, Cochran also focuses on the fact that his program differs from many Division IIIs in both its level of play and its Division I-type atmosphere. "We're in a unique situation that we have a lot of flavor of a Division I," he adds. "We fly all over the East Coast playing games. That gives them a flavor of Division I. If you talk to some other Division III schools, they don't have the opportunities that we have where they're flying all over. I think that makes a difference." Winning four national titles also makes a difference.

Not only do Division III coaches have to recruit without scholarship money, they must wait until spring for a prospective student-athlete's admissions and financial aid packages to come through. This can be exasperating, especially when the applicant's other choices are Division I and/or II institutions, perhaps pressuring her to make a decision in the fall. However, as Rueck assures, "I really am sold on DIII with the exception of maybe that whole process, waiting for financial aid." By its very nature of being nonscholarship, Division III possesses a different team dynamic. "I like the fact that we don't give scholarships because I have to treat that student with respect," Rueck states, "and I believe that it develops proper relationships between player and coach. If I don't treat that player with respect, she's gone. So I feel that it gives them the best environment to play in." Nonetheless, especially with the cost of a small private college education skyrocketing, Division III coaches can find themselves powerless at the mercy of financial aid offices and of families seeking free college educations.

Academics, Admissions and Financial Aid Influences on DIII Recruiting

In Division III recruiting, academics first is often the mantra. With the strict grade and test score requirements for admission at many Division III schools, the academic factor alone can narrow a coach's prospect list right at the beginning. Although a high school player can be a wonderful person and athlete, a perfect fit for a program, her transcript must be up to snuff as well.

Because of the lack of a National Letter of Intent and the necessity to wait for admissions and financial aid decisions, Division III's recruiting schedule differs greatly from that of Divisions I and II. A coach could be the best recruiter in the world and could have convinced a top prospect that this is the place for her. However, those efforts will prove in vain if the prospect does not get into the college or if her financial aid package is not sufficient.

According to NCAA regulations, Division III coaches cannot have any influence whatsoever on an applicant's admission or financial aid package. The most that the NCAA allows them to do is check with university officials to see whether a student's application for admission or financial aid is complete. "It's kind of a frustrating process for everybody because we don't control the finances," states Rueck. "It's totally out of my hands. I have no idea what's going to go out to the kid, and a lot of times they will know before I do. So I'm at the mercy of our financial aid office. I don't know what their parents make, I don't know what their taxes look like, and so I don't know what their financial aid package will be, completely. That's frustrating for me.

"The time frame is frustrating for the students," Rueck continues. "Let's say they're applying to George Fox, Pacific, Winfield — they have to get all those packages back before they can make a decision. Then if you're doing what I'm doing, which is trying to get these kids that are being recruited by higher-level programs, DI, DII schools, they put deadlines on them. I'm at the mercy of financial aid and how they process, and they're supposed to be treated like any other kid and they are. They're in that process where they could be buried under a hundred different kids, so it's not going to be two weeks until they can get to your stuff. Well, Western Oregon needs to know if I want that scholarship, by Saturday. That's a tough spot to be in. Where does that put us? Just the fact that it's not a full ride and there is going to be some financial commitment, that's stressful in itself."

Although some acknowledge that they have heard of Division III programs wielding more influence than they should in the admissions and financial aid processes, no specifics bubble to the surface. In 2001, the NCAA's Division III committee adopted a bylaw that in part reinforces the idea of providing aid to athletes and non-athletes in a consistent manner. Athletes and non-athletes admitted to a school must have the same range of test scores, receive the same financial aid in similar circumstances, and so on. As of winter 2001, a proposal on the table would require Division III athletics programs to hire an outside party to perform an audit of their financial aid processes every year.

"I wish we had some interaction with financial aid, but we really don't," Cochran comments. "They turn in the paperwork to financial aid, and we're pretty much totally out of that loop. Let's say, for example, if they see that the kid's a women's basketball player, something, a football player, they could call us up and say, 'Hey Steve, such-and-such doesn't have all of her forms in for financial aid. Can you call her and tell her to send in the forms?' That kind of communication takes place. Same way with admissions." It still behooves Division III coaches, then, to become friendly with the admissions and financial aid offices at their institutions, to make sure those lines of communication stay open.

Coaches cannot tell admissions or financial aid officers that they must admit a certain individual or that they must grant her a certain financial package. However, this does not mean that coaches do not frequent those two offices. "We have very open communication between admissions and our program," explains Metcalf-Filzen. "I have one or two people that I connect with there. We are able to provide information regarding the student-athletes and how we see that they would impact our program, those kinds of things, but that is just part of their file that helps to make the decision. Ultimately, if they're not academically qualified, they're not going to get in."

"Admissions knows who my top 10 are," adds Rueck.

For some, financial aid requirements, restrictions, and protocol often turn out to be the highest recruiting hurdle. "My biggest challenge is that at Carleton, every bit of our aid is based on financial aid," says Metcalf-Filzen. "We have no funny money. We don't have presidential scholarships, we don't have anything. So when I go to recruit against other programs, and other programs in our conference, they have presidential scholarships so they are bringing a kid in who meets a certain standard. Maybe it's a kid who gets a 25 on the ACT. They can automatically give them $10,000 when they walk on campus. We can't do that . . . Ours is strictly need-based, and in that sense, it doesn't feel like a level playing field." It will be interesting to see what impact the proposed financial aid auditing system has on NCAA Division III athletics.

The most that many coaches do once students have sent in their applications is sit and wait, while talking to admissions and financial aid officials as often as they can without making enemies. "As far as the financial aid part," Goodenough muses, "I will go over and the give them a list of my kids and say, 'have you been able to package her award letter yet?' I just try to keep my players' names in front of them all of the time, so they will package their letters and I will quit bothering them." Coaches try to make sure not only that recruits have completed all necessary forms but also that university workers keep up with their own paperwork. However, many coaches still give admissions and financial aid their lists of recruits so that they can be notified if something is missing from an application. Even if they have not been overtly pressured, officials nonetheless have those names in front of them when reviewing applications.

A Different Timeline

Division III coaches' recruiting hinges on May and April. They could be jetting off to high school and club games and calling girls' homes every day until they make their decisions. However, they do not, for three main reasons. One, their budgets restrict many to analyzing via videotape. Two, their staffs, most of which are part-time, cannot handle the workload. Three, most seem to realize that some of the recruiting rules imposed on Division I and/or II coaches make sense for them, as well — for the prospective student-athletes' sake.

Budgetary constraints limit many to focusing their recruiting regionally or locally. "The summers for us are . . . getting out to recruiting camps, showcases and stuff, pretty much in our area," says Metcalf-Filzen. "We have a Minnesota elite camp that we hit. Otherwise, Wisconsin has a couple of club tournaments." This summer scenario may change as Carleton College has begun to draw more national interest. However, in that case Metcalf-Filzen would need to make up elsewhere in her basketball budget for increased recruiting expenses.

For Rueck, whose recruiting is regional as well, summer recruiting means attending one large team tournament in Oregon. "Because that tournament comes to us every year, I can pretty much do what I need to do," he comments. "I don't know that I'd do much more."

Partly because of money, recruiting is much more localized even for some top teams. At Hardin-Simmons, most of the squad hails from a 200-mile radius. Goodenough relies on the phone and e-mail in addition to a mass mailing for recruiting contact. Her recruiting travels consist of watching tournaments on several summer weekends. "During the summer, with the national AAU tournaments, BCI, that sort of thing, unless they are in Texas I probably would not attend because of financial reasons," she adds. "I think it would be helpful to be able to do that. We get postcards from kids a lot, saying, 'I'm going to be playing in Colorado Springs in July and would like for you to come' or whenever. Financially, I am just unable to do that." During her own season, she does not venture out to watch games often, instead sending her grad assistants to contests close by.

Fahey and Cochran get out quite a bit during the summer, seemingly more so than many of their Division III colleagues but not as much as some of their other recruiting competition. "It would be nice to travel more, but I don't feel held back," says Fahey. "For Division III we're actually in a good situation. So in comparison to Division I, yes, I do feel held back, but in reality, we're in a good situation . . . I certainly wouldn't suggest that this place is holding me back. It's quite the opposite." The Washington University staff travels as far away as the July AAU national tourney, held on the East Coast.

One advantage Division III coaches do have in recruiting is the absence of quiet and dead periods. They often encourage recruits to visit their campuses in August, before the back-to-school rush begins. In this way, in addition to the fact that they may speak with players and parents when out watching them play, some feel that they can develop more of a personal relationship with prospects.

"I think recruiting is different for different Division III institutions," acknowledges Metcalf-Filzen, who says she calls recruits less than once a week. "I talk to other coaches in our conference who are calling kids, or I talk to kids that we're recruiting and, coaches from our conference are calling very frequently. Once a week regularly, that kind of thing. Especially the student-athletes that we've gotten, we kind of talk through and debrief them on the recruiting process once we have them, not specifics but in general what was your feeling? One of the things that they say to us is, we like the fact that you didn't call us all the time."

Division III coaches do not do home visits, they rarely board a plane when recruiting, and they watch a lot of video. Many must balance recruiting with other non-basketball duties at their schools or elsewhere. Budgets limit their recruiting areas, and they can feel immobilized during the admissions and financial aid processes. What's more, Division III is not best known for its athletic prowess, and many of its institutions are smaller and more specialized academically. The result is a recruiting atmosphere that may not be as stressful overall but that can be every bit as exasperating for coaches.

Student-Athletes' Knowledge of the Rules

While Division I and II coaches find that many prospects are uniformed about some of the most important NCAA recruiting regulations, Division III coaches observe a different problem. Some prospective student-athletes assume that the rules they have learned apply to all three divisions. Therefore, students think that Division III coaches violate the rules when they call them more than once a week or approach them after their games.

A few have even turned in coaches for recruiting actions that are not violations in Division III. "We have to do a lot more educating because it's different," Fahey admits. "We'll try to talk to someone, and she'll go, 'Well isn't this a quiet period?' We'll say, 'No, we don't have that.' We have to educate them more that we're not doing anything illegal. Somebody reported us one time, and we're like, we can do that. They're not used to seeing Division III out there, so we have to educate even some other coaches."

While she feels that in general students and families are knowledgeable, Goodenough adds that many do not realize certain other Division III distinctions. "A lot of the kids that we recruit don't realize that we don't need them to register with the Clearinghouse," she states. "For our situation, I think it's just difficult recruiting against scholarship schools that are right in our area. But rules and everything, I feel like we have so much freedom with recruiting." Many DIII coaching staffs do not have the resources to do things that would prompt a more complex system of rules.

Some of Division III prospects' confusion may stem from the fact that for many high school athletes of every skill level, Division I is all that they focus on. "Kids that are looking to be recruited, many of them are looking to be recruited at the Division I level," says Metcalf-Filzen, who also served as an assistant at the Division I level. "At that level, there are so many rules, that I don't know how anybody [remembers all of this] . . . We used to take tests on that stuff. People still claimed ignorance. I just think it's a lot for a high school athlete to take in, and so there are times when they will assume that Division III is under the same rules as Division I. I still do that occasionally. I'm thinking, wait a minute now, can I send out a multi-colored . . . and I go through this whole thing, and then I go, there's no rule there for us." As with most recruited athletes, many Division III prospects rely on college coaches to know the regulations.

In some areas of the country where Division III ball is not as prevalent, coaches have had to correct some major misconceptions, beginning with the fact that not every college recruiter has athletic scholarships to offer. "That has been a little bit tough to educate parents on, that this isn't that different of a thing, a student loan isn't the end of the world," explains Rueck. "'It's 20-what? It's $20,000? We need a scholarship. Your daughter's going to qualify for a scholarship." According to Rueck, it's up to the high schools to bridge that knowledge gap for high school student-athletes.

High School and Club Coaches

In Division I recruiting, and many times in Division II, club ball is a major component. However, Division III coaches tend to deal more with high school than club coaches in recruiting if the two are different people. Many Division III coaches do not spend June and July watching countless games, where they might have conversations with non-scholastic coaches. Many log the bulk of their recruiting conversations during the academic year, when contact with the high school coach seems more logical. Still others who have initiated contact with club coaches have been shunned, due to the stigma of Division III as not good enough for a certain summer coach's players.

The preceding scene has even occurred at Washington University, which is about as high-level Division III as it goes. "We will talk to some club coaches, and they go 'Oh, DIII,' and they kind of go, and you're like wait a minute," comments Fahey. "That makes it a little difficult on us because you have to go through the explanation of, 'Do you know this player?' We have recruited her. And they go, 'Oh, really?' So we have to do some more educating ourselves." Only when she convinces the coach that she attracts good players does she become worthy of his or her time. Cochran does always try to talk with both the high school and club coach of a prospect. When you compete with scholarship schools for players, the summer period becomes that much more important.

Prep-level coaches who have been through recruiting with other players, perhaps at Division I or II, may not give their all to help their athletes find suitable Division III programs. "The kind of kids that we're looking at, often times our players don't want the club coaches involved, or they'll give me information and I'll call and visit with them," says Metcalf-Filzen, who deals more frequently with high school coaches. "But the club coaches don't see this kid as being a kid who's going to go Division I or that kind of thing, so it's a little bit more low-key. I think that club coaches are out there pitching those kids who are going to get the high-profile scholarship kinds of stuff. I do think there are club coaches that are really in the experience because of the kids, and they believe in the kids, and they are looking for the best place for them. I think that there are definitely people like that out there. I just think they kind of get lost, for the more aggressive, verbose kind of people who just want to see their kids go into Division I.

"That's the same way with the high school coaches, sometimes at the expense of the kid," continues Metcalf-Filzen. "I can say I sent three of my kids to Division I, but they might be in Left Overshoe whatever on a $500 per year scholarship and sitting on a bench and never playing, where they could have been an outstanding player at the Division II or Division III level." Division III coaches play off that last scenario when talking to athletes with several collegiate options.

For some of these reasons, and because of the setup of the recruiting schedule itself, many Division III coaches do not contact club coaches. "When I am recruiting someone, I usually do not talk to the club coaches unless they call me," says Goodenough. "I usually don't get many calls from club coaches, unless they're calling about their daughters."

Advice for the Consumers

Aside from making informed decisions, Division III coaches encourage prospects and their families to remain open to the possibility of college basketball at any level, and to make sure they ask detailed questions about the school's academics. Once they explore all areas of college life, they may find Division III to be a positive and workable option, despite the seemingly steep price tag.

"Keep open the options to every level," Rueck says. "Of course I would say that, but there are a lot of things at DI that aren't a lot of fun. A lot of kids go that route and say, man, this wasn't what I thought it was. You hear those stories all the time, and the longer I've been around now, I hear them more and more. One example is a kid I did a home visit with that the University of Portland was looking at. Well, they called her and yanked her scholarship and their offer. There's all kinds of things like that, and don't shut the door on a level because you think you're better." Recruits who rejected Division III coaches 10 months prior could find themselves seeking out those very same coaches later.

Although they must be proactive in recruiting by marketing themselves, students and families also need to recognize the important role of the high school coach. "I would strongly recommend for the parents not to get involved with selling their daughters and calling and sending all of the newspaper articles out to coaches and that kind of thing," Goodenough states. "I think high school coaches are probably the best resource as far as recommending a player to a college coach. I would put more clout with the high school coach than with what someone's dad says. The parents are great, [but] I think the coaches are going to be a little bit more honest with you about the player, and that is the relationship that I am more interested in, not that dad-daughter relationship but the player-coach relationship and how this player has worked for this coach."

No scholarships means somewhat of a recruiting power shift. Unless they receive significant academic or need-based aid, student-athletes basically pay to play in Division III, and they should not hesitate to ask any question at all. As with any major purchase, they and their families want to make sure that they make the best possible decision about where to spend that college money. "The thing that I would say to high school student-athletes is, understand that you are the consumer here," says Metcalf-Filzen. "They are in the driver's seat. Don't be afraid to ask very specific, very probing questions. How many students from your school apply and go on to medical school, and what is your acceptance rate? Or, I see that you bring in 30 kids a year, and you don't have any seniors on your roster, and only one junior. Where are those kids? Stuff like that.

"I can see it when they sit in my office," Metcalf-Filzen adds. "It's like they're waiting for me to give them the information, which is very much the case, but they are the ones making the decision. I tell them that there is not a question you cannot ask me. In fact, if you don't know what to ask, let me give you a list of questions. These are questions that you should ask me but that you should also ask every other coach that you're talking to. They should be able to answer this because this is an investment — at least at our level it is." Not only is the monetary investment often large, the promise to invest time and effort in basketball also deserves consideration. While athletes do not usually miss classes or have to enroll in summer school, many do lace up their kicks for several hours a day, six days a week. Division III basketball is a big-time commitment, and choosing the right program is a big-time decision.

5

Recruits' Point Of View:
High School Class of 2001

For the girls themselves, the college recruiting process is often overwhelming and unpredictable as well as just plain stressful. Researching schools, talking to coaches, and visiting campuses is quite an undertaking in and of itself, without the unexpected and embarrassing mishaps that may occur along the way. Duke University assistant coach Gale Valley remembers one such recent incident. "We had an unofficial visit, a junior, on campus," Valley says. "She ended up going to this anatomy class, so they had the bodies out there. She passed out in class. She was pretty mortified by it, but how she handled it was great. She was telling everybody all about it and everything like that. I guess that class wasn't a good one to take her to." In the anatomy of the recruiting process, this athlete had the right perspective of realizing that the unforeseen will happen and going with it.

■ ■ ■

Selecting a college will be the first major life decision for most recruited student-athletes. Many have made sacrifices for a whack at playing college ball. This could be their first serious encounter with adults outside of their families, some of whom they will have to disappoint. From the most highly-coveted recruit who sees her name up in lights on official visits, to the athlete choosing between Divisions I and II, to the Ivy League or Division III hopeful who was promised nothing more than a chance to compete for a spot on the roster, all of these teens enjoy the attention of being recruited — at first. As the process continues, the letters, phone calls, and praise become tiresome. For those considering scholarships, signing early becomes a priority.

What's more, female athletes may progress through high school with the belief that if they play well and get exposure, colleges will come to them. However, in an environment with more and more quality high school girls' basketball players, this may not happen. In the case of Chelsea Wagner, the 2001 *USA Today* Oregon Player of the Year and a *Street & Smith's* Honorable Mention All-American, what began with boxes of recruiting letters in her freshman and sophomore years led only to being all but passed by until the end of the late signing period, not to an early signing with her school of choice. "As an athlete, not only are the schools trying to sell themselves to you, you have to sell yourself to them," Wagner states. Aside from the top four or five players in the country, the Springfield High grad says, every prospect must promote herself.

For most everyone, what begins in excitement ends with anxiety and then relief, not necessarily relief about their choices but simply that the process is finished. However, it takes most at least a few years for them to determine whether they have made the right decisions.

The Club Scene

College coaches believe that summer basketball is important to the recruiting process. Club coaches certainly say so. Many parents consider it a worthwhile investment in the future. As for the players themselves, their specific reasons for participating may vary. However, they realize that in order to get a collegiate opportunity, they must get seen, and that club basketball is one grand avenue for exposure. Many female prepsters have caught on to this summer phenomenon, and summer opportunities for girls now abound.

"When I was in elementary school up until junior high, it was definitely that you are supposed to be playing on travel teams," says Azella Perryman, a two-time Alaska Player of the

Year from Anchorage's East High who signed with NCAA Division I Stanford University "This is what you need to do because this is what will get you better. I wasn't really enthusiastic about going, and I didn't raise any money for it. My parents paid for everything. When I got into high school, it was more, if you want a college scholarship, you're going to go out in the summer because that's the only way you're going to get one. Coach [Dorena] Bingham believed that, and she has been doing it for a long time." Bingham coached both Perryman's high school and travel teams and served as a crucial element in her exposure and recruiting. Furthermore, Perryman credits summer ball with the huge skills improvement she made between her freshman and sophomore years.

Participation in club basketball can depend on the sports culture of the player's town and region. 2001 Naismith National Player of the Year Shyra Ely, who began playing basketball as a fifth grader, joined her first club team the next year and continued through her junior year in high school. "When I was younger, I thought that that's what you were supposed to do is play AAU," the Indianapolis Ben Davis High alum states. "After you're out of the school season, you go play AAU. I think that's what you have to do if you want to continue to go at a higher level, do something to help your game in the summer . . . It's different from your high school team so you're not playing with the same people all the time, but people who are at the same level that you are." Ely's club squads advanced to the AAU Nationals and U.S. Junior Nationals, two of many college coaches' regular stops on their July circuits. However, Ely would not have gone unnoticed by college coaches even if she had played on a poor summer team. She signed with NCAA Division I University of Tennessee.

Some prospective student-athletes have heard the rumors of how girls' summer ball is following the course of boys'. They've heard about, or may have had, less-than-ethical girls' coaches who favor and do more to help certain players, on the court and in recruiting. "I was really against AAU in the beginning," comments Missy Traversi, whose three-year journey with club ball began her eighth grade year. "I had heard a lot of bad [things]. I don't mean to badmouth it, but it's very rare that I had heard of good AAU programs. There were so many different coaches out there who had different styles, and I wasn't really hearing positive things. I had the mentality like, OK, these kids are going to go to school, come home, go to practice for 4–5 hours, be exhausted, and eat, sleep, drink basketball. In a way, that's what I wanted — I wanted to be focused on basketball. But I didn't want it to get to the point where it wasn't fun for me." Traversi faced the NCAA Division I/Division II dilemma during her tenure at Attleboro (Mass.) High. She opted to go DI, choosing the University of Maine over Bentley College.

Not only does summer ball often require a time investment on the part of the athletes, participation can be quite pricey. Depending on the organization, the flat cost for tournament fees, uniforms, and travel may or may not be offset by fundraising and corporate donations. While some players compete for free, others pay upward of $2000 for one summer. Clovis, New Mexico, native and 2001 Gatorade New Mexico Player of the Year Cisti Greenwalt recalls the cost being as much as $1500 for one team, then substantially lower for her second team. "They have a booster club, people who give us money and stuff, and we didn't travel as much . . . "comments Greenwalt, who now plays for NCAA Division I Texas Tech University. Perryman was a fundraising dynamo one summer, selling more than $3000 worth of raffle tickets for her travel team. She covered her own expenses and helped out teammates as well. While NCAA Division I Duke University player and Holy Innocents Episcopal (Atlanta) grad Wynter Whitley remembers the cost being around $350 per summer, her mother says that she never paid to play. Ely always played for free as well.

The number of games played can jump as much as the cost. Hallie Belleau estimates having played in 25-30 games per summer, with a tournament every weekend; Belleau, who played for the outstanding Pickerington, Ohio program, was recruited by top NCAA Division III schools but ultimately decided not to compete in college. Abby Everitt, a Middlebury, Vermont, native who signed with Bentley College, guesses that she competed in 40-50 contests the summer between her junior and senior years of high school. However, the burnout factor never kicked in for her. "It was hard to say it was too many games because I had a lot of fun doing it," Everitt enthuses. "Being there and being with my team was a lot of fun, and you don't really think about it like oh, man, it's another game."

In the summer of 2000, Ely played half that many games in one week. "We went to Las Vegas, and myself, Ashley Allen [a former Ben Davis teammate who signed with Ohio State] and Jackie Batteast [a native of South Bend, Indiana, who signed with Notre Dame] played 24 games in one week, five days," she says. "At one time, we had five games in one day, and that was really tiring." Other than feeling fatigued that one day, Ely has nothing but positives to say about that summer team experience, when she was home for about three days total. "I think it was fun because I was playing basketball every day, but at the same time you miss home and you get a little homesick. I enjoyed it a lot." During that crucial summer recruiting period, Ely and teammates had plenty of opportunities to showcase their stuff in front of colleges, who had heard of them before.

While many club teams hold tryouts, some tryouts do not mean much. Sometimes everybody who shows up makes the team, and the coaches add teams to allow for increased participation. Other times coaches invite the best players in the state, or out-of-state, to "try out" and play on the team. "I never had to try out for any of the AAU teams — I was invited," says Ely. However, she adds that it was not only the chosen ones who played in her club organization. "During the year, we'll have open gyms where anybody can come and play who wants to play. If they want to play AAU, they can join a team. But so many people can be on a roster. If there are more, then he'll make two teams." Even if the coach does not exclude anyone from participating, he or she can certainly divide the teams up at will. The better the players, the farther they will advance and the more college exposure they will probably get.

However, there are exceptions to this theory. Wagner played on stellar club squads, especially during her junior year spring and the summer before her senior year. Oregonians Kara and Kim Braxton, both highly-touted recruits who signed with NCAA Division I Georgia, competed on her team. That crew captured the title at a national spring tourney in North Carolina, winning the championship game by 30 points. "We went to all of these tournaments," Wagner states. "Every summer, we went to, there's the Colorado Springs tournament, the Las Vegas tournament, the Oregon City tournament, and the Deep South Classic, and that San Francisco, the Bay tournament. Those were the major national tournaments, and every summer I was at at least one of them. Most of the time, two of them." However, her recruiting stock plummeted after her junior year, which still baffles her. When asked how she played that summer, she says, "I feel like I did OK . . . Obviously, I wish I could have played better at some of the tournaments, but for the most part I think I did well. I made tournament teams."

Club and high school coaches' involvement in a particular player's recruiting process depends on a number of factors. For example, Traversi's junior summer coach, who happened to be a former college coach, provided all of the advice and guidance that she needed. "[My high school coach] didn't play a big role because it was basically during the summer of my junior year where the coaches were really there," Traversi says. "He was only with me during the winter, so it was already done by then. They did talk to him, but that was about it." Everitt also relied heavily on her club coach's expertise. Ely, Belleau, and Stevenson High (Ill.) grad and NCAA Division I Depaul University athlete Jenni Dant, on the other hand, played high school ball for successful teams and experienced coaches, and those coaches tended to be more involved. While Greenwalt says that her high school coach was not closely involved, he attended all five of her home visits. According to Whitley, who verbally committed to Duke over the phone in July after her junior year, neither her high school nor her club coach played a large recruiting role. As for Perryman and Anne Schwieger, high school and summer coach were one and the same, both experienced in the recruiting realm. Schwieger played under

Tony Pappas at Waterloo, Iowa's West High and signed with NCAA Division I Ivy League Cornell University.

Then there's Wagner, for whom neither of her coaches factored heavily. "I don't want to bash [my high school coach] because I love him to death and I think he's a wonderful person and a great coach, but I don't think he knew really how to recruit me or any of my other teammates," she says. When no big-time NCAA Division I colleges came calling for her in the fall, she decided to really try to pick up her game and also market herself. During her senior year, she sent out packets to 30 schools, with stats updates as her season progressed. However, once the late signing period loomed in the near future, she contacted Oregon City High co-head coach Brad Smith, who she knew through different tournaments and players. Smith connected her with his coaching buddy, Oregon City's Carl Tinsley, who immediately made some calls. "By no means did I realize that he was going to pick up the phone and call schools," she comments. "Within two days, I had 15 schools." She had only wanted advice about how to contact colleges.

For girls serious about playing college basketball, summer means working on your game and getting college exposure. Many players attend camps run by universities or by camp companies, which can provide them a chance to improve their skills and to interact with college coaches and players. While colleges use summer camps partly as a recruiting tool, the tool of choice for student-athletes seems to be club ball. A successful summer can raise a prospective student-athlete's recruiting value exponentially. However, a sub-par summer can send it into a nose-dive. Hopefully, the dollars spent on non-scholastic basketball will pay off in a promising college opportunity, but if not, at least a fun few months.

On the Horn

The direct relationship between a recruitable student-athlete and a college coach often begins on the phone. The coach introduces himself or herself, attempts to establish a relationship, and may present an opportunity, all over the phone. A prospect may reveal her college decision over the phone as well.

The official recruiting process, in a sense, begins and ends over the phone line. What's more, the way in which a coach presents him or herself in those conversations could make or break the college's chances.

Many teenagers have trouble holding conversations with any adult, let alone a college basketball coach. However, many athletes do not really need to learn the art of conversing maturely with adults because the coaches do most of the talking. Whether long-winded or good listeners, coaches' true personalities seem to come through to the girls during the course of these conversations, even over the phone.

For the highly recruited, June 21st of the junior year is a day spent fielding or avoiding calls. Call waiting, voice mail, and time zones make the day interesting. As much as players' club and/or high school coaches may have tried to prepare them for that first day, many still find it overwhelming. And after the phone rings a few times, the talk all starts to sound the same.

Despite previous warnings from Bingham, Perryman nonetheless thought she would have an easy first day of calls. She found out otherwise bright and early in the morning, when her phone first rang at eight o'clock. Between talking to coaches and catching up with messages, she didn't get off the phone until over twelve hours later. Although she appreciated the attention, Perryman soon caught on to the pitch. However, as Bingham had insisted that she keep every option open, she remained polite and collected on the phone the entire time. "It was cool," says Perryman, "but it got so old because everybody was just like hi, we are so and so, we would like to give you a little bit of information on our school. We are this, and this, and this — we are the top and this, this, and this. It just seemed like everybody was a champion, and everybody was the best academically. Everybody was up and coming athletically, and it was just like, OK, you said the same thing that the last three people said. But you couldn't say that. You had to act interested. If you don't act interested, they are not going to think that you want them and they are not going to recruit you."

Greenwalt's phone rang off the hook beginning at 6:30 that morning. She, too, had been advised but was still unprepared for the deluge. "They had told me it was going to be bad once that day came, but we didn't really think it would be like that, you know," she states. "And it was bad." While she knew that she would never attend some of the universities that called, she felt reluctant to be that honest with coaches on the first day. Looking back, she says she would probably handle that differently. "No, I didn't tell anybody that first day that I wasn't interested in them," she admits. "That was probably a mistake. I should have." Greenwalt might have spared herself and the coaches many phone conversations that she knew had no potential.

For Wagner, June 21, 2000, proved awful as well but for the opposite reason. While she had been anxiously expecting many phone calls, only a few came. "I tried to keep myself busy, and I try to forget about that day," she says. "After I realized what was going on, I don't think I ever really necessarily got down, though. That's one thing that I feel lucky about. I never got down and upset about it. It just made me work harder because I knew that something was going to happen because I worked way too hard for something not to happen. I got a couple phone calls from some schools, none of which I was really excited about. But I still felt, well, I guess there's at least some people who still like me."

After that initial call, NCAA Division I and II coaches are allowed to call recruits three times in July with not more than one call per week, and once per week from the beginning of August until the athlete signs a National Letter of Intent. NCAA Division III, NAIA, and junior college coaches can call as much as they like, but most do not call more than once per week. As students juggle school, activities, and family commitments, many quickly find the phone calls tiresome. "They called at probably the worst times, I must say," Traversi comments. Some even enlist family members to tell the coaches they are not home. "I would screen the calls," explains Ely. "I hated the whole thing. I hated talking on the phone. That was the worst part, I think. If it was a college I was interested in, it was cool, but they would just call all the time — all the time, all day. It just took so much time, and it gets overwhelming." The student-athletes appreciate coaches who ask if they are calling at a good time and who keep conversations short.

For Belleau, the phone talks became repetitive, even though they were usually brief. "We basically talked about the same things," she says. "They'd ask how I was and stuff, and family life, and then they'd want to know if I was still interested and how my season was going and things like that." While the conversations only lasted for 5-10 minutes, they got old nonetheless.

During the fall of Dant's senior year at Stevenson, about 15 colleges called her every week. Unlike some peers, if she was sure that a school was not on her list, she told the coach right away. "The ones that I was interested in, I did call back," she explains. "I tried to get back to them as soon as possible. The ones that I wasn't as interested in, I would try to get them on my free time or if I didn't, I would leave a voice mail and say I wasn't interested when I did connect with them." Dant eliminated three or four schools early on this way.

Students can find themselves in the midst of a frustrating game of phone tag when the once-a-week calling begins. Schweiger spent about 2 ½ hours a week on the phone with coaches, with many messages in between. "I would never be home when they'd call, and I'd try to call them back and they wouldn't be there," she recalls. "It was just playing phone games. I got kind of tired of it, and I wasn't even that heavily recruited, so I can't even imagine what it would be like for someone who is a top prospect."

Just as college coaches repeat themselves time and again over the phone with recruits, girls find themselves repeating their words over and over with coaches as well. Everitt offers the following perspective: "It's exciting. Having someone call you and say, I think you're amazing, and feeding you all these lines, you're like, cool. But after a while, I began to feel bad because I'd be saying the same thing over and over again and I wouldn't remember what I was saying."

A college coach who expresses a desire to listen as well as

talk scores big points. For Greenwalt, who had 20-25 schools calling her weekly, the phone contact quickly became "annoying. I hate talking on the phone usually . . . especially when you don't really have anything to talk about. You're just listening to them talk about what's so good about their school." Like many athletes, Greenwalt arranged her after-school schedule around coaches' calls. "Certain schools did want to hear what I had to say," she continues, "but then there were certain ones that just talked and talked and talked. Then they would ask me, 'OK, now what do you think?' Well, you talked for an hour. I don't really remember all of it."

Whitley, on the other hand, had already picked the Blue Devils before the fall. However, she had previously discovered in conversations with the Duke staff, when she called them, that they were truly interested in her as a person. "Duke talked more about me and how I can help their program," she comments. "Some of these other schools sent stuff like, look at us, we're blah blah blah. Look what we've done. Look what we've accomplished. Duke did that more, look what we could accomplish with you. We could have a national championship with your help, stuff like that. So it was more about how I could help their program than about, look what we've already done. That was a really big positive, and that stood out a lot." On the first day of official calls, she remembers being completely straightforward with coaches. As she already had a list of potential finalists at that time, she mustered up the courage to tell those who did not make the cut. "I just wanted to tell them if their school wasn't right for me so they could move on to their next recruit," she explains. "I didn't want to waste their time." Whitley didn't waste any time either, as she made her decision in July.

Throughout the process, many prospects keep listening and talking to college coaches whose schools they know they probably will not attend for another reason. It's hard enough for a teenager to tell an adult no about anything, but to turn down someone with whom she may have developed a relationship can be devastating. The fact that she next has to call several other coaches that she may really like and let them down overshadows the excitement of calling the coach of her chosen school. Those calls can be the most difficult part about the entire recruiting ordeal. "Telling people no was so hard," admits Perryman. "I actually didn't decide very well. I had 10 home visits. I don't even remember who it was I first called to say no. I think somebody called me, and I had to tell them. It was the worst feeling in the world. And they were very nice about it. They were like, 'OK, if you ever change your mind we're still here.' They were really nice about it, which made it a lot easier." Ely adds, "Turning down coaches is tough. It takes so much time. You want to make the right decision, and so it's stressful."

Even after they've been shot down, some college suitors can be persistent, even bordering on harassing. Once Perryman called Stanford, she then told her other finalists about her decision, all of whom stopped contacting her except for one. "One coach in the PAC 10, I told her, and she said, 'OK, but can we still send you stuff? Can I still call you?'" Perryman says. "I said, 'Well, I don't know what kind of point that would be. I don't think I'm coming to your school.' 'Well, I just would like to keep in touch, and I'd still like to call you every week.' And I said 'Well, I don't think I'm coming to your school, so . . .' She said, 'I'm still going to try to come up for a home visit.' I was just like, 'Leave me alone.' She called the next week." As for Greenwalt, she waited until late September-early October to come up with her five finalists. When she told the others that they did not make her short list, a few kept calling her every week anyway, to make sure that she had not changed her mind.

Due to the other limitations of the recruiting process, much of the contact between athletes and college coaches occurs by phone. Some student-athletes enjoy the conversations, and others try to avoid them, but they do provide the backdrop for the two parties to feel each other out. As a result of this talk, both make decisions about whether to pursue or thwart the relationship.

The Real Deal

Some say that youngsters are the most astute judges of character. In order to commit to a college coach's program, a prepster must trust that coach. From prospective student-athletes' own views, women's college basketball coaches give them the real deal many times but not always. Many girls seem perceptive at distinguishing the sincere effort from the sales pitch.

Though Wagner believes that the college coaches who recruited her were honest, she also remembers that they accentuated only the positive. "I was just thinking about all of the fun things," she comments. "But I didn't really register how much hard work it is going to be because they don't make you think about that when you're there. They just make you think about the positive things and how much fun it's going to be and all of the wonderful things. It's not that you need to think about the negative things, but you also to need to realize that you're going to be far away from home. You have to do things on your own. You have to grow up. And they don't go over that."

These days, more girls are shrewd enough to ask college coaches where they stand on their lists. They say they can tell when a coach hesitates to divulge information. "Some people would be straightforward with me, and the people who were straightforward with me, I'd want to continue the conversation," Traversi explains. "I'd be more interested because they were honest and they were up front with me. When they were honest and up front, immediately they'd answer. They'd say, 'OK, you're our three.' If they were shady about it, some would say, 'You're in the top five, but more in the upper half.' I'd say, 'OK, there's five spots — upper half?' That's one or two, and it was two and a half. That made me think, OK, you're not being straight with me. You're not being honest with me."

For those in the top one or two, it's not an issue — if those athletes show interest, coaches will extend a scholarship offer. However, if the top two or three decide to go elsewhere, coaches' focus turns then to numbers four on down, who have suddenly jumped in priority. "I think that most of the time for the most part, the college coaches were being honest, as honest as possible," says Dant, who was also recruited by Indiana University. "I know that with the Indiana situation, they had told me the whole situation where there were people ahead of me that they had already previously talked to before they even saw me or got interested in me. I was happy that they were being honest. I didn't want them to sit there and lie to my face. But at the same time, I thought, maybe they're not too certain about my skills. They are just jumping on the bandwagon." For that reason, Indiana never stood at the top of Dant's list.

Some colleges and universities do not use the ranked list. As a result, the timing of the decision-making process can be different for athletes. It can also mean increased pressure. "Stanford, their whole thing was, they didn't have a number one, number two, number three, number four recruit," Perryman states. "They recruited a certain number of people, and whoever said yes first, that's who they were going to take. They needed somebody at whatever position we all were. So it was a matter of, if you don't sign now, I'm not saying that your scholarship won't be here, but there's a possibility that it won't be here in two weeks when you come back from Rutgers." She had scheduled an official visit to Rutgers after her Stanford visit.

"Bingham was like, if you want to go there you have to tell them now because what happens if you get back from Rutgers and it's gone?" Perryman continues. Even though she loved Stanford, part of her felt that she should still visit Rutgers. However, she never made it to New Jersey. "It was definitely stressful to know that if you don't decide now, somebody else could decide tomorrow morning," she comments. "Then you won't have a scholarship anymore. They really didn't say it in a mean way. They were just very matter of fact. They said, 'We want you, but we also want other people, too.'" Three days after she went to Stanford, Perryman made her final decision.

Sometime during the course of conversations between recruit and coach, the topic of the prospective student-athlete's perceived role in the program, if not the subject of playing time, often arises. If they find themselves up against stiff recruiting competition, some coaches use playing time as a bargaining point. However, while they may think girls will be impressed with a promise of quality minutes, these comments actually diminish the college's stature. "There were a couple of schools that said I would come straight in and start and play for them," recalls Greenwalt. "If they would already say that to me, you know, as a freshman, they probably aren't that good or they don't have any posts that are good, if they would go ahead and tell me that I was going to get to come in and play without coming up there and working with them first." Statements intended to impress might end up haunting college coaches.

While student-athletes admit that most coaches that they dealt with were honest during the recruiting process, many of the same girls also point out at least one coach who was not. "Most of the coaches were very up front with me and told me where I stood," explains Everitt. "I think all of them, except maybe for [one] coach . . . I went there early on, just to visit, on an unofficial visit. The coach told me that she had a scholarship for me if I wanted it. It was the first school I visited, and I was really excited. I talked to her a little bit over the summer when I could. I didn't hear from her for a while. Then she called me one day, and we talked for a while, and she said, 'We'll call you in a couple of weeks and we'll arrange your official visit.'" Everitt never heard from the coach again, however, and she describes what happened simply as a "weird situation."

In recruiting, like any other negotiation, each party wants to know where it stands with the other. While the players interviewed admit that the college coaches they dealt with were straightforward overall, they also found that a few held back. They warn against the recruiter who makes promises about a season that is still far in the future.

It's Official

The campus visit seals the deal for many prospective student-athletes. They may have previously visited schools on their own, unofficially. Perhaps they have watched some college teams in action. College coaches have seen them play, and they've talked on the phone. If a college coach offers an official visit, it means that he or she is fairly serious about the recruit. If the recruit takes an official visit, it means that she is fairly serious about the school. The NCAA allows Division I coaches to offer 12 total official visits, and Division II and III coaches can offer unlimited official visits. Prospects who are high school seniors can take five official visits each. During the visit itself, both factions try to impress, but college coaches usually have much more to impress with.

Getting a taste of team and school life factors heavily in recruits' decisions. Some make up their minds right away, on campus, during official and unofficial visits. However, others enjoy all of their visits such that they find it that much more difficult to pick from the finalists. In any case, coaching staffs may give them the royal treatment while they are there, and women's basketball coaches have become more creative with these tactics. While the girls know it's all in the name of marketing, they still appreciate it. Though the special attention does not often make or break a decision, it does not seem to hurt.

Coaches pulled out all of the stops for Ely. "All of my official visits, the schools were great," she remembers. "I think that after I left each one of them, I said I was going to go there . . . All of the schools made up a uniform for me, and they put my name up in lights in the gym." She received the same star treatment over and over again on campuses, and even though she knew the reason, she enjoyed it all the same. "When you go into the gym and see your name up in lights, it gives you goose bumps," Ely continues. "I really wanted to be there someday. But you have to look at it like they're advertising and they're selling their school, and you have to look past it. In the locker room, they would have my locker and stuff like that. They would make up a newspaper article, and my hotel room was decked out. It was really nice. They would put in a whole bunch of clothes, apparel from their school, and a whole bunch of banners, things like that." Even though she couldn't take any of the swag home with her, Ely definitely appreciated the trouble the coaches went through to make her feel wanted.

You don't have to be the National Player of the Year to receive such treatment. Greenwalt saw the sneakers, the uniform. Her favorite display of attention was sitting in the college gym with the lights out, listening to the end of a play-by-play with her scoring the winning basket. "I thought it was pretty awesome," she enthuses. "That one was the best. They had the lights going everywhere and stuff. It was really cool." Texas Tech just happened to be the college with the dazzling electric show.

Dant also saw uniforms and her name up in neon. While she knew the motive, she still enjoyed the attention. "I knew it was a marketing technique," Dant states. "It was very nice of them, I thought. It was more personable than, you should come here, this is what your classes are going to look like. It was more detailed, but at the same time, they were going to do it for all their recruits, so I wasn't dumb about that."

For many players, the special treatment and compliments that they receive during the recruiting process will stand out as the years progress. Many will never feel so wanted again in their lives. This sentiment is perhaps echoed most clearly during the official visit. Logic tells the girls that college coaches make up uniforms for all of their recruits, as they see when they progress to their second, third, and fourth visits. Even so, it's still flattering. After all, who wouldn't enjoy seeing his or her name up in lights?

Decision Time

More frequently, prospective student-athletes make up their minds before the beginning of the official recruiting process. Others pick their colleges in the summer after their junior years, before official visits can occur. Still others decide during the early signing period, and some during the late signing period. And many NCAA Division III recruits make their final selections during late spring. Whatever the timing, in determining that best match, personalities matter to students. If a player bonds with a coaching staff and team and finds on her campus visit that it just feels right, she often knows at that point that she has made her choice. Just as recruiting is not a science for coaches, it is not always based on reason for student-athletes either.

When she got her first letter from Duke, Whitley had a negative reaction. "I thought, I'm not going there, please," she remembers. "I don't know why, that's the weird part." However, after thinking about it, she realized that the distance from home, class size, and the type of program all suited her. "I wanted to go to a program that wasn't already a built dynasty," she says. "I would rather go with girls I don't know and build it as the years go. It also came down to the coaches' personalities, and basically, academics too . . . In my heart, I always knew, once I started the process, that Duke was way above everyone else. When I went to Duke, I don't know, I just felt like I was in the right place." Whitley definitely did her homework well ahead of time. She went on several unofficial visits during her junior year, as she knew she did not want to face the stress of the recruiting process as a senior. As a result, she had no home visits. She took one official visit, to Duke, after committing.

Similarly, Wagner never thought she would end up spending her collegiate career at NCAA Division I University of Hawaii. Before spring of her senior year in high school, she had only drawn intense interest from lower-level NCAA Division I and Division II institutions. After she had a strong senior season and with Tinsley's intervention, she made two campus visits. "As soon as I went to Hawaii and I liked it so much, I was just like, I'm done," she says. "I was going to go visit Tulsa, and I was also talking to Iowa and some other schools, too. But I just felt that, I felt really good about this place, and I thought, you know what? I am being given this chance to go to a great school, and I'm not going to pass it up. So I felt blessed, and I said I'll take it." Indiana was her second choice, but the visit to Hawaii made up her mind.

Where would Wagner be now had she not had such a terrific final high school outing? She would still have her eyes on that dream of big-time NCAA Division I hoops, probably stopping for a year at the junior college level. "I feel that I'd probably be just at a junior college, doing the same thing," she states. In fact, after her 2001 postseason accolades, several NCAA Division I colleges scrambled to find a way to fit her into their plans. Although they had their rosters set for 2001-02, some encouraged her to play junior college ball for a year and then sign with them. The University of Nebraska even arranged a full scholarship at a top junior college for a year, assuring her she could then transfer to Nebraska on scholarship. Although Wagner definitely considered that option, she held out for an immediate opportunity at a quality program. "I had my goal set, and that's what I was going to do," she continues. She adds that at the end of her junior season, she did not play well in her final tournament matchups, which may have hurt her recruiting. "I played a terrible game, but that never really bothered me. I knew that happened, but I just kind of let it go and was moving on. So if I had a bad game here and there, I just kind of let it go. I didn't have time to let it bother me. I didn't have time to think about the mistakes. I just had to get better. I didn't focus on anything negative that year, because if I did, I felt like I was just going to die and hit the ground."

To help them make their choices, some girls actually do make a list of qualities that a college must have. Dant, for example, had some definite specifics heading into her search. "The most important thing to me was that I wanted to be able to play basketball there and have a more diverse city than I had at Stevenson," she reflects. "I chose DePaul because they have a good coach. I heard a lot of positive stuff about him. But it was also, again, the diversity, like I said. I wasn't going to go to an all-black school, but at the same time I wasn't going to go to the same type of school environment that I was in now. I decided to change that."

"The main reason I chose Texas Tech is probably because it is close to home," explains Greenwalt. "All of my family can go watch. But I like the coaches, and it's an awesome atmosphere. The fans and the gym, and it's just awesome. The coaches and the players, I get along with fine. They're like family — that's how they treat you." Greenwalt also chose Tech over the University of New Mexico because of its higher status.

Even for the elite, the final choice may not have even been on the first list. "For a long time, I thought I was going to go to Purdue," Ely comments. "When I was in eighth grade, I went to the Purdue Elite Camp. I loved Carolyn Peck and her whole program, and that's where I thought I wanted to go. Then I got some interest from Tennessee and Georgia and things like that." After years of being the go-to player, Ely felt ready for an environment where she would have to work her way up. "I wanted to go to an already-established school," she continues. "I didn't want to have to create a dynasty or whatever. I wanted to go somewhere where I wouldn't have to be the only one doing everything. I didn't want to be the superstar. I wanted to go somewhere where I would have to work hard." In the end, she chose the program with the staff that she thought would challenge her most.

Although Schwieger had scholarship opportunities elsewhere, it was all about the Ivy League, which cannot award any athletic aid. She visited Harvard, Yale, and Cornell in search of the right blend of academics and athletics. Specifically, Cornell has an interdisciplinary major combining human biology and societal influences. "It was a perfect fit academically," Schwieger states. "I really couldn't have asked for a better combination of a school and a team. The coaches . . . are wonderful. They're just very nice people, and I felt comfortable with them." Two days after her Cornell official visit, she made her decision.

For those choosing between divisions, the decision can be more complicated. In some cases, the colleges themselves influence the choice more than whether they compete Division I or II. Bentley was not even on the radar at first for Everitt. "I was actually on the way home from a tournament, I think, and my parents said, 'We're going through Boston. Let's just swing by,'" she says. "I definitely thought, I don't think I want to go to school here. My parents said, we'll just stop by so you can cross it off for sure. But as soon as I stepped foot on campus and as soon as I met [the coaches], I knew I was in love — this is where I want to go. So I was really, really fortunate."

Although extremely pleased with her choice, Everitt admits that she is still aware of the Division I-II issue. "In all honesty, the Division I-Division II thing's always going to be there," she continues. "I'd like to be able to say I am playing DI. But what I really realized is that I'm not going there to play basketball so that other people can know I'm playing DI. I'm going there because I want to play basketball. I began to realize that if I did go play DI, I wouldn't be going to play at UConn or Notre Dame or something like that where I'm going to beat everyone. I'd be playing at a small DI, like a lesser one in a smaller conference, and I would never be able to compete with them. Bentley, who could probably beat a lot of DI schools, is going to go for that and compete for a national title."

For Traversi, who also drew attention from Division II schools, the number next to the division definitely played a part in her decision. "That was hard for me because I had dreamed about Division I since I was little," she says. "Division I was it. So that definitely did play a key role. The fact of the fan capacity at UMaine, that blew me away, and that added to it. And the fact that I was taking a chance on Maine. It was more of, I didn't know what was going to happen, and it was like I was taking a chance, but in a good way." During her recruiting process, many friends, acquaintances, and family asked her about the Division I-Division II debate. "I knew I could have an impact at Maine, but I still looked at it as it's Division I-Division II level . . . I would be competing with the best, and only by competing with the best, I would hopefully become the best," she adds.

You don't often read about the many girls who compete in high school ball, are recruited, and decide at the end of the recruiting process to retire from the sport. Belleau, who drew notice from such esteemed NCAA Division III institutions as Baldwin-Wallace, agonized over her decision not to play. "Deciding was very hard," she says. "I just sat down and I'd been debating it all year, whether I really wanted to go through a whole other four years of playing basketball. I really do love basketball. Playing at Pickerington, it's great, but basketball is life. You don't have very much free time to do other things, so I really wanted to just get out there and experience life without basketball." Instead, Belleau chose to enroll at Ohio University, where she says she just felt at home when she visited the campus.

Athlete or non-athlete, any high school student faces the daunting challenge of finding the right match in a school. For athletes, that challenge can be either complicated or simplified

117

by universities that show interest in them. As shown by the many who transfer each year, the real-life experience of attending is the only sure-fire way to test a choice. The most that prospective student-athletes can do, then, is to try to make the most informed possible decision ahead of time and then wait and see.

Looking Back

For anyone involved, going through the recruiting process can be an enlightening experience. For parents and athletes, who usually have one shot, the learning curve is huge. Even those pleased with their decisions admit that there are things they wish they had done differently. Given the chance to go back to the beginning of their high school careers, most would change at least one area of how they handled the recruiting process, from the most trivial to the most significant.

"If I could go back, I would probably try and enjoy it a little bit more," Perryman reflects. "It was really hard to try and just enjoy being wanted." At the time, she could really only think about making a decision and making it right then. All she could see was the pressure to make her choice. Also, trying to balance her 10 home visits and her classes proved difficult.

Although she only had four home visits, Ely scheduled them all for the same week. "If I could go back and do it again, maybe I wouldn't have all of my home visits in one week, four in a row during the week," she says. "I think I was taking in so much information, and they were one right after the other. I think I probably just needed time to think about each one instead of hearing one thing and the next day, hearing the same thing but maybe in a different way." The week after the home visits, Ely and her mother asked college coaches not to call so that they would have a period of time to think about the finalists without being disturbed.

Even though they may have thought about college choices ahead of time, many recruitable athletes wait to see which universities show interest in them and select from that list. In retrospect, some wish they had been more proactive in dealing with college coaches. "Maybe email coaches more and call them, because they say you can call us," Schweiger comments. "I was always afraid that maybe they're just saying that. Maybe they don't really want you to call them." Before making their final decisions, some girls feel so anxious about deciding that they can only concentrate on the colleges that had previously shown interest.

"If I could do it again, I think I would probably start a little earlier with the process and go out and see more schools," says Traversi, who did do one unofficial visit her junior year and four at the beginning of her senior year. While Traversi would have begun the search earlier, Greenwalt would have narrowed her list down earlier. She did not compose her list of final schools until late September. Two weeks after picking finalists, she had chosen Texas Tech.

As more girls go through the recruiting process, there are more high school and club coaches, parents, and athletes sharing experiences with others intent on playing in college. Accordingly, the girls' basketball community as a whole is more educated about rules and regulations, questions to ask, and overall progression of recruiting. However, even though they have been told ahead of time what to expect, student-athletes cannot really be fully prepared for the ins and outs of the process.

"I wish in the beginning that I had known just how intense it was and what it was really like so I could have been prepared and maybe done it a little differently," comments Everitt. "I might have looked at schools a little differently. But there's really no way you can know that. You can't know how intense it is until you actually go through it, so I don't know . . . I think I would have put more time into researching different schools and picking out ones that I really, really would have been interested in, instead of letting them come to me and having to deal with the fact that I really didn't want to go to their school. Then having to talk to them for hours just to end up saying, 'I really don't want to go to your school, I'm sorry.'"

From these reflections, the players express several common themes as advice to girls about to enter the recruiting process. First and foremost, begin seriously thinking about college well before the summer of your junior year. Visit some universities unofficially as a junior or even a sophomore. Narrowing down choices early on will make things easier on you and the coaches, so don't be afraid to turn a coach down. Overall, don't be afraid about hurting someone's feelings. Take a more active role in your own recruiting, instead of letting people come to you. Enjoy the attention while it lasts, but do not string a coach along merely for that attention. Once you have your final list, allow yourself ample time to reflect on the pro's and con's of each option. Finally, realize that no matter how ready you feel for the recruiting process, you will never really be totally prepared. The most that you can do is prepare yourself to make an educated decision.

Perhaps the most essential advice comes straight from the mouth of Wagner, who is definitely qualified to dish it out. "I think everyone told me never give up," she ponders, "but you don't really understand what those words mean. Those are just so important. You just really cannot give up . . . I could very easily have given up. I could have just been done. Don't give up on your goals and your dreams because they're always there. Some people just can't achieve their goals. I probably, I have these dreams and hopes of playing in the WNBA. Who knows if I will ever reach them, but I will never give up until I'm too old to play basketball. So I'll move on to different things. But just definitely, just don't give up. If you don't give up, and if you keep working harder and harder, good things will happen." While pertinent to recruiting, these words would be well heeded by readers in any life situation.

The All-America Survey

A few days before the 2001 Phoenix/WBCA High School All-America Game, the 20 elite high school seniors selected to play filled out a short survey created by the author of this book. The survey focused on the college recruiting process. The athletes, all of whom signed early with NCAA Division I schools, did not know the purpose of the survey, and each filled hers out anonymously. The survey's 20 items were presented either in a fill-in, multiple choice, or short-answer format. Questions focused on what actions they took during the recruiting process, how they made their decisions, how stressful the process was, and what advice they would give to others. Three of them were also interviewed in detail by the author for the first portion of this chapter.

While these student-athletes definitely represent the upper echelon of girls' basketball, they present some sound advice applicable to anyone interested in college ball. Below are their names, hometowns, and high schools, as well as the colleges they signed with.

Name, Hometown	High School	College/University
Ashley Earley, Memphis, TN	Briarcrest	Vanderbilt
Shyra Ely, Indianapolis, IN	Ben Davis	Tennessee
Katy Flecky, Highlands Ranch, CO	Highlands Rach	Notre Dame
Cisti Greenwalt, Clovis, NM	Clovis	Texas Tech
Brittany Jackson, Cleveland, TN	Bradley Central	Tennessee
Bethany LeSueur, Garden City, NY	Garden City	Virginia
Cappie Pondexter, Chicago, IL	Marshall	Rutgers
T'Nae Thiel, Weatherford, TX	Weatherford	Stanford
Angelina Williams, Chicago, IL	G. Washington	Illinois
Courtney Young, Ventura, CA	Buena	Tennessee
Genesis Choice, Orlando, FL	Maynard Evans	Florida State
Monique Currie, Washington, DC	Bullis School	Duke
Liz Dancause, Nashua, NH	Nashua	George Washington
Clare Droesch, Rockaway, NY	Christ the King	Boston College
Loree Moore, Carson, CA	Narbonne	Tennessee
Chelsea Newton, Monroe, LA	Carroll	Rutgers
Shawntinice Polk, Hanford, CA	Hanford	Arizona
Katie Robinette, S. Sioux City, NE	South Sioux City	Nebraska
Kendra Wecker, Marysville, KS	Marysville	Kansas State
Wynter Whitley, Kennesaw, GA	Holy Innocents	Duke

These standouts are no strangers to the hardwood. Seventeen of the 20 had been playing basketball for at least eight years when they filled out the survey, while the other three had been playing for 4-7 years. In addition, they had logged significant time competing on non-scholastic teams. Twelve had played club ball for 7-9 years, five for 5-6 years, and three for 2-3 years.

In high school and even earlier for some, the 2001 All-Americans became well-known public figures. All but four were in junior high/middle school when college coaches first expressed interest in them. Three were freshmen in high school, and one did not receive any college attention until her junior year.

One might expect the top prep players to be knowledgeable about NCAA recruiting regulations. Then again, if they knew that they were going to be sought-after, perhaps they did not feel they needed to learn the rules. When asked how well they thought they knew recruiting rules and regulations prior to the beginning of the process, the players' choices varied. Over half of the participants felt comfortable with their knowledge of recruiting rules, while 30 percent said that they knew some things, and 15 percent said that they knew a little bit about recruiting but were by and large uninformed. The percentage of girls who said that they were knowledgeable about recruiting regulations on this survey is probably higher than the national average because of the caliber of players; however, even at this level, the rules remain somewhat elusive. Looking back, 70 percent said that they did not think the process should begin earlier than it currently does.

Although coaches at all levels encourage prospects and families to contact the NCAA for information on recruiting, these athletes employed a variety of sources. Choosing from a list of options, the girls were asked how they learned about the NCAA's recruiting rules. Forty-five percent indicated that they had read NCAA materials, and 40 percent learned the rules mainly from workshops at camps, clinics, or tournaments. Thirty-five percent mentioned their high school coaches helping educate them, 20 percent mentioned their club coaches, and 10 percent mentioned both coaches. Twenty percent said that their parents were a main source of knowledge about the process, and one pointed out her high school counselor.

The NCAA places restrictions on phone calls in recruiting, but none on email. By definition, the NCAA considers it the same as snail mail. College coaches can technically send recruits a hundred email messages per day, or vice versa. How often did these players use email to correspond with college coaches during the recruiting process? Less than one might think in today's connected society. Forty-five percent responded "only every now and then" while 30% said "pretty often" and one-fourth said "very frequently." Perhaps they were too busy, or perhaps college coaches as a group have not embraced email as an inexpensive and instantaneous way to check in with recruits.

Any fan knows that the top players, and many at all levels in Division I and II, sign early. This group is no exception. Three out of four made a verbal commitment prior to the early signing period, and all of them signed a National Letter of Intent during the early signing period in November. They were asked to choose from among four selections the most important reason why they signed early. Half indicated that they they just wanted the recruiting process to be over so that they could enjoy the remainder of their senior years. Forty-five percent said that they had known for a long time where they wanted to go to school, so there was no reason to wait. One wanted to make sure she got her top choice.

The number of unofficial and official visits taken by these athletes varied. Two of them did not take any unofficial visits. The remaining 18 took anywhere from one to eight. As for official visits, 30 percent went on only one, while 35 percent took two, 15 percent took three, and 20 percent took four official visits. Several had scheduled more official visits than they actually took because they ended up making their decisions before progressing through all of them.

This particular group did not emulate the Jackie Stiles technique of having 16 home visits. Today's high school stars must be listening to the Vinny Cannizzaros of the world telling them to narrow their lists down to three or four before the fall. Most of the players had between one and five home visits; interestingly, one did not have any home visits. Asked who else was present at the home visits besides themselves and the college coaches, 30 percent said that only their parents, other family members, and/or family friends were there — no high school or club coaches. Forty-five percent said that only family members and high school coaches attended, while 20 percent said that both high school and club coaches were present.

These All-Americans were also asked if they felt that they spent too much time on the phone talking to college coaches during the recruiting process. Forty percent definitively said yes, and 20 percent said no.

In an era when some believe family life to be deteriorating for a number of different reasons, these twenty student-athletes indicated that their parents were very significant factors during their recruiting and decision-making processes. When asked to choose from a list, 70 percent said identified their parents as most helpful to them while they progressed through the process. Thirty percent said that family friends were helpful, and 35 percent mentioned their high school coaches. Only one singled out her club coach, and one indicated another family member.

Perhaps most surprising was the student-athletes' response to the question, how did you decide which colleges you were interested in at the beginning of the recruiting process? Many could probably have picked a college ahead of time, contacted that school's coach, and, grades notwithstanding, gotten a full ride. However, not one indicated that she did research ahead of time, made a list, and contacted the colleges, which was one of the answer choices. Two said that their parents told them where they thought they should go. One indicated that both her parents and club coach told her where they thought she should go. A whopping 90 percent chose the response stating that they had some ideas in their heads but that they waited to see who showed interest in them.

Their Own Words

The survey completed by the 2001 Phoenix/WBCA High School All-Americans concluded with two open-ended questions. First, if you could tell college coaches what they could do to make the recruiting process easier for prospective student-athletes, what would you say? Second, now that you've been through the recruiting process, what advice would you give to other prospective student-athletes about to enter the process? The comments that flowed from their pens and pencils are succinct, funny, and enlightening.

Advice to College Coaches

- "Talking on the phone is great but not for longer than one hour, please!"
- "Ask what would be a good time to call."
- "Don't hold us on the phone for so long."
- "Don't call 24-7."
- "To be more considerate of the time(s) they call our houses."
- "Don't pressure players to talk on the phone for a long time. Make the conversations brief."
- "If someone turns you down, stop harassing them; just say OK."
- "I would try to say don't ride them so hard, and if they really want them to talk to them in person or over the phone and write to them personally."
- "Give us more time to think about it."
- "Give us a little space, time to think."
- "Don't push an athlete to make a decision too quickly."
- "Don't talk so much."
- "Just be as honest as you can and let the athletes know where they stand."
- "Don't be fake, tell the truth and not what you just want to hear."
- "Tell the truth."
- "Be honest."
- "Get to know the person. Don't be funny. Keep it real."

Advice to other Prospective Student-Athletes

- "Look at the long term and decide where your future will be and find the one that 'feels good.'"
- "Make a positive/negative or pros and cons list."
- "Find out as much info as possible before the fall starts (w/officials, home visits, etc.)"
- "Tell the people who you are not considering that you are not interested early in the process."

- "Get as much information as you need and use your heart."
- "Take as many visits as you want. Make sure you look at everything."
- "Make your visits early."
- "Don't wait."
- "Take it as slow as you can, don't let anyone tell you where you should go, follow your heart!!"
- "Take all your visits."
- "Take their time and make sure that the decision is completely what they want."
- "Don't wait to make decisions. Call your top choices before they call you."
- "Sign early!"
- "Do not get caught up in all the fairy tales the coach tells you. They tell everyone the same thing."
- "You need to look at every option you have. Make sure you like the town, coaches, and players. Look everything over very good."
- "I would tell them keep their options open for other colleges and to really look into them and make sure that they have all that they need."
- "Don't put too much pressure on yourself."
- "Don't let it stress you out."
- "Have fun with it."
- "Make sure the choice you make is the right choice for you. Make sure you're comfortable with the coaches."
- "Go where you feel comfortable."
- "Go with your heart."

6

Keeping it Mum:
Parents' Involvement in Recruiting

Oregon City High co-head coach Carl Tinsley estimates that he has sat in on over 150 home visits. His tally would be 17 higher had he not missed out with a former player. "One of our kids whose father decided to do the recruiting process instead of me, the father set up 21 home visits," Tinsley remembers. "Literally, people were waiting in the car outside the house for the home visit to be over." After 17 of those home visits, the athlete's family pleaded with the father to cancel the remainder.

While a few parents of prospective student-athletes like to handle recruiting themselves, many welcome expert help. Even those who have been previously educated by their daughters' high school and/or club coaches or others find the recruiting process overwhelming and unnerving. However, once recruiting begins, parents may acquire some of the shrewdness possessed by recruiters, high school and club coaches, and players alike.

In the confusion and excitement that can drive the recruiting process, different parents assume varied roles. Overall, those who talk to other parents with experience find themselves much better off. Some have more contact with the college coaches than others. While college coaches, high school coaches, and summer coaches might have other agendas, parents usually have only their children's best interests as their guiding principle in recruiting. Although coaches can help with determining the right collegiate level, progressing through the recruiting calendar, and information-gathering, parents will be the only ones close by when their daughters make their decisions.

Reality Sets In

Just like their children, most parents do not know what to expect from recruiting. If lucky enough to have the benefit of an experienced high school coach, club coach, or other parent, they will receive a general overview and will be warned of the pressures to come. However, even parents of the top high school players in the country, whose daughters have already attracted college attention, are shocked once the official process begins. Despite the fact that colleges may have shown interest in their girls for several years, nothing can really prepare them for the actualities of recruiting. Many parents do not realize what they or their daughters are in for until the phone rings with the first college call.

"I knew that Shyra was good, and I kind of thought that every Division I school in the country, every no-name school in the country, and everyone who thought they were a big-time school would be contacting her," states mother Jean Ely. "But I guess, the magnitude of it all, it just hit me in the face on the first day that they could actually call her. It was quite overwhelming. I didn't expect to be as overwhelming as it was." Ben Davis High coach Stan Benge had already had meetings with the Elys, trying to ready them for the onslaught of phone calls and visits.

Needless to say, calls poured into the Ely household right from the beginning. Benge had told them that in order to make the process manageable, they would have to eliminate schools right away. That meant telling people no on the first call. "Shyra handled the first call very well," Jean comments. "It was a call from California. She said, 'I really appreciate you calling, but I'm not sure I want to go that far from home...' I was just so impressed with her ability to start out and let them know what her interests were. The coach told her that she really appreciated her being up front with her, and she wished her well and said that she would continue to follow her because she was such a good player. After that, I thought, she's going to be OK. The next call came, and she did the same thing." Before that first day, Shyra had a list of approximately 20 colleges. Immediately afterwards, she cut it to ten so that with the next round of calls in July, she could indicate that she had narrowed her choices.

Terri Greenwalt cannot even guess how many times the phone rang on June 21, 2000 with calls for her daughter Cisti. She had to step in and screen calls later in the process. While talking to other parents helped Greenwalt gather tidbits of extremely helpful advice, she also relied on another source to answer specific questions. "We're real good friends with the athletic director here," she explains, "and I'd call him and say, can we do that or can we not do that, or can they do that?"

Not only can parents band together during the process, the inexperienced can talk to recruiting veterans beforehand to get a jump start on how recruiting works. Sandi Everitt learned multitudes talking to other parents in the bleachers during her daughter Abby's club games. "As parents, we were completely in the dark about all this stuff," she admits. "Some of the other parents with the really top-quality players, like nationally-ranked players, were very motivated. They knew all the ins and outs of this whole thing. They knew what needed to happen. They knew that the girls needed to go to big tournaments." It didn't hurt that two of the people she chatted with were the parents of Ashley and Morgan Valley, both of whom now play at the University of Connecticut.

For the many, many parents who do not have the advantage of other experienced parents, it takes initiative and effort to learn the ropes. "I didn't really feel prepared going into the recruiting process," David Belleau confesses. "Quite frankly, I had to get the rule books and stuff. I started to be concerned about, well how many visits can we do, and so on and so forth. I found out in asking myself those questions that I didn't know anything. So I thought maybe it was time to get the right information and read through it so I knew what we could and could not do and so on and so forth. It took some time to go through that and figure out what's what." Even coming out of a top high school program, daughter Hallie and her father had to do some of their own research. Fortunately, they became knowledgeable enough about the rules and calendar by doing their own homework.

Parents' Interaction with College Coaches

Although ultimately the choice is usually the student-athlete's, her parents' opinions count, even when they make it clear that the decision is entirely hers. College coaches know the importance of establishing good rapport with parents. In the recruiting process, parents have varying levels of contact with college coaches – at the very least, perhaps chatting with them for a few seconds when the phone rings. Overall, these conversations are positive, according to the parents interviewed for this chapter. However, parents also could perceive which coaches truly wanted to get to know them, as opposed to those who thought they had to in order to win their girls over.

Like their children, parents of recruits are impressed by the attention at first. However, many soon see through the compliments. Seasoned high school and club coaches talk about the importance of asking college coaches the tough questions. Mark Traversi, father of Missy, had no qualms about doing just that. "I did speak with college coaches when they called . . . I talked and I'd ask questions," he says. "Where was she on your list? Some were vague when answering that. Some wouldn't tell you. They might not get who they want; that kid might want to go to another school. They've got to have a backup. They probably would be 100 deep on each position, and hopefully they wouldn't have to go any deeper than five." Knowing why coaches held back in responding, he would press on. "How badly do you want her? Where is she on your list? They would beat around the bush on that. That's the biggest one. That's the key because everybody wants to play. Nobody wants to sit out." Mark says that his coaching background as well as his and his wife's experiences working with children helped them imagine the different recruiting situations college coaches faced.

Overall, the Greenwalts were excited throughout the process and when talking with college coaches. However, Terri wondered about the candor of a few who called on her highly-recruited daughter. Several coaches made promises that she found difficult to believe. "There were a couple that told me, she didn't even have to take the ACT to go there or anything like that," she says. "I'm thinking, OK, now how come a Division I college can tell me that when I know good and well she does. I'm thinking, how can they get away with that?" As some student-athletes have noted, these comments also lessen colleges in parents' eyes.

Parents accompanying their girls on campus visits can also play an active role in getting to know coaches. For example, Belleau talked with several coaches while Hallie was off having lunch with or getting a tour from members of the team. This provided him an up-close opportunity to ask questions on his own. "We talked about everything, from what type of game do they play, what type of practice . . . just trying to get an overall feel for how they run their program, how intense it is," he says. "What their practice schedule is like, and so on and so forth, really just trying to get a feel for the coach and what their temperament is." Between his conversations with coaches and Hallie's discussions with players, David felt that the coaches were completely frank about what to expect.

In discussions with coaches, parents find themselves doing a lot of listening, sometimes on topics intended to impress. "It didn't hurt their selling point by any stretch of the imagination, but . . . [Georgia head coach] Andy Landers, all he could talk about was Teresa Edwards," quips Norma Whitley. "We don't care about Teresa Edwards. Sure, she's done a lot, but it was like, so what? Not to diminish anything about the pioneers . . . but the whole thing was like, she's never been one of my top 10 favorites. But you use what you have to try to pique people's interest. And Tennessee, talking about Holdsclaw — sure, but it just didn't mean anything to us." Whitley encourages college coaches to focus on the recruit herself as opposed to those who excelled before her in the program.

As with their children, parents who form bonds with college coaches during the recruiting process have a difficult time as the process draws to a close. This situation intensifies when your daughter, one of the country's most sought-after recruits can basically pick her collegiate institution. "I love them all, and I became just good friends with the coaches," says Ely. "It was real hard for me, I guess, because you talk to these people every day, and you just form a closeness with them."

However, Jean knew that a few coaches would not stop calling after being turned down. In fact, she had to step more than once and say to them, "Please respect the fact that you're not on her list and she is moving on now." On the other hand, the Elys were also spared uncomfortable discussions about how many prospects were ahead of Shyra. No matter what the level of recruitment, some parents have a difficult time ending their relationship with college coaches.

High School Coaches, Club Coaches, and Summer Ball

Some high school and club coaches inject themselves into their players' recruiting processes, others offer to help if families come to them, and still others do not express a desire to be involved. While the right coach can be a godsend for parents in the recruiting process — evaluating skills, asking difficult questions, and offering advice — parents can easily become confused about who should be involved when. Rivalries, coaches' willingness to help, and the desire to avoid hurting feelings can complicate this dilemma.

The Greenwalts had a hard time deciding who to include in home visits and at other recruiting events such as Cisti's Letter of Intent signing. Cisti had had two club coaches that she really liked, and they also felt that they should show loyalty to high school coach Dale Severson. "We didn't really know who was supposed to be here and who wasn't," Terri says. "We didn't really know who to ask, or sometimes when we'd ask Severson, he didn't really give us an answer, so we didn't really know a whole lot about who could come and who couldn't come and who should come and stuff like that." The clan became more concerned about pleasing others than about who they really wanted there. While Severson had offered to help in any way, he also made it clear that they needed to come to him.

Because they did not specifically seek out Pickerington High coach Dave Butcher, David and Hallie Belleau also endured much of the process alone. "I'm not knocking Coach Butcher," David comments, "but I think, with Coach Butcher his approach is this: look, if you want to play, then you come and talk to me about it, and I'll help you do whatever you want. But unless you tell me that, I've got other things to do." Also, Hallie had decided beforehand to wait and see which colleges contacted her. If it were up to her father, and if he could start over, he would probably do more to market her by looking into sending out tapes and other methods of promotion.

Although Hallie received college exposure through club ball, David believes that her last few years of participation may have contributed to her not hearing from more NCAA Division I institutions. While she did get seen, fatigue may have been a factor. "It was a lot of games," he says. "Hallie was tired. I think that there were . . . games that she played in AAU ball that I'm sure that there were coaches watching, and because of the cumulative effect of playing so much basketball, she did not play the type of basketball that she was capable of playing. And so I think that some of those games, the fact that she was playing and got that exposure probably hurt her some ... I think that by and large it was just too much basketball, too intense, the basketball that she was playing, and some of that may have hurt her." Most girls' summer teams play at a higher level than their high school teams, but the reverse might have been true for Hallie.

However, Abby Everitt's non-scholastic team played at a much higher level than her high school squad. Her high school coach, who Sandi says never believed Abby would get a scholarship, was not really involved with their recruiting process. Sandi describes the involvement of Kara Leary, Abby's club coach, as "indirect," explaining that she was busy promoting a few other high-profile players. However, she harbors no resentment at all. "When you say that, it sounds like a negative thing," she says, "but . . . I think if we had felt we needed her to do something for us, she would have done it. But she also had, in particular, one girl who is a really good player, but she had some personal family issues and some lifestyle issues. The coach, I think, felt it was her responsibility to supervise this girl as well as try to get her off on a good footing in this whole thing. On the other hand, I think that the coach saw that Abby had two interested parents who were going to be helping her and talking with her and guiding her. This girl didn't have that, and I think the coach felt that she needed to do that."

For the Traversis, the most helpful person was a family friend, former Boston University coach Chris Basile, who coached Missy's club team in summer 2000 and also gave recruiting seminars. "She just said to us, you need to learn," mother Sue Traversi remembers. "You need to read. She threw a couple of books my way, but it wasn't until she sat with me and went through an outline of what she went through in a typical visit with a player that the education started. Mark and I really started seeing what we had to do. It was good because as much as we didn't get directly involved like Missy did, we knew a lot of what was going to come." Basile was there every step of the way, sitting in on home visits and offering counsel after campus visits.

While Shyra Ely's recruiting process was indeed hectic, it could have been much more so without Benge's efforts. Since before Shyra's high school career began, he had been collecting mail from college coaches. During her junior year, he sat down with mother and daughter to discuss how to handle the volume of contacts that would soon barrel their way. "Coach Benge was very, very involved," says Jean. "He did everything he could to prepare us for this. In the beginning, we talked about, do you want all of the contacts to come through me? How do you want to handle this? I just told him, 'You have been doing this, so you tell us what you think is best, and that's what we'll do.' He came to every home visit, he and her conditioning coach, Coach Vanderbush, who is wonderful." Jean credits Kevin Vanderbush, also Ben Davis' strength coach and Benge's assistant in 2000-01, with helping Shyra settle into narrowing down her choices. "Shyra, when she got off track, she eventually got to a point where she didn't want to make a decision," Jean continues. "It was like, this will go away if I just stick my head in the sand. Vanderbush would bring her back to reality every time. He has just been great. She was able to talk to him and let him know her feelings. He would just bring her back to reality — 'Shyra, this is not going to go away.'"

Before Wynter Whitley verbally committed to Duke, she received many letters and did plenty of research, preferring to decide before school started in the fall. NormaWhitley's late husband, Wilson, played in the NFL, and some former pro buddies gave mother and daughter advice on recruiting. In addition, Wynter's former high school coach helped with some of her early homework. As a junior, however, Wynter relied most on her mother when thinking about her decision and making unofficial visits.

Wynter's former high school coach, who Norma would not name, did not coach at Episcopal during Wynter's senior year. She appreciates his early advice and efforts, as well as the fact that he let Wynter choose which college camps the high school team attended in the summer. However, she says that he had a strong opinion about where Wynter should go to school. "When it came to the recruiting process," says Norma, "[Wynter] did not make him part of it because he wanted her to go to Georgia, and Georgia only. When we started reading letters in the beginning, he wanted to see every letter that she got. For years, letters had come to him and we didn't even get them. He started a book he kept for her for years, until we could start getting the letters. In the beginning, I tried to Xerox letters for him, but then it got so crazy that I couldn't do it. There was too much mail coming in. As the process got down, and he would say that we shut him out of that after everything he had done for us, but it wasn't about that. It was a family decision. She needed her own head and mind to do this decision, and he had only pushed her toward Georgia." Georgia ended up Wynter's second choice, and unfortunately, because of what had transpired, the relationship with this coach ended poorly.

Norma also says that she saw firsthand the close relationship between some non-scholastic coaches and scouting report organizers. After neglecting her high school team for several summers, Wynter decided to attend a team camp with her high school team instead of a different one with her club team. As a result of this choice, says Norma, her daughter dropped from number three to 17 or 18 on a major report. "I said, you know what, when you don't do what people want you to do sometimes, they can hurt you," Norma states. "It didn't stop anything from coming to this mailbox and to this porch when we came home from work every day, so it worked out OK." At the same time, Wynter never paid a cent to play club ball. Her mother, admittedly "jaded" by her daughter's club experience, gives it no credit for college exposure. The college notice began, she says, when Wynter attended a camp run by the WBCA at age 13.

Many college coaches believe that whether they like it or not, they must depend on club coaches as a primary recruiting contact. However, if those interviewed for this book are any indication, parents and prospects rely sometimes on high school coaches, sometimes on summer coaches, and sometimes on neither of the above. At the same time, it also seems as if many parents would not mind prep coaches' checking in with them unannounced during the recruiting process.

Special Treatment Wows Parents as Well

Like their daughters, parents quickly catch on that if every college they visit makes up a uniform, they must do that for other recruits as well. However, also like their daughters, parents still are affected by these measures, although they know the reality behind them.

"Every time she saw a uniform with number 43 on it, she was ready to go to that school," Jean Ely says. Despite this realization, Jean enjoyed the efforts as well. "Ohio State even had a picture of her superimposed on a uniform, and it was really neat. They had a film — technology today, I tell you — because they used clips from their workouts or games, and they showed a film with them. They were using their names, and it was just really neat. They got a kick out of that. It was just really neat to hear their names on the film, like they were on the team." All of the colleges chasing Shyra were determined to find out what measures their competition took to woo her. While both mother and daughter understood the reason for the repetition, Jean was still impressed with the thoroughness of staffs' research.

Aside from some of the above, Missy Traversi saw her name in a made-up article about a college's Final Four trip. Although these efforts may not make a student-athlete change her mind about a school, they absolutely make her feel wanted. "I think it makes an impression on the individual," states Mark Traversi. "I don't think it made her decision, but I think it definitely, at that particular time, makes you stand up and take notice. I think it makes the kid more aware of that school. But I would hope that when it comes time to make a decision, they make their decision based more on what's the school going to give me if I get hurt, for one thing."

Some parents can be as star-struck as their children upon receiving special treatment from coaches working toward that big commitment. "It was awesome," enthuses Terri Greenwalt. "They did it at UNM, and they did it at Tech, but UNM, I mean, it just wasn't as neat because Tech has been there. They were doing it at a national championship game, and that was what was so cool. They had another little recruit there too, and she signed, too . . . And they had their names, you know, going on the floor and everything and the lights, with the lights out and everything." With the exception of Oklahoma, every school Cisti visited did some of these things. When a parent already likes the college, those extras make the school that much more notable.

"Of course, I think the official visits are pretty pressured situations," says Sandi Everitt. "People are putting out a lot on you. They're taking you to dinner, you're meeting a lot of girls that you like at the different schools, you're having a good time with them. They want you to choose them. You know you are going to have to say no to somebody, to several somebodies."

Few students or parents choose a college program because its coaches make up a personalized uniform and a newspaper. However, these steps do not lower a college's reputation. Unless a coaching staff philosophically opposes these efforts, these parents provide enough evidence for them to keep it up.

Parents' Reflections on the Process

Parents' analysis of the recruiting process is similar in ways to the comments of other involved parties, but with a different focus. "In the beginning, it was exciting," says Sue Traversi. "I don't know how she got through the decision. I think that must have been really hard for her. I would say it was very stressful."

Two adjectives, "overwhelming and awesome," come to Terri Greenwalt's mind. She says that she and her husband expressed more excitement than Cisti did about all of the attention. "Cisti is one that just doesn't ever get real emotional and doesn't get real excited," Terri explains, "and so we said 'Oh my god, look at this one,' and, 'Look at that one,' and she would go, 'Oh.' But I think she thought it was really neat."

For someone who had thought she might play NCAA Division III hoops, Abby Everitt found herself confronting the unexpected. According to her mother, by the time she recognized that she had some top-level Division II as well as some Division I opportunities, Abby felt the strain. She also did not have any close peers in similar situations. "I think by the end, she was crazy," Sandi comments. " I think it was very hard. First of all, there were her friends from her AAU team, but some of them had committed. Others weren't really getting offers, legitimate offers that they were happy with. Abby was getting offers that she thought she could see, but she didn't have anybody similar close by that was going through this experience with her. I think by the end, the pressure of dealing with so many phone calls from coaches was beginning to be hard. And of course, none of her friends, they were just doing the beginning, I've got to make a decision about college, I've got to make some lists out. She had to make a decision. I think it was hard."

For Hallie Belleau, the stress did not come from college coaches and players as much as it did from her local community. "There were a lot of people who wanted to help her try to get to the next level," David says. "She felt a lot of that pressure . . . Being in Pickerington and being a pretty decent player, it's just expected that you're going to go to college and play basketball. There were a lot of people who were pushing her to do so. A lot of her actions, I think, in some of the initial recruiting process, were to appease other people because she thought that's what she was supposed to do. Then our discussions, she and I, our discussions were, look, this is your life. You've got to live it, and you've got to do what you think is best for you." It took Hallie quite some time to face those expectations and imagine a fulfilling collegiate tenure without basketball.

For everyone, the recruiting process produces anxiety. However, for the most elite, even with the help of an expert high school coach, it becomes all-encompassing. "It just cut into every aspect of her life," comments Jean Ely. "She came home from school, and by the time she got her studying done and got her shower and talked to the coaches, she was exhausted. She had no social life . . . Her life was consumed with recruiting." However, Jean also does not see how anyone could have made the process easier. She knows that college coaches were doing their jobs, and she does not want to seem ungrateful. "I feel badly saying that it was overwhelming, and I wish this, and I wish that," she adds, "because this kid, as long as she's playing and playing well and doing what she needs to do, she doesn't have to worry about her education."

While they explain how nerve-wracking the recruiting process was for their girls, parents neglect to include that it is stressful for them, too. Between mail, calls, and visits, recruiting disrupts any family's life. Parents' commentary also brings to the forefront that in general, even though college coaches may find it important to butter up parents, the decision really is up to the recruit alone.

Parental Advice

Parents indicate that talking to parents whose daughters had already been recruited was extremely helpful and reassuring. Here, they offer their own recommendations on everything from approaching recruiting to surviving the stress to making a sound decision. Perhaps most remarkable are their comments regarding specific actions that they took pertaining to academics as well as athletics.

Before the Everitts road-tripped it to look at schools during Abby's junior year, Sandi asked Abby to think about her college major. That provided them with a definitive yardstick with which to compare schools that they visited. After Abby decided she thought she wanted to specialize in business, off they went. "That allowed her, every place we went, even unofficially, they set up a thing at their business school so she could see what the business school programs were," Sandi explains. "That, I think, was very helpful. She had a comparison in the field she was interested in of all the different types of schools she looked at . . . She could really then, when we said, if something happened and basketball was out of the picture, which school would you want to be at doing business, assuming that she even stayed in business. That really helped her delineate a lot." It also logically led them to place Bentley, known for its business focus, on the list. Even though she had never thought about Bentley before, her desire for a business concentration kept the college in the running until she realized that it was a fit, athletically and academically.

Among the extraordinary efforts that Shyra Ely's college suitors put into courting her, setting up academic meetings meant the most to Jean. School after school arranged get-togethers with doctors, counselors, and students in the pre-med program. "All of the schools that we visited . . . had the director, the doctor who oversaw their med program, meet with her," says Jean. "A med student who was almost done and then a student who was just going in on the basketball team who was just starting also met with her. I think at that meeting, there were about 12 people there. Everyone talked to her about what to expect. It was just very informative and a great meeting." Colleges went out of their way to arrange meetings for Shyra. However, any family can take the initiative to suggest that visiting an academic department of interest be part of every campus visit, official or unofficial.

Assessing your child's basketball talents objectively can be extremely difficult if not impossible. However, Mark Traversi thinks there is a way. "I would just say, be honest with yourself. Is my kid really that good? If you look at enough basketball, you can see. If not, don't go that route." He also warns of burnout in an age where girls and boys specialize in basketball earlier and earlier. On Missy's club team, Mark saw several athletes who he says could have gotten college scholarships but grew tired of the game. "These kids are going one sport all year long," he adds. "I think that there is more to the kid's development socially, to develop the whole person. I think a lot of these kids are getting shortchanged. They're not getting to develop the whole person, the social side of things and what they are supposed to be doing at the age of 13, 14, and 15. You're not supposed to be in a gym eight months of the year."

As women's hoops becomes more cutthroat, a college opportunity becomes more a matter of connections and of being seen. Some parents argue that this can be more important than actual skill level. "What's amazed me is that if you can get exposure, you don't have to be the best player," Belleau comments. "If you get exposure, and we've seen it at Pickerington, you can get a lot of money to go play basketball somewhere even though you may not be the best player that is out on the market. It's almost become a marketing game." To capitalize on this theory, more recruiting service-type companies have emerged that promise to promote student-athletes to colleges for a fee. However, many college coaches do not rely on these services. After all, anyone who pays can register with many of them. If someone that the coach knows and trusts vouches for on-court abilities, that means much more.

In an age when women's basketball is beginning to emulate men's in terms of outside parties involved in recruiting, a prospect can easily become confused about her loyalties. Parents think that girls should depend on those who know her best and who put her interests above all. "Don't trust the people who are trying to motivate and get themselves further, and trust your heart," Norma Whitley cautions.

To illustrate her advice, Norma remembers when Wynter gave her verbal commitment to Duke. As expected, Wynter had a hard time telling the other coaches that she had chosen another school. "One coach, who will remain nameless, one assistant coach called, and Wynter said, 'I have already committed,'" Norma remarks. "'Well, who did you commit to?' 'I committed to Duke.' 'Duke?! Wait a minute. I think coach so-and-so would want to speak to you.' She puts Wynter on hold, and the coach gets on the phone. 'Wynter, this is coach blah blah from blah blah. What do you mean that you have committed?' 'I committed.' 'Well, have you spoken to your AAU coach?' Wynter said, 'My AAU coach had nothing to do with my decision.'" Girls who have a strong parental presence throughout recruiting are better equipped to distinguish those who want to help from those with other motivations.

Once the initial excitement wears off, recruits can be bogged down by the disruption of phone calls and visits as well as the intensity of the decision. Terri Greenwalt advises all to take a step back during the process and appreciate the results of sacrifice and hard work. "Enjoy all of it you can because it doesn't last," she states. "We let it last as long as we could." Even the Greenwalts, who repeat that they were keen on the attention that they received, could not endure the process longer than two weeks before the early signing period.

Parents would much appreciate college coaches' explaining to them, during the recruiting process, what their daughters' lives will be like as members of their programs. This includes the daily schedule, overall expectations, and the grim realities of how tough it is to play college ball. Greenwalt encourages college coaches "to be sure and be honest with the way they coach and what they expect, and just lay it on the table right straight out, what they expect, and for the girl what the girl is to expect when she gets there, and not sugar-coat everything. To me, if you want to play, you're going to play whether they sugar-coat it or not." Instead of scaring off prospective student-athletes, says Greenwalt, coaches' bluntness will confirm girls' dedication to the sport.

Depending on their daughters' levels of recruitment, parents have different recruiting concerns. However, their best suggestions apply to every situation. Thinking about criteria ahead of time, talking to other parents, picking a loyal recruiting teammate of their preference, watching prospective teams in action, and asking questions can give families an edge. Listening to experienced high school and club coaches about their daughters' ability and which levels they should pursue can result in a more targeted and realistic college search. But while coaches with the know-how should be present during visits, the ideal decision-making environment consists of players and parents alone. With those ideas in mind, parents can help their daughters progress through the recruiting process, not easily, but as easily as possible.

7

Go-Between: The Complex Role of High School and Club Coaches

Undoubtedly, high school and club[1] coaches can play a large role in the recruiting process. While many do everything they can to promote the student-athlete and help her make the right decision for herself, some can be a bit extreme in their attempts to control the process. "I've heard of AAU coaches who have timed coaches," comments John Feasel, director of *Ohio Girls Basketball* magazine and scouting service and a former club coach. "Fifteen minutes on the home visit. I had an AAU coach here in Ohio that timed them on a visit. You've got 25 minutes, and then sat there with them. That's not a lot of time in which to convince a kid to go spend four years of her life. No, it's not — it's crazy, too, is what it is."

■ ■ ■

In some states, high school and club coaches could be one and the same, while in others, high school coaches are not allowed to coach summer teams. As girls' non-scholastic basketball becomes more popular, and club coaches become increasingly involved with their players' college selection process, friction arises between the high school and club coach. Who has more influence overall in recruiting? The coaches' experience,

---

1. Once again, the terms *club, non-scholastic,* and *summer basketball* can be used interchangeably to mean any organized basketball played outside of the regular scholastic season. Although AAU is a specific organization, some use the term as a substitute for one of the other three expressions.

connections, and relationship with the prospect as well as the level of recruitment all affect who's involved.

Many high school and club coaches' involvement in their athletes' recruiting processes comes about because of their willingness to help their players to make the best college choices for themselves. However, even in girls' basketball, a few coaches are in it for more self-serving, personal reasons. Even if they do not have allegiances to certain college coaches, they may still steer their charges toward specific schools, knowingly or unknowingly.

Those prep-level coaches in the recruiting mix can have a tremendous amount of power. After all, college coaches cannot talk with prospective student-athletes until the end of their junior years unless the student-athletes call them or they attend the college's summer camp; however, college coaches may contact their current coaches as early and as frequently as possible. Many high school and club coaches educate players about recruiting ahead of time, trying to give them a sense of the general rules and what to expect. They attend home visits and help girls evaluate them. Before and during the official process, they relay thoughts and inquiries from college coaches to recruits and in turn tell college coaches prospects' latest thoughts. They can serve as the ultimate intermediary in recruiting.

State of Affairs

Across the country, state high school associations or federations determine whether a high school coach may coach a club team, as well as the number of athletes from a particular high school who can play together on one club team. In some states, high school coaches can legally coach their players in the spring and summer. In others, they cannot. In Oregon and California, high school coaches are allowed to work with their teams. In other states, however, "percentage" rules apply. For example, New Hampshire high school coaches may coach club teams, but while the school year is still in session, no more than 25 percent of their teams may be from their high schools. In Massachusetts, on the other hand, the blanketing rule is 50 percent, whether school is in session or not. In Texas, high school coaches cannot coach their athletes at all outside of the high school season.

As a result of these varied regulations, some squads are at an advantage when different non-scholastic teams compete against each other in the club circuit. Nationally-ranked high school teams may be able to play together all spring and summer in club tourneys with their high school coaches at the helm. This will help them both during the club and high school seasons. Other teams could be a combination of All-Stars from a region.

The better teams advance farther in the various non-scholastic tournaments held around the country. Players on these squads have more opportunities to showcase their talents in front of college staffs and that increased exposure makes a difference.

High School Coaches in Recruiting

High school and club coaches should serve the same role in the college recruiting process. Although some do not want the involvement, most high school coaches think that helping players and families through recruiting is part of the job description. Overall, they should be as involved as the individual athletes and parents want them to be. When speaking with college coaches, they should pose the questions girls and their parents are afraid to ask. When players ask which colleges they think would be best for them, coaches should toss their own preferences aside and help determine the best fit, even if it is not NCAA Division I.

Some high school coaches see their main role as helping both college coaches and prospective student-athletes sort through background information and small talk. "I just try to find out what their interests are," explains Dale Severson, who spent 22 years as head coach at New Mexico's Clovis High School. "I tell them to weigh both the positive and the negative and then those questions are usually brought up to me, and I just bring them up to the recruit . . . find out what's going through her mind, is she even interested, is it worth the trip." When players fear expressing their true thoughts or hurting college coaches' feelings, high school coaches should be there to tell them that it is OK to say no up front. They assure athletes that college coaches have been rejected many, many times.

"The way I look at it, my role is to do anything possible to help my players play at a level that they're capable of playing," states Suzie McConnell-Serio, former WNBA standout and Penn State alum who has coached at Pittsburgh's Oakland Catholic High School since 1990. "Sometimes, if a player is highly recruited, you may just help them evaluate each school. Then that helps them make a decision, the pros and cons of each place and what they're looking for. Really just guide them if they're being heavily recruited. I think if they're not heavily recruited, they don't play AAU, they haven't been seen, then you take on a different role where you help find a school for that player." McConnell-Serio, whose squad captured the 2001 state title, estimates that she has helped 35 players through the process since taking over the helm.

Keeping parents and students informed forms the basis of the high school coach's role. "Besides gathering information, I think the job of the high school coach in recruiting is obviously letting them know the rules and letting them know the process itself," says Stan Benge, Indianapolis' Ben Davis High School head coach. "A lot of it depends on how active the parent is. There are some parents who are very, very active. My assistant coach's daughter got recruited, so basically he took care of it. I didn't have to do a whole lot there because he was very, very knowledgeable. Some parents have never gone through the process. That's a different story." Unlike many other high schools, Ben Davis has counselors who educate students about recruiting as well. Combined with Benge's experience in over 16 years of coaching at the school with over 30 recruited athletes, this makes for a knowledgeable crew of girls' basketball prospects.

Education about the intricacies of recruiting, both before and during the process, is the basis of how coach Tony Pappas helps prospective student-athletes at Waterloo, Iowa's West High. Pappas, a 20-plus-year veteran who has produced many All-Americans, works as floor director at the Nike All-America Camp each summer. He travels the country year-round giving coaching clinics and individual instruction to high school, collegiate, and WNBA players. Well-connected with college coaches, he has his own recruiting booklet as well. Each of Pappas' players gets a 70-page handbook that he assembled which outlines the process. "Make sure they have the NCAA handouts, rules and regulations," he comments. "I am going to oversee to make sure that they are taking the right academic classes, which is a big problem, by the way. I'm going to make sure that if I feel that they're going to have problems with a qualifying test score . . . Then I'm going to keep them informed, and I'm going to try to stress to them because it can become such pressure, you're going to be well-prepared. You're an elite person here in our school of 1800. There aren't even a handful of others who are being recruited like you are, and at first it may seem like a lot of fun but it's going to wear on you."

High school coaches who have recruitable athletes are surprised when they are not contacted by college coaches. "I really believe that high school coaches should be involved in recruiting quite a bit because we see them a lot," explains Lori Elgin, head coach at Alabama's Hoover High School and a former NCAA Division III coach. "If a college coach really wants to know what a kid's like, I would suspect they would call me as far as basketball and even as a person," Elgin adds. "I did that when I was recruiting. I talked to the high school coaches a lot more than what I have ever been called on. That's kind of weird to me." When parents look to Elgin in recruiting, she accepts that responsibility. "Everybody wants their daughter to play basketball in college and be recruited," she states. "Well, they all look at me like, what are you going to do about it? I have always felt like it was my responsibility to get the ball rolling, and then whatever happens happens, but it should be part of the job." Even after 10 years of coaching, Elgin is still trying to figure out the intricacies of recruiting in her area. She says that each time high school coaches change schools, they must adjust to different recruiting environments.

Sometimes egos become more important than who knows the student's skills, background, and personality. Although high school and non-scholastic coaches can contribute positively in recruiting, rarely do the two work in harmony for the athlete.

"I'm offended when a college coach calls me, and this is a player that I have been coaching for three years, and they tell me that they've spoken to the AAU coach first," says McConnell-Serio. "I see them basically year-round. I know that player as a person, and I know them as a player, better than an AAU coach will know them having had them for a month. When you're on an AAU trip or you're at a tournament and a college coach has questions about, what's this player like with this team, and it's questions like that, then I think that's appropriate. But I think when college coaches call AAU coaches first instead of the high school coach, I just think that they don't know them as well as their high school coach." McConnell-Serio used to coach club teams. When college coaches contacted her in that capacity regarding players, she would give them her evaluation. However, she would add that she only coached them on that summer team and that their high school coaches would know more about them.

Even the most well-known high school coaches whose grads go on to successful collegiate careers could be ignored in recruiting. "There are coaches who have recruited my players and who have never talked to me once in this whole process," remarks Dave Butcher, head coach at Ohio's Pickerington High School. "It's not many, but they're still out there. For a high-profile program like us, I find it amazing that they're actually going through without talking to me. From my point of view, I do not like it when they supercede my authority and talk to an AAU coach. It doesn't happen a lot, but I think it happens. It does not happen to me personally, but I think it happens a ton." In this situation, high school coaches cast the blame on club rather than college coaches. However, if the non-scholastic coach can bring about a match between a player and a college during the summer, providing the coach with enough background information, perhaps that athlete will verbally commit during the summer. Practically and unemotionally speaking, this eliminates the need for the high school coach's involvement.

Conflicts between club and high school coaches in recruiting can produce more tension for a student-athlete in what is already a stressful time. Instead of helping her through the process, trying to make it as easy as possible, this can compound the pressure. "And so now all of a sudden a club coach has developed a kid for a couple of years, and now that kid's going to get recruited, and then all of a sudden the high school coach wants to step in, where they haven't been there for three years," says Brad Smith, Oregon City High School co-head coach. "Hey, I'll coach you from October, November, through March, and then go do what you want to do, and stuff, and so they haven't been a part of the process at all. Then all of a sudden the club coach has done it, and if you're the club coach you're thinking 'Hey, I've got some ownership here, too.' That's why to me, it should be one of those that the club coach and the high school coach need to get along. And if they don't, then the kid has divided loyalties, and now the kid's got a problem, and so does the school and everybody else because who do I listen to?"

Joe Lombard, head coach at Texas' Canyon High School, has seen nine state titles in almost 25 years of high school coaching. Over 50 of his athletes have gone on to play at all collegiate levels. "As high school coaches, we would like to help and be a positive influence and to be an asset to that player and to that player's parents," Lombard explains. "Maybe a go-between. If the parents ask for advice, I will give advice, but they know that the decision is entirely up to that player and the parents. They know that I won't tell them where they need to go, but we will maybe talk about the pros and cons. Help them understand . . . do you want to go to a Division I school? What are your chances of playing? How important is it to you? Is playing the most important thing, or do you just want to be in a great program? Can you sit on the bench that freshman year?"

More so than parents or family friends, high school coaches can provide a reality check for prospective student-athletes. "Sometimes I think the kids, they forget that these recruiters, they're looking out for themselves first and not so much the kid," says Frank Mattucci, head coach at Stevenson High School in Lincolnshire, Illinois. Mattucci, who has 20 years of experience, coached WNBA athlete Tamika Catchings during her first two years of high school and her sister Tauja for her entire high school career. "Sometimes I think it's up to the high school teacher or coach to keep things in perspective for them and keep a little reality base going — either way, so that the kid doesn't get too high, too excited about a possible scholarship, or get too down if someone says to them, 'Well, now we don't want you,'" he continues, adding that helping athletes "sort out a priority list" is also important. He has his recruited athletes work their lists with pen and paper, comparing each college visited with the established criteria.

High school coaches' assessments should include an honest evaluation of players' college potential. Although players may not like hearing that they are not NCAA Division I-bound, a coach's honesty could prevent future disappointment. "I think the role of the high school coach should be to let the kid know what her options are and to be honest with that kid," says Dorena Bingham, head coach at state champ East High School in Anchorage, Alaska. Bingham, who assumed her post in 1993, also leads a successful travel team. Between the two ventures, almost 30 of her players have been recruited. "We've got so many kids here, and I'm sure everywhere," she continues, "who think they're the top Division I recruit and if they just have good seasons, everybody will come after them. It doesn't work that way. I think they need to sell themselves and not be afraid to sell themselves, but they also need to understand their limitations and what they're going to be able to do as a college player. Don't go to a place that runs if you're slow."

Many high school coaches, for sure, face the situation of a student-athlete and/or parents who think that she is definitely Division I material, when the coaches know otherwise. Some choose not to break the news themselves, letting recruiting take its course and deliver that message. Even before the official recruiting period begins, this scenario can create tension between high school coaches, parents, and athletes. "What I tell our players, and I think it's really important, I may get 25 letters a day but a lot of those are form letters," says Butcher. "A lot of those are letters to the kids that you know as a coach that they have no opportunity whatsoever. I don't think you want to create false impressions because in a lot of ways that's going to hurt you individually. Say you've got this kid, and I'm getting form letters on the kid, and I'm sitting here thinking, golly, we've had 30 kids play Division I. I know this kid's definitely not a Division I player and may not even be a kid that's going to start varsity for us, and I'm giving her these letters and things. Then all of a sudden it comes back on Dave Butcher. Why aren't you starting my kid? So you've got to be careful what you do." Many times these letters and questionnaires arrive at the high school coach's mail slot early on in their players' prep careers. In abiding with NCAA rules, he or she would only be able to pass fill-in questionnaires along to the student-athlete prior to her junior year.

"I let the colleges tell them," Bingham says. "In other words, I basically don't burst their bubble. I let it be burst by the colleges. It's interesting because you get situations like one I have now, where the parents blame you because their kid is not being recruited like they thought she should be. You just have to have broad shoulders and move on." Although some players slip through the cracks and are underrecruited, this is the exception. Nowadays, most quality high school girls' players will be seen by college coaches. While nobody can blame parents for being their daughters' biggest fans, for athletes serious about playing in college, an impartial opinion is essential.

From the rookie to the National Coach of the Year, high school coaches should only be as involved in the process as the player and her parents wish. Ultimately, the college choice is a decision that the family will have to live with. "I become involved in the recruiting process when a parent asks me to," quips Butcher. "I did not want to be the person who steps in and says, 'Hey, listen, I think you should go to this school,' and all of a sudden a kid goes to that school and they hate it. So I think you've got to educate before, when they're younger, provide the information to the students, provide information to the parents. Then, when you get to that final recruiting process, if my players want me to sit in on visits, I will. If a player wants to come in and pick my brain in my office, I will. If a player or a parent wants to give me a call and talk and ask what do you think about this program, because I know just about everybody, I'll do that. But I'm not going to give that final piece of the puzzle to them unless they ask for it because I just think it basically comes down to a player-parent choice." In almost 20 years at Pickerington, Butcher has seen many former players, including Ohio State star LaToya Turner, sign Division I scholarships.

Just as college coaches sell their programs, many high school coaches see it as their responsibility to help promote their players. "Our job is almost like a salesman," declares Carl Tinsley, co-head coach at Oregon City High School. If high school coaches recognize the business aspect of women's basketball, they can see how they can contribute to the business model. "Our job is to make sure that people know about our product, that being the player," continues Tinsley, who also organizes the End of the Trail summer tournament. "People that can purchase that player, in other words in this case, they'll recruit that player — I'm using analogies — but they would be able to get the opportunity to know about our product and then see our product and see whether or not that product fits their needs. We're not going to hard sell a kid like you might a car, but we're going to say hey, this kid . . . When I call somebody, I think it's important that I'm fair and also that I know what's going on. We should be contacting these people. We should get film to these people or get them to our games and give them an opportunity to see the kid play."

Taking an active role in recruiting requires time, effort, and patience. Unlike the coaches interviewed for this chapter, many high school coaches find it difficult enough just to plan and coach practices and games in-season, let alone work with players and parents on the recruiting process. Some relish their off-seasons and do not want to have much to do with basketball from April to November. As with any job, others go through the motions to supplement their incomes, uninterested in putting forth extra effort. Some want to help but have no idea what to do. A good start would be attending clinics and talking to colleagues who have experience with the process.

"I think that the purpose of the high school coach is to allow the player to make the right decision for that player, and not the right decision for what the coach thinks, and not the right decision for what everybody else thinks, but what is best for the player," asserts Smith. "I think sometimes that the high school coach, you've got to take the emotion out, and you have to ask the tough questions at the recruiting thing. If there's a place that the kid just, it's just bam, point blank, I love this place, I think it's the job of the high school coach to say, that's great. Let's look at some possible negatives. Make the parents and the player weigh both sides. We've had kids that have done it all — gone to a school because their parents wanted them to, felt the pressure to go there, picked the school because of who the coach might have been, all of those things." Smith has seen recruiting from different approaches; in 1998-99, he took a one-year hiatus from the high school ranks and served as an assistant coach at Vanderbilt, where his daughter Ashley played.

There may be a difference between what people believe the high school coach's duties should be in recruiting and what they actually are. The high school coach should be an educator, an objective evaluator, a facilitator, a liaison, a listener. Those about to embark on the college recruiting process for the first time may find it difficult to assume these responsibilities. However, by researching and communicating, and above all remembering that the girl and her parents are the focus of the process, the high school coach can be a key player in helping athletes choose the right college match.

Club Hoops and Club Coaches

Where does club basketball fit into women's college basketball recruiting? "It's huge," says Kara Leary, president and coach of the winning New England Crusaders club. As NCAA recruiting regulations have become more stringent, the three-week open window in July is for all practical purposes the recruiting period in women's basketball. Many prep players do not play with their high school teammates and coaches during that time. They join with athletes from their area, and sometimes outside their area, to play on what are called traveling teams, club teams, AAU teams, or any other term used for a non-scholastic team. Due to all of the above, club coaches have assumed more importance in recruiting — perhaps too much, and in many cases more so than the high school coach. It's no secret that boys' club coaches do not have a positive reputation these days, as some have made headlines for acting as agents and profiting from their players. While the money does not exist on the girls' side, the stigma attached to club coaches certainly does.

Though club ball is not an absolute necessity for those who want to compete in college, girls need some method of being seen by college coaches. "I don't think student-athletes have to play on a summer team if they want to play in college, but I think the benefits of a good traveling team are worthwhile," states John Coffee, who coaches with the AAU Dayton Lady Hoopstars. If players' high school teams do not advance to state tourneys, and if they do not attend individual summer camps or clinics, non-scholastic competition may very well be the only source of needed college exposure.

While the shift in recruiting power toward girls' club coaches can in part be attributed to personalities, it can also be attributed to changes in the NCAA recruiting calendar. "The early signing [period] has made a huge change in recruiting because it made summer important," Tinsley states. "Literally, the recruiting is done mostly in the summer now and not in the high school season. So that, then, gave the club coach much more influence on the recruiting process than the high school coach. It took the process away from the high school coach and put it in the hands of the club coach. That is who the college coaches will contact in the summer when they're recruiting. Because of that, the high school coach has been eliminated from the process in the summer. Not in our case, but in most cases."

The pressure on athletes to perform well in front of college coaches can be significant during the month of July. College coaches try to watch as many games as they can during that three-week span, and they may try to see prospects they have their sights on in several different tourneys. If a girl has a bad game, sometimes it's no longer just a bad game that she needs to shake off. "We had some kids in our organization who very definitely felt that they had 25 days to prove to these coaches that they could play, especially kids coming out of our area where it's not normal for a coach to be out since their freshman year, watching them," says Leary, who also coached two seasons at New Hampshire's Nashua High School. "But then we have kids who just play and it doesn't matter . . . They have the right perspective. They just go play, and if things work out, great. If they don't, that's fine too. We have very definitely had kids who were just like, if I don't play well, I don't know what I'm going to do. We give them the opportunity." Leary keeps roster numbers down to give each player ample chance to be seen.

Different non-scholastic coaches have different goals, be it just giving girls a chance to play and improve and have fun, winning championships, and/or amassing scholarship opportunities. Those who care mainly about victories may not be as concerned about promoting their athletes to college coaches. "There's a lot of garbage in AAU," comments James Anderson, head coach at state champ Narbonne High in Harbor City, California, and director of the OGBL club program. "AAU basketball is based on having the best players and winning games. A lot of those coaches don't care if their kids get scholarships. For me, it's based on how many kids get scholarships. To me, that makes your program look better.

"I think you have two different philosophies," Anderson continues. "Are you doing it to win AAU trophies for your program, or are you're trying to get scholarships, and that's going to accentuate your program? For me, it's the scholarship part of it."

The makeup of non-scholastic teams and tournaments varies, as does the level of college exposure garnered by a single squad. Certain summer tournaments host only certain types of teams. For example, the AAU only allows AAU teams to play in its state and national tourneys. A single AAU team based in a particular state can feature only players from neighboring states. However, other summer tourneys, often privately-run, accept any club team, allowing coaches to stack their squads on an invite-only basis. "There are coaches out there who will put together a team, like, we go to Junior Nationals every year in Washington, and they'll put together a team with a kid from Oregon, a kid from Puerto Rico, a kid from New Hampshire, these kids from all over, and they'll try to go to these tournaments and win," explains Jill Cook, assistant coach at New York's Christ the King High School and president and coach of the New York Liberty Belles club. "They can do that because it's not a national tournament event. It's just like, I feel like running a tournament. You would be allowed to do that in a private tournament. We never got involved in that because our focus for the summer is really on the kids from our area getting exposure to colleges. We're not trying to win a tournament title. We like to win, but that's not the main focus."

In order to get exposure, a student-athlete obviously has to get some playing time. On club teams, athletes used to lots of minutes with their high school squads could be faced with sharing time or even with warming the bench. This creates conflicts with players and parents, many of whom consider their monetary investment in summer ball a guarantee that when college coaches are in the stands, their daughters will be running the floor. "Parents are paying money, and now they expect their kids to play," Leary explains. "We have had situations where parents haven't been happy. We sit down, and we try to figure out whether they need to go play somewhere else for the rest of the summer. I know quite a few people in the area who I can place them with, if that's what they want. But it's kind of like a double-edged sword. These kids want to be on the floor all the time, but they also want to play with the best players, but they may not be the best player. They don't want to go play on this team over here because maybe all of the college coaches aren't following that team, but they would be on the floor and may be the reason why these college coaches would follow."

When a player's high school coach and club coach are two different people, she might feel caught in the middle in recruiting. Who will she go to for advice? Who will attend her home visits? Who will she call after visiting a campus? Perhaps she has known her high school coach longer, or perhaps she has a closer relationship with her club coach. "The reality is that the club coach is not 'for' the high school coach," Tinsley muses. "In some cases, they're against the high school coach, and they're battling that high school coach for that kid in the summer. What happens is that kid is now drawn between her loyalties. Now the club coach is telling her, 'Hey, you hang with me and I'll get you a scholarship.' The high school coach is worried about winning games during the regular season. Well, the kid's worried about a scholarship, and it becomes a selfish kind of thing and they start to worry about, well gosh, where am I going to play in college? Then the club coach is just going to get that kid.

"Sometimes they're not going to help them make the best decisions," Tinsley continues. "There are some quality club coaches out there, quality, that do the right thing by their kids. There are some club coaches out there that do not do the right thing for them." If a student-athlete draws attention during summer ball, chances are that her non-scholastic coach will be involved with her recruiting process. In recruiting utopia, high school and club coaches work together. In real life, however, they sometimes compete for a prospect's attention and services during the summer.

In addition, because of the negative label placed on club coaches in general, some college staffs like to interact only with high school coaches. Even when non-scholastic coaches may be more knowledgeable and connected, the overall reputation prevents some from getting involved. "The reality is, a lot of college coaches prefer to deal with the high school coaches," Leary comments. "But there are some AAU coaches out there that are good. From what we hear from coaches who deal with our organization, I have high school coaches who don't know a lot of things, and what we try to do is educate them. But I have a lot of kids who prefer me to be a lead in their process over the high school coach. You know how that goes. The high school coaches need to be educated. In a lot of situations, they have one player who goes in 20 years." As club basketball con-

158

tinues to evolve, perhaps high school and club coaches will work harder on collaborating to help their common recruitable players. However, this will require compromise from each party, especially with different experiences and motivations.

In terms of recruiting, summer basketball may benefit mid- and lower- level colleges and prospects the most. "AAU is a financial boon to colleges, simply because they can go to one event and see a number of athletes who would qualify from an ability standpoint to play at their institution," explains Eddie Clinton, AAU senior sport manager. "If you go to a high school game, you're lucky if you see two that would fit into that category. It's just an economics thing where you can make one trip and see a lot of different kids. The biggest beneficiary, however, is the mid-level . . . The top 100 kids, I don't care what sport you're in, they are going to pretty well have a pick of where they want to go. It's the ones who are playing along with them who go to mid-level and low-level Division I or Division II or Division III or NAIA schools that still get scholarships, still have the opportunity to be student-athletes. Those are the real beneficiaries, in my opinion — those almost superstars, the kids who have ability but may not be the top two or three percent of their age division. Because they are playing with the other kids, and you get the very best . . . the coaches see the other kids and it's just a win-win situation." While Clinton specifically mentions AAU, his comments apply to any non-scholastic basketball.

Because of concerns over the influence of summer ball and club coaches in college recruiting, a growing group believes that the NCAA should take club basketball completely out of the recruiting process. In other words, college coaches would not be allowed to watch summer tourneys, and they would not be allowed to interact with club coaches.

However, according to Clinton, even if the NCAA did eliminate the summer evaluation period, club basketball would still play an important role in recruiting. "The summer program — kids are going to play," he asserts. "It's not going to go away. If they shut down the recruiting, basically all we'll do is we'll tape all of our events and then sell them $500 a tape. Coaches need to have the information that we have, and kids are going to play in the summer regardless of what the NCAA does or the high schools do." For coaches who shell out thousands of dollars for recruiting expenses, an additional $500 seems like small change.

The Prep Perspective on College Coaches in Recruiting

Of the different parties involved in women's basketball recruiting, college coaches and prospects' current coaches often interact the most. No rules restrict the frequency or start of their communication. By the end of the process, recruits' current coaches could know the college coaches better than the recruit and her family do. While most do not see college coaches trashing major recruiting rules or flat-out lying to players, they do acknowledge that college coaches sometimes play the game of not being completely up front, just like other recruiting participants.

"College coaches are being as honest as they possibly can under the situation," says Benge. " I guess we get into different shades of honesty, and I've been very, very impressed with every coach that I've dealt with. As far as the honesty, I don't feel anyone's just completely lied. A long time ago that happened to one of my players, where she was going to go to a university and the coach called up the day before she was supposed to sign — she had not looked for over a month — and the coach said 'Well, we lost a scholarship, so we're not going to offer one now.' That just was not true. We ended up getting the player another scholarship, but if they had been honest right up front . . . That's the only time. But what I mean by shades of honesty, it's like, they've got one scholarship to offer and they've got four kids they're looking at. So you're the fourth kid. They're not going to tell you that they don't want you and they're not going to tell you about these other three kids." Combined with the fact that most girls do not like to ask these questions, this can leave players in quite a conundrum.

Offering an additional perspective on the degrees of honesty, Cook explains that a college coach's reluctance to fully answer a question shows that the athlete does not top the recruiting list. As only a handful of teens can hold that first slot, this discussion is frustrating for the majority. "If the kid is their number one choice, they're going to come right out and say, we want you right now," she says. "If you tell us you're coming, we're dropping everyone else. If they're kind of between players, or the kid isn't your first choice, they'll try to really not answer your question. They'll say the thing that drives me crazy about college coaches. They'll say to you, 'We're as interested in Mary as she is in us.' So I always say, 'Well, she wants to come, so does that mean you're going to take her?' And then they kind of won't answer you. My feeling is you either like the kid or you don't. Her level of interest in you, to me, should be irrelevant if you really like the kid. But if they dodge the question they'll say, you know, we're going to have three kids come to campus and we'll talk to our players and see who they like, and they're going to evaluate exactly what they need. They just give you standard lines, I guess."

Although high school and club coaches can be as star-struck as their players at receiving attention from big-time colleges, this feeling wears off with experience. Anderson, for example, has coached many NCAA Division I prospects, including Loree Moore, who headed off to Tennessee in 2001. Accordingly, he fields lots of calls, often when college coaches just want to know who he's got in his pipeline. Astute prep-level coaches know why college coaches establish these relationships. "I like Pat Summitt, and I enjoy Pat Summitt," begins Anderson, "but Pat Summitt calls because we have pretty good basketball players. I can say that, and Pat's a great person." Although some college coaches may want to stroke egos, high school and club coaches should know that these compliments are not as important as helping their players make the right decisions.

In a way, going through the recruiting process is much like being on stage, with all trying give a great performance. This analogy certainly rings true for college coaches. "Every coach who comes in wants to let you know that they're at the top academically, or they're at the top. Whatever it is, they're at the top of," states Smith. "And I think it's up to the high school coach to be able to know that and to know that everybody can't be up at the top. Somebody's got to be at the bottom . . . College coaches come in and they're just like highlight films.

I'm never going to see the mess . . . When they say 'Hey, call anybody you want to call,' well, your best bet is, make sure you find a kid who quit three years ago or a kid who never played two years ago."

"The majority, and not all of them," adds Pappas, "come in and they are one way in the visits, home and college and on the phone — and once you get there it's a whole different person that you see. Do you understand what I'm saying? Fun and games are over, baby. Now we're going to put the pedal to the metal." Talking with players and observing coaches in action will help prospects and families distinguish between the "recruiter" and the "coach."

Other times, college coaches have forgotten that high school and club coaches are usually advocates for their players; they will notice if college coaches seem fatigued or unenthusiastic. "I was put off by some college coaches at times when I met with them," states Michael Deady, head coach at Massachusetts' Attleboro High. "Put off in the sense that I felt on occasion when I talked to coaches at the games . . . I got the impression a lot of times that they didn't want to be there. Maybe they were tired or something like that." This would be the last impression that college staffs should want to leave with student-athletes and their families.

Although high school and club coaches do not see college coaches blatantly breaking significant recruiting regulations, some say that college coaches may try to get around other rules. "I think there are college coaches who are bending the rules," says Bingham, who has seen college coaches passing notes, even after 1996, when the NCAA made it a recruiting violation to do so. "I remember when they stopped letting you pass notes. You can't pass notes anymore, and there are people still doing that kind of thing and acting like they didn't know, and it's kind of funny." When college coaches used to be able to write personal notes to individual students at games, club or high school coaches would pass them along. After contests, college coaches would stand in line for the summer coach, waiting not only to talk to him or her but also holding a handwritten note for a recruit.

Prep-level coaches have seen evidence of the increased recruiting pressure in the number of their players making decisions well before the early signing period. "I think college coaches are pushing very much harder for kids to come in earlier, big time, way more than they used to," comments Tinsley. "There's way more kids committing now even before September. You never used to see that, and now you see it all the time. You've got kids now who are committing as juniors in high school. You didn't used to see that. A lot of that has to do with college coaches cranking that up because now it's important for them to win, all of them. I think what's happened is they're now putting more subtle pressure, if not outward pressure — hey, if you don't sign we're going to take the next kid. There have been some huge changes in recruiting in the last five years just because of that. Some kids are like, if I don't sign here I'm not going to get that scholarship I wanted."

These days, some like to speculate on the similarities between men's and women's basketball in recruiting. While people will always disagree, few could currently present hard evidence condemning women's college basketball coaches for their overt disregard for important recruiting rules and all-out dishonesty in recruiting. However, as some high school and club coaches point out, college coaches do play mind games, avoid questions, and apply the full court press in recruiting. Nonetheless, others do have only the best of intentions. Hopefully, the prospective student-athlete has a savvy coach to help her and her parents make sense of recruiting's many twists.

Recruiting As Seen by Prospects' Current Coaches

High school-level coaches are uniquely positioned to see what the recruiting process is like for prospective student-athletes. Perhaps better able to describe recruits' perspectives than the subjects themselves, they may also have more of an insiders' view than college coaches.

"I think the hardest part of recruiting for student-athletes is when they start being able to talk to coaches," says Bingham. "I think the phone calls are tough because they don't know what to say. I think if you're really highly recruited it's very strenuous. You've got your homework and you've got everything else, but you're still trying to make sure you make contact with everybody." Simply conversing with any adult is enough to make many teens cringe, not to mention talking to a coach with an interest in their futures. No wonder, then, that so many recruits pick a college based partly their perceptions of the coaching staff.

"Each kid deals with it differently," states Benge. "Some of them try to avoid it, and they don't want to talk about it. Others just totally stress. I know the day Ashley Allen [a 2001 Ben Davis grad who signed with Ohio State] was going to announce what college she was going to, she couldn't make up her mind between two colleges, so we had to postpone the announcement. It was very tough. It's a lot of pressure on these kids. You know, they don't have all the information they need. They can't go to every practice . . . They get a feel and they get as much information as they can." Doubt plagues many right up to the eleventh hour, and even afterward.

Student-athletes' reluctance to turn college coaches down is compounded by some college coaches' reactions. "It's difficult to tell someone that you've spoken to three or four times a week, it's difficult to tell them no," says Cook. "But at the same time it's exhausting. It depends on the personality of the head coach whether there's a lot of pressure. Some schools are really understanding . . . You have people react in a positive way and wish the kid good luck, say if you need anything I'll be there. And then we've had coaches who are kind of jerks about it. I understand from their point of view they've put in a lot of time and effort, but it's not always the best reaction when you tell them you're not coming."

"I can tell you about another coach who I don't want to name, who called Jenni [Dant] and just said, 'Hey, we didn't want you anyway,' when Jenni told her we're not going to accept the scholarship," Mattucci states. "Now what is that? That's childish. My girl was as kind and as up front and straightforward as any 17- or 18-year-old can be, and then you've got some supposed adult head coach telling her we didn't want you anyway. Is she just supposed to make her feel bad? That to me is unethical." These experiences could leave students with a bad feeling about college coaches and about college basketball in general. At the very least, it takes away from that feeling of excitement about being wanted, about being rewarded for hard work.

With the increased attention some college coaches lavish on girls at young ages now, it can be easy for players to be misled about their basketball potential. "I think a lot of these kids are disillusioned because of all of the letters they get at early ages," Severson comments. "They're 12 and they're 13, and they're all form letters. They're not personal letters. We're going to follow your AAU as you go through, and these kids they get their heads way up in the clouds right away because they think they're going to play at UCLA, and they think they're going to go to Notre Dame and stuff like this. So I think that the idea of the form letters is great, but there needs to be a way that these people are informed that that's all they are." Even in high school, players draw the false conclusion that if a college sends them a letter, that college is actively recruiting them.

What begins as a whirlwind of exhilaration progresses to be an exhausting and nerve-wracking process, as prospects, parents, and high school and club coaches will attest. Even the most prepared high school athlete with the most knowledge-able coach(es) will be overwhelmed. "I think the hardest part for student-athletes is meting out the hype from the truth, fig-uring out the frill and the thrill from the real and the deal — what is really going to happen," Mattucci reflects. "That's the toughest because they're impressionable kids. They're not dum-mies but they're impressionable." These comments provide yet more proof that even the most perceptive prospects need help throughout the recruiting process.

Changes in Recruiting

According to prep-level coaches, the many changes in women's basketball recruiting range from the overall atmo-sphere to the attitudes of college coaches and of student-ath-letes. They generalize that the process has become more na-tionwide, regulated, and concentrated. As they note, recruit-ing now poses completely different challenges and dilemmas.

"Recruiting has become much more intense," Pappas states. "When I first started trying to place my players 21 years ago here, I would just make the contact, and then they would kind of call and talk to you and get some ideas, maybe send a videotape. If they liked what they saw, they would maybe go on my recommendation a little bit or maybe they'd come to one game and see them, and that was it. Then you go to the other end of the spectrum where they're spending anywhere now from $10 to $20,000 to recruit one kid. They're following them all over the world, and the contacts are incredible, the amount of time and effort, whether it's producing their own jerseys with their names on them and taking them into the coliseums or wherever they're at, and the writing and the contacts."

Pappas saw evidence of this in the recruiting of 1999 West High grad Nina Smith, a National High School Player of the Year who attended the University of Wisconsin for two years before transferring to Iowa State. "I think one time Nina got 27 letters from 27 people from the same institution in one day," he remembers. "They had alumni, department heads, players, coaches, president, governor. It impressed her a little bit." What's more, college coaches spent thousands of dollars to follow Pappas and Smith to Paris during two weekends for an international tournament and to see Smith play in Russia during the summer. Additionally, the prominence of all levels of Division I has increased. "I think just in the last few years," Cook adds, "I've seen the mid-Division I schools and the lower Division I schools seem to take a more aggressive approach on recruiting, rather than you just hear about the big names that are out there and have the big budgets. I think AAU has obviously helped consolidate all the good players in one area. Maybe that's helping the mid-level schools get their names out there and become more familiar with the kids." The fact that any college coach can attend a handful of nationally-known summer tourneys contributes to this phenomenon. In effect, any college coach from any division can attend the Nike All-America Girls Camp in Indianapolis, which features 80-something of the country's top players. Even if the coach recognizes that the chance of roping in a prospect from one of these elite events is scarce, attending nonetheless helps publicize the college program.

In fact, many staffs at all different levels focus on recruiting, which most coaches now see as a major component, if not *the* major component, of their jobs. "You used to get contacts from a number of schools but now, even the smaller DI schools and DII and DIII are making contact with the coaches and trying to identify and get lists of the players as soon as possible," Butcher says.

Many of the ways in which women's college basketball recruiting has evolved came about because of changes in women's college basketball in general. "It's become more competitive, and it's become a national search," says Tinsley. "It used to be that the best players in Oregon and Washington would probably be signing most of their letters of intent in the Northwest, and now they're signing them all over the country, and vice versa. So you see now college programs all over the country that are smattered with all kind of different kids, and now you're seeing the foreign players really come into play."

Furthermore, several new influences play a role. "I think you've got to look at the shootouts and the portfolios that they're selling and the money that's involved," Butcher says. "There are a lot of differences that were not there 15 years ago. You're looking at the people who run the camps, who run the shootouts, who are compiling the information for the coaches. I think from the college coaches' viewpoint, anybody who can make their jobs easier with the constraints they have now, they're going to deal with." However, Butcher does not know whether these outside parties and their contributions add up to an overall plus or minus for recruiting.

In an effort to minimize a coach's chances of gaining a recruiting edge, increased regulations may unfortunately have damaged the chances for a close coach-recruit relationship. "I think that with a lot of the recruiting rules changes, the coaches and the players both don't have a lot of opportunity to get to know the kids as well, so there's not as much of an opportunity to see if there's a fit," Leary comments. She believes that this absolutely relates to the large number of women's college hoopsters who transfer each year. "What do you do when you see a kid in mid-July for the first time, and you really like her," Leary ponders, "and your top two choices who may be local kids who you have followed since their freshman year because of geography, and the reality is that recruiting is still very geographically-based because of budget. You have since found out that they are looking elsewhere. So now you see a kid just like her in the middle of July, so instead of having two or three years to watch the kid, you watch her from July, you maybe see three or four more games, and then you've got to try to sign her. So you'll see her three or four more games, and that's all you're seeing of her because she's not starting to play her high school season until December.

"On the flip side," Leary continues, "that same kid is now getting interest from you, and she hasn't seen your college team play or practice, those sorts of things. It's hard. But that's the way it goes, I guess. A lot of the measures put in for recruiting are cost-containment issues. You've just got to make sure your kids do their homework. We tell them that you never know, really know, until they get there." In fact, Leary's own sister, Michaela, transferred from the University of Michigan to George Washington (both NCAA Division I colleges) after her freshman year in 2001.

The increased transferring also reflects a change in student-athletes' mindsets. No matter the perspective, all seem to recognize transferring as a reality of collegiate athletics in general. "You can get recruited, you can go to a school, and if you don't like what's going on, you just leave," asserts Deady. "In the past, like when I was a kid, it was almost like if you did something like that, you were going back on a commitment. It was viewed as a negative thing. Now people say that's just the way it is. The last thing coaches want, they don't want a kid around who's miserable. They want people who want to be there." Does this philosophy take some of the pressure off student-athletes? Does transferring factor into college coaches' recruiting plans? Perhaps the ever-growing transfer tally is also indicative of today's society, with divorce much more commonplace, with the average person switching jobs with much more frequency than a generation ago. Both examples provide teens real-world evidence that no decision is final, regardless of its significance.

Girls' attitudes toward recruiting and college ball have changed as well. "One of the things that I've talked about with a lot of college coaches lately is how kids are more demanding now than they used to be," Cook says. "Kids want to play now in a new arena, and they want to play in front of 7,000 people. If a coach has an old gym and they draw 1,200 people to a game, they feel like they're at a real disadvantage. When I played and I got recruited, that wasn't even an option in your mind because it just wasn't what was happening in the world of women's basketball."

Of the many changes that have taken place in women's basketball recruiting, some are concrete. Rules are more stringent, college coaches devote more time and money to recruiting, more prospects sign early, the summer period has become significant, and competition is greater. Other differences are intangible. The atmosphere is more intense, it seems harder for some athletes to find the right match, and conflict can arise between high school and club coaches. In this ever-evolving environment, high school and club coaches wrestle with their roles.

Preparing Student-Athletes for the Recruiting Wars

Though coaches have different tactics and advice for helping their charges in recruiting, their experience with the process benefits the athletes. Some educate their players as a group about recruiting early in their prep careers, whereas others hold individual meetings. Still others do not do much advance preparation with families, preferring to deal with individual tribulations as they arise.

Some coaches have contacts in the college coaching realm and experience with recruiting. Prospective student-athletes on their teams are lucky to have them as resources. While they agree on major aspects important to students and parents, they take different approaches to helping out. Some do not become involved unless specifically asked, whether or not they school the masses on the process.

Severson, for example, subscribes to this approach. "I tell every one of my kids that I will do everything in my power to get you a college scholarship if this is what you want, but I am not going to start any process until I hear from you people that this is what you want to do," he explains. "I don't really, unless they come to me and they say, 'Coach, can you help me find a place to play?' I say, 'You bet, I'll be happy to do that.' Then I'll start calling people." He does not talk to families ahead of time about the process unless parents call him with questions. McConnell-Serio also tells athletes that she will be involved as much as they want her to and will gladly send out tapes and contact coaches.

On the other hand, others have established systems of educating student-athletes about recruiting. Aside from guiding her athletes throughout the process, Bingham requires all team members to carry a notebook featuring a section on the NCAA and recruiting — articles, pamphlets, and so on. Those who do not have the notebook with them at all times, or at least whenever they see her, will run at practice. During the process, she checks in with recruits frequently to see if they are filling out their questionnaires or how a phone call or campus visit went. Pappas, a seasoned recruiting veteran with many contacts in the field, is also very involved, armed with his 70-page recruiting handbook. Anderson, who says he fields 20-30 calls every week from college coaches, sits down with his entire team each spring to discuss recruiting.

"Our kids at Christ the King know the process," says Cook, "because we really try to educate them from the time they're a sophomore in high school. We make sure they know all their requirements, they know everything they have to fulfill, they do their paperwork for the Clearinghouse. Our sophomores see the process our seniors are going through, coaches coming to practice or home visits, campus visits and all that stuff."

Handling recruiting on a case-by-case basis also works for some. In any case, when they do get down to talking specifics with families, coaches might first ask questions to help create a list of colleges. How far away are you interested in going? What major(s) interests you? Are you more interested in being part of an established program or one that's up-and-coming? What style of play do you prefer? What type of coaching? Do you have particular schools that you are already interested in?

When the recruiting process actually gets going, many see it as their responsibility to interact with college coaches, either after games, on the phone, or most often at home visits — where families will hear comments first-hand. They ask questions that they feel are important but that parents and students may not know to ask or may be afraid to ask themselves, as they have such a personal stake. Where does she stand on your recruiting list? Are you ready to offer her a scholarship right now? How long to you plan to stay at the school? What are your requirements academically? What are your program's graduation rates? Where do you see her fitting in? If you are not nationally competitive, how do you plan to get there? How do you treat your players?

"Oh, they've got their pat answers," Pappas states. "'Oh, you're at the top of our list.' 'We wouldn't be here if you weren't at the top of our list.' Sometimes they're honest, and they just say, 'We're making a home visit. We're not going to give you a scholarship.'" Pappas points out that college coaches have their tough questions as well, that often come up during the home visit. "'Are you ready to sign right now?'" he offers as a prime example.

As a practical bit of advice, Anderson says that when it comes to campus visits, recruits should always schedule their top choices last. This was the case with Moore, considered by many the country's top high school playmaker in 2001. "We always leave the number one school as the last campus visit because you're trying to find a reason not to go to Tennessee now," Anderson explains. "There has to be a reason why you don't want to go there, and if you can't find any reasons, then that's the school we end up going to. [Loree] took the other trips, and she loves Duke and Notre Dame, but when she got to Tennessee, there was still no reason why she shouldn't go to Tennessee. That's how we figured hers out." For those so inclined, if they take the necessary steps, not only will they be in a position to get a scholarship, they will also have choices.

Although everybody knows that research plays an important part, students and parents need to make sure their research focuses on the right areas. "They need to know what the rules are," says Butcher. "No matter what, there's a lot of great academic institutions in the United States, but you're going to have to deal with that coach, with those assistant coaches, with their rules and their setup . . . The type of players they recruit, the style of basketball they run — that's something you need to research. I think you need to be realistic on this whole situation. I think somewhere you've got to be realistic about the level of athletics that your daughter can play at . . . I think you need to have done your research before they try to sell. Then you know what questions to ask."

Helping student-athletes analyze the nature of recruiting also plays a part, in addition to specific and practical preparation. "You've got to work hard, both in the classroom and outside the classroom," says Pappas. "You've got to take these next three months and prepare extensively for this week in July when you're going to be seen by the college coaches. We're going to develop a move that will stand out that will make college coaches snap their heads if they see you make this move and write down your number and things of that sort."

"Don't take anything for granted," Anderson advises. "You have a lot of kids who, I got a letter from here, and they always say, I am being recruited by — no you're not. You got a letter from there. That doesn't mean anything. I would say, take it slow. For one thing we always tell our kids, it's the kid's decision. The kid has got to be there for four years, not the parent, but the parent is there to advise and give information . . . I would tell them to ask every question, even if you think it's a stupid question or a question that's going to cause tension. Don't wait and find out later it was something you wanted to know and you didn't find out about it."

To keep up with the Joneses nowadays, women's college basketball coaches need to have multiple backups on their recruiting lists. Athletes who may have thought they would play at a certain level of college might not end up at their dream school, or even at that level. However, as there are many merits to different levels of college ball. "Don't be set on DI, or don't think you can't play DI," Elgin states. "Just keep all of your options open. Make sure you're filling out everything and sending it back so you have options." The main reason college coaches send out forms and questionnaires, after all, is not to find out the requested information about a student; college coaches could easily pull up their stats and hobbies from other sources. A returned questionnaire indicates a girl's interest in an institution.

Sometimes the most useful suggestion is the simplest. McConnell-Serio always makes sure to pass along to her recruitable players the memorable suggestion she received as a high schooler. "I think the best advice I was given, and I know it's common advice," she muses, "but when you choose a school, you're playing basketball for four years, and I'm sure the basketball program is what's attracting you to that school first and foremost. But when you make your final decision, if you got injured your freshman year and it was a career-ending injury, would you be happy being there as a student for four years?"

Although no student-athlete can know the reality of recruiting until she actually begins it, this does not mean that she should sit idly by until the phone rings in June. "I'd say the big thing is to find out exactly what's going on ahead of time and know what you're looking for," Benge insists. "Don't just say, 'Oh, whatever college wants me,' or 'I don't know where I want to go. I'll just look at one college.' Let me know what you want your college experience to be." That way, when coaches begin to show interest, girls can compare each school's qualifications to their criteria instead of having no base of comparison. This will make the decision more logical and less emotional.

While seeking advice is helpful, having more than a few involved parties could compound an already-perplexing situation. "Don't listen to everybody," quips Mattucci. "If you listen to too many people, you're going to be more confused than you ever were before. You need to decide who do I trust and who do I not trust. I point blank, I bring that up with my kids. If I'm not the one you want, then let's not seek out my advice. Let's find some people and then you listen to those people only, no more than three . . . Because if you start listening to everybody else, they're going to want you to go here, some want you to go there, this cousin said this school's better, you're really not going to play, blah, blah, blah." Even after a student chooses her allies, she should realize that the ultimate decision is hers to make, as much as she may want her coaches, friends, and parents to tell her where they think she should go.

Smith offers a frank analysis of the transition from prep to college hoops, in terms of both level of play and atmosphere. "College and high school are totally different," he says. "Be prepared for the differences in college. And each level of college is different. Division II, Division III, NAIA, are totally different than Division I. The higher you go, the more it's going to become, everybody says a job, but the more it's going to become harder work without the same payback per se, emotionally. There's going to be a lot more responsibilities thrown on you. Your time is going to be regulated a lot more. It may not be that everybody's worried about how you're feeling. Where if you're in high school, or lower levels and stuff, people might be feeling, they're concerned about how you're feeling. That's an overgeneralization, but I think that's the thing you've got to be careful of."

Sometimes the pressure and other negative aspects of recruiting overshadow the fact that it can be fun if students allow themselves to step back. "It is a once-in-a-lifetime opportunity," says Tinsley. "Instead of worrying about it and fretting, enjoy the process and then, there are no bad decisions. . . .When they get all stressed out, we try to tell them most people in the world in the school you're in do not have this horrible decision to make. Most of the kids in this school sitting here right now will not have that opportunity." At the same time, it will not always be fun. "I just think that adults and outsiders and college coaches should understand that these are kids," Cook reflects. "It is a stressful thing at that point in their lives to go through this whole process. As much as people think, oh they should appreciate it and enjoy it, it's not always enjoyable to be put under that kind of pressure as a 17-year-old."

Some girls' basketball prospects go through the college recruiting process without the assistance of their coaches. However, others either seek or are offered help by their high school and/or club coaches. Though coaches may have the right intentions, sometimes they do not want to spend the extra time to help or are mostly concerned about their own self-esteems. Even if coaches are recruiting rookies, at the very least they can help with research and provide another perspective. For coaches who do have experience, recruiting can be a much less overwhelming and traumatic process for their prospective student-athletes, perhaps with a better outcome.

8

The Exposure Biz:
Recruiting Reports, Shootouts, and
Exposure Camps

Until recently, not many people other than some college coaches could make a living solely from women's basketball. However, a growing number now earn their keep in women's hoops without ever having to pick up a clipboard; they have made exposure for high school girls' basketball players their business. While some operate recruiting services or scouting reports, others run camps and exposure events for high school girls. Some do both of these things, and sometimes they also coach a team on the side. The sneaker giants even sponsor some of them. Their motivation could be any number of issues, from teaching girls to growing women's basketball to making money to helping college coaches build winning teams.

Whatever their driving forces, exposure camp and scouting service directors have become increasingly important to women's college basketball recruiting. They have not been around long enough yet to acquire quite the same bad rap as their counterparts in boys' basketball. While they do have their proponents, even those who may not be their biggest fans admit that they serve a necessary component of women's recruiting.

Scouting Services: An Overview

Recruiting reports or scouting services exist primarily for the benefit of NCAA Division I college coaches. They should be distinguished from other so-called "recruiting services" that charge athletes to register with them and sometimes also charge college coaches to look at their listings. These recruiting services, some of which cover multiple sports, market themselves primarily to high school athletes, promising exposure. Most will create an individualized listing for any player with the cash, no matter the skill level.

Simply put, recruiting reports that charge college coaches provide names and other details for those the directors consider college potential. While some rank players, others list them in alphabetical order, or in no particular order. Many offer additional details on a group of prospects, saving coaches time digging up the information — home address and phone number; high school team, coach, and coach's number; club team, coach, and coach's number; parents' names; academic background and interests; basketball strengths and weaknesses; and so on. Some also offer individual consultation, where subscribers can call directors toll-free to discuss players.

These recruiting reports may come out as infrequently as twice a year or as often as every other month. Some are sent out via email, others via snail mail. Some offer special reports including camp or tourney wrapups or profiles of individual players. It seems that every year, more women's basketball scouting services pop up as more people jump on the growing women's hoops bandwagon.

National Scouting Services

Though many services are regionally-based, some cover the national scene. In general, however, they are relatively small operations, regional or national. Some directors say that they are out watching players more than they are at home, their schtick being that they have seen every single listed athlete in the flesh. Others rely more heavily on a network of contacts.

The triumvirate of Joe Smith, Mike White, and Mike Flynn dominates the national arena. Smith and Flynn have been around women's hoops for 20-plus years, with White the relative newcomer, a convert who crossed over from men's basketball in 1994. While Flynn and White currently coach, Smith has never coached. All three operate basketball businesses that do more than just evaluate high school players, and all three proclaim themselves experts on the national recruiting scene.

Though he had to be dragged to his first women's game at Queens College, Long Islander Smith was instantly hooked on women's basketball. He and a pal compiled national stats for the AIAW, the predecessor to the NCAA for women, for several years. Then he started attending summer girls' basketball tourneys, from which Women's Basketball News Service was born. "A few college coaches said, maybe you can put together a list of people you saw who you really liked," Smith recalls. "For the longest time, I didn't do it for money — I did it as a favor. And then basically [Louisiana Tech head coach] Leon Barmore said to me, 'You've got to charge for this. It's ridiculous for you not to charge.' And so I did." The scouting service portion of *Women's Basketball News Service* comes out semi-annually, pre- and postseason. A one-year subscription to the report costs around $125, and Smith has over 140 subscribers, all NCAA Division I schools. He considers himself a small player compared to White and Flynn.

While Smith does not coach or run tournaments, his service goes beyond his high school listing for subscribing college coaches. He also does pre- and post-season All-America teams for the high school and college levels, which are picked up by newspapers and magazines. These duties, supplemented by some freelance writing, comprise his income. His basketball travels take him to everything from national summer tourneys, to fall shootouts, to holiday tourneys featuring nationally-ranked teams, to state tournaments.

"I think I'm probably very much on top of the recruiting process," Smith states. "I know it from the coaches' standpoint, the high school and club coaches' standpoint, and the players' standpoint. I like the fact that I get to know a lot of the players, so I feel I have a good handle on how things are with it." Smith definitely watches a lot of games, including following his favorite local girls' squad, Christ the King.

While Smith is almost a one-man show, he does consult others in making his lists. "I have people in the field who provide information on the scouting service side of things and then input on the various All-American teams," he explains. "Some are college coaches, some are writers, and on the high school level, club coaches also." He says he has tried to stay small in an attempt to avoid politics. At this point in time, Smith has no corporate sponsorship.

Mike White, on the other hand, is an Adidas man who has a hand in several women's basketball ventures. Adidas does not give him money, but the company allows the Floridian to use its name alongside the camps and tourneys that he runs, and it supplies gear to his campers. The scouting service side of White's business, *All-Star Girls Report*, has over 200 NCAA Division I subscribers, as well as a few from other levels. *All-Star Girls Report* puts out top 100 and top 250 lists, preseason and postseason, and it also includes college signings and ranks colleges' recruiting classes. In addition, White compiles a list of the top 1000 junior college players. He took on a partner, Bret McCormick, in 1998. When not evaluating talent or running tourneys, White focuses on his newest enterprise, an exhibition traveling team composed of ex-college, ex-WNBA and ex-ABL athletes. The team, which debuted in 2000, provides preseason competition for college squads.

In the early 1990's, White coached boys' club basketball in Florida. Among his charges were several who he calls big-name high school players. He says that he was "a direct route for a lot of the players, just getting exposure in front of college coaches." This led to an introduction to Sonny Vaccaro, an infamous figure in the Nike and Adidas wars. After serving as a basketball consultant with then-Adidas' Vaccaro while also assistant coaching at a junior college, White decided that his chances of advancing in Sonny's ranks were slim. "So I elected to take a glance at this women's basketball, and I did that for a while, and I said, 'Well, you know what, there's growth in this,'" White comments. He then helped boys' recruiting guru Bob Gibbons for a year, learning the trade before launching his own service on the girls' side. The camps, tournaments, and teams came later.

"I hate to say this, because a lot of my friends make jokes about this," White comments, "but a lot of high school players that are turning pro, and they're getting these commissions and things like that — you know, I had a lot of those players. I could have been a major player in the men's side, but I elected to go into the girls, and I missed my fortune. But maybe my calling is making the women's basketball game really big."

At the same time, White contends that his main motivation for the gender switch was "a land of opportunity." He seems to have involved himself in just about every possible angle of that opportunity. However, he still touts his scouting service as his mainstay, professing to help college programs win. "I'm about publicity of rating players," White says, "and getting them into the service so they can be recruited. If I can't see them, then that affects where they might be in the service or how they're going to be recruited by Division I programs, if they're not put in the right scene. That's really my only concern." Between White and McCormick, *All-Star Girls Report* tries to cover every single major top-level girls' event.

Also well-known as a national girls' basketball recruiting expert is Mike Flynn. However, Flynn's current marquis is his globe-trotting Philadelphia Belles club organization. In addition, with Blue Star Basketball, Flynn produces the *Blue Star Index*, which provides several rank-numbered listings, including top 100 seniors and top 80 overall. *The Blue Star Index* has between 30 and 40 subscribers, half at the NCAA Division I level and the other half divided between NCAA Divisions II and II and junior colleges. NCAA Division I subscribers pay $495 per year, while all others pay $275. Subscribers also receive the biannual *Blue Star Report*, which contains articles, college signings, and rankings of high school teams and college recruiting classes.

Blue Star Basketball also runs a series of exposure events. Furthermore, Flynn is affiliated with the U.S. Junior Nationals, one of the stops for many top-level college coaches on the summer recruiting circuit. He wears the Nike swoosh; his Belles are a Nike-sponsored team; he helps select Nike Girls All-America Camp invitees, and he keeps his eyes peeled for potential prep-level Nike teams.

In the late 1980's, Flynn became the first person to do *USA Today*'s girls' basketball rankings. He came recommended for the job by Dave Krider, who was compiling football and boys' basketball rankings for *USA Today* at the time and later took on the girls as well. While Krider did *USA Today*'s rankings for over 20 years, Flynn only did girls' hoops for a handful of seasons. At that time, Flynn had already started Blue Star Basketball and the Philly Belles. His Blue Star Camp in Terre Haute, Indiana, used to be considered the only premier summer event for college coaches. Like White, Flynn is involved with several different areas of girls' basketball, and like White and Smith, he has a large address book. Many major colleges and universities subscribe to the *Blue Star Report*, as they do *Women's Basketball News Service* and the *All-Star Girls Report*.

Flynn was contacted numerous times over a span of more than five months to be interviewed for this chapter. However, neither he nor anyone from his staff returned any phone calls or email messages.

Whether coaches approve of them or not, many Division I colleges subscribe to these three reports. Some look at them hoping to find rising talent who has gone largely unnoticed thus far. Others use them primarily as a checklist, just to make sure they have not missed anyone. They compare them with each other, knowing that an athlete ranked in everybody's top 10 is a keeper. According to a study released by the WBCA in fall 2001, the average recruiting budget across NCAA Division I women's basketball in 2000-01 was $40,282. Why shouldn't coaches spend some of that to make sure they've exhausted every avenue in their quests for potential players?

Regionally-Grounded Recruiting Reports

While it has the potential for more broad-based publicity, scouting talent across the entire nation takes a lot of time, travel, and contacts. However, aside from Smith, White and Flynn with their national focus, a number of regionally-based women's basketball recruiting reports have surfaced. Once again, these are not the recruiting services that charge student-athletes a fee in exchange for exposure but reports that charge college coaches.

Though some regional recruiting reports cover single states, others tackle a specific area of the country, and still others deal with other countries. Many of these recruiting report directors combine their scouting services with other duties, basketball-related or not, for their careers. While NCAA Division I coaches comprise most of their subscribers, a larger percentage of Division II, III, and other levels of college subscribe as well. Two of the more well-known regionally-based efforts in the states are *Ohio Girls Basketball* and The Corwin Index.

Having produced such stars as the WNBA's Katie Smith, Semeka Randall, Brooke Wyckoff, and Georgia Schweitzer as well as college sensations Tamika Williams (UConn) and LaToya Turner (Ohio State), the state of Ohio cultivates much girls' basketball talent. Nobody knows that more than John Feasel of Ohio Girls Basketball. In 1994, Feasel started *Ohio Girls Basketball Magazine*, a publication that goes out six times a year, mostly to parents. In 1998, Feasel added the recruiting report arm, Ohio Girls Basketball Scouting Service. Now, he also has shootouts and tournaments going, in addition to an exhibition team featuring a few WNBA and mostly ex-college players. He has one partner, Tom Jenkins.

"This is Tom's living and my living," states Feasel, who also dabbled in coaching girls' club teams. "He stopped being a lawyer so he could do this. I'm not saying we're getting rich, but the scouting service is a good money-maker. It's mostly labor-intensive. It's not really big costs that are involved in it. We're not getting rich, but we do a lot of things. For us to stay alive, we do a lot of different things."

As Feasel focuses only on Ohio and includes upward of 200 players in each issue of the report, not all of his listees are NCAA Division I prospects; however, he considers all of them college-level material. His subscription base has grown from 25 to over 120 in 2001. Feasel estimates that 65 percent of his subscribers are NCAA Division I coaches, 5 percent Division II, and the remainder divided among Division III and junior colleges. A yearly subscription to the scouting service costs around $250.

Feasel does not rank his players. Instead, he rates them A-K, according to where he believes they will fit into the college scene. Whereas an A could contribute to a top 25 NCAA Division I team as a freshman, a K might make the roster on a low-level Division III or junior college squad. "What we do is we give colleges home addresses and phone numbers and schools and GPA's where we can and test scores and everything," he explains. "We do rate the players where we think they can play, just so when Duke gets our scouting service, they're not sending letters to every girl in Ohio to find out who the best ones are . . . This is so that they're not sending letters to girls who can't play their level. It's good for the smaller colleges, too, because Division III schools get our service. So a Division III school like Wilmington is not wasting their money here in Ohio sending letters to Barbara Turner, one of the best recruits in [the high school class of 2002]. So it's kind of helping both ways." Feasel and Jenkins refuse to rate athletes that they have not seen personally. While they will list the girls' other information, an NR will appear in the rating column.

Although some recruiting reports number players in what they perceive to be order of ability, others stand vehemently against the concept. "I just think it's impossible to rank a girl one to 100," Feasel says. "To one school, yeah, they might need a point guard real badly and that was their high priority, so that might be the best player that they see out there. But another school might need a post player, and so that might be their most important thing. The one to 100 thing just drives me nuts." Whether or not reports rank athletes, they can differ greatly from one another.

Whatever the focus, national or regional, report directors tend to be on the phone a lot — with college coaches, prep coaches, parents, players. As relationships develop, and especially as parents and students grow to value their expertise and inside knowledge, they are asked for advice. Like trusted high school or club coaches, their opinions definitely count. "I don't ever steer anybody toward a school," Feasel vows. "I find that gross. It kills me because some guys will do that and say, 'Hey, you need to go here, or you need to go here.'" However, he does have certain loyalties. "I like to see them go to schools that are subscribers, I'll tell you that right now," Feasel adds. "I would love to see them all go to schools that subscribe to my service. That would make a lot of other people go, oh, wait a minute. But I'm not going to say, don't go to this school because they don't get our service. We don't do that. I might say, if it came down to Dayton and a school that didn't get our service or something, I'd go, 'I just know that the Dayton guys are really nice because I know them, and I work with them personally.' But I'm not going to say, 'Well, that other school, they stink. You want to stay away from them.'"

Putting out The Corwin Index is not Bob Corwin's day job. For the past 20 years, the Floridian has worked for the U.S. Department of Agriculture's marketing service, fruit and vegetable market news division branch. As someone who monitors fresh fruit and vegetable prices and movement, he says he finds what he does in basketball similar to what he does for the DOA, "except instead of analyzing basketball players, you're analyzing . . . the price of a particular commodity at a given time."

At about the same time that Corwin started his scouting service in the late 1980's, he was also assembling girls' traveling teams in Florida. Like Smith, he cut his teeth in girls' basketball watching high school and club teams play. He continued with the traveling teams for 10 years, until he says the fundraising got to be too much for him. Since the late 1990s, he has focused on his scouting service, in addition to his DOA job. The service is now almost 100 percent email-based.

The Corwin Index, which began with Florida players only, now covers the Southeast. Corwin has about 150 subscribers paying about $85, each ranging from NAIA schools to top-level NCAA Division I. He has clients across the country, with the heaviest concentration in the South. Corwin's various reports fall into different categories. Events reports give coaches a heads-up on what tourneys would be good for them to attend in the area over the winter holidays, for example. Player analysis events, which Corwin says are the toughest to do, consist of his take on every single team at a major tourney such as the 15-and-under AAU nationals. His class lists include name, school, height, a comment or two, address, and phone number. Each year, his Corwin Index Awards feature his outstanding performers in the state. He also adds to award listings and sends them out, where he will take something like an All-State list and add information that may not otherwise appear in an announcement, such as grade and height. Lastly, as Florida boasts many junior colleges, Corwin also does a comprehensive report on the 20 Florida jucos.

Corwin has devised his own rating system based on which collegiate level and even which conference he thinks best suits each student-athlete. "I have a different view," he comments. "I always am very fascinated by these people who rank people, one, two, three . . . You're player number 77 — you're better than 78. I look at kids on a scouting viewpoint as, where can you play? In other words, are you a kid who can play in the ACC, the SEC, Big Twelve, Big Ten? Or are you a kid who maybe who can play in one of the smaller, non-major Division I conferences? Or are you somebody, let's say, who could play in the lesser level, but maybe you could play a little bit higher, or maybe you might be a developmental player in the upper level, but maybe could get more time a little lower?"

Recruiting report directors have some of the same problems college coaches have when assessing talent. If attending a huge national event and intent on seeing as many girls as possible, they do not have much time to watch any single player. If a student-athlete does not dazzle during her few minutes under the evaluator's watchful eye, the analysis could be skewed. Corwin is one of few who acknowledge this reality. "If you go to certain events, you only watch a kid for a short period of time, and you only get a snapshot impression," he says. He illustrates his point by explaining his 'Snapshots from Georgia' report. "It was the case where I was analyzing over 100 kids who I had each seen maybe play for about five minutes. That's about as dangerous as it gets. You can be really off.

"I remember one kid," Corwin continues, "and I was joking about it, I rated the kid like L plus. That means somewhere in the smaller DI range, maybe up into the middle level eventually. The kid's a major, major Division I player, will play in the majors, and is in junior college today. I remember laughing over it, but hey, you saw her one or two times going up and down the court. Maybe she didn't finish or looked a little raw.

185

Hey, missed evaluation. You're not going to get every one right, especially under those circumstances. Most people, I would say, probably value my Florida evaluations more than some of these others, simply because I'm more familiar with these kids and make it a point to really have a pretty good line on the Florida kids. The kids out of state that we go to these snapshot events, shotgun evaluations — well, it's another opinion, but it can be as wrong as any other opinion."

College Coaches Give the Skinny on Scouting Reports

The Duke University staff subscribes to four or five different scouting reports. "It really just checks our list that we find over the summer, just to make sure we're not missing kids," states Duke assistant Joanne Boyle. "If we find a kid that's ranked in the top four in a scouting service, and we don't have her anywhere in our database, we'll follow up and check out that kid. We just really want to make sure the kids that we have in our database and that we've seen over the years are the same kids these people are seeing, because we're at the same camps, to make sure that we're on the same page."

Just like any other ranking comparing teams or individuals, scouting service lists attract heated deliberation. Some coaches even believe that they are not the primary audience. "The recruiting reports are a subjective opinion," says UConn associate head coach Chris Dailey. "It's more for media. It's not for us. I would not want the job of having to say, number one, two, three, four. I think that's really difficult to say and it's very subjective. I use it as a guideline. I use it sometimes as comic relief, just to kind of chuckle at some of the bizarre things people will write and do."

However, Dailey also gives report directors credit for covering a broad base fairly well. "If I was just looking at the list to get an idea of who the top players were, I think in the general vicinity they are accurate, but I wouldn't necessarily agree with the numbers." Furthermore, once coaches have signed players, the reports can provide evidence of a signee's merit. "Sometimes it helps you with your AD," Dailey adds, "like oh, we had the number one recruiting class. I heard somebody was getting a bonus if they signed a top 25 player. I was like, that is ridiculous — whose top 25?"

Personal connections and preferences can also play a role in the reports. Take the case of UConn standout playmaker Sue Bird, a Christ the King High alum. "When Sue was a junior, one of the lists did not have her listed in the top 200 players in the country because our kids don't go to this particular guy's functions because they don't need to," remembers Jill Cook, assistant coach at Christ the King. "The next year, after Sue went to the Nike [All-America] Camp and she talked to the guy who wrote the list and he found out, oh, she's a nice kid, the next year she was number three. So she went from being not in the top 200 to number three."

If nothing else, the reports spark some lively debate. "We have some players who we go, how could that kid not be in the top 100?" says New Mexico Head Coach Don Flanagan. "We kind of laugh at them, but at the same time we subscribe to them. You're just trying to make sure that if there's somebody that maybe you didn't get to see and they're close by and you've got to make a call on them. It's just another way of making your own list." At the same time, Flanagan says that he might be disappointed after finding one of his own recruits on the list; being ranked means that she will surely attract more attention, throwing more recruiting competition into the mix.

In addition to providing a cross-check among current recruits, the reports can also be a first alert regarding next-generation talent. "I use them a lot for young players, like rising sophomores, freshmen," explains Mickie DeMoss, Tennessee associate head coach. "There will be maybe five freshmen that are on every list. I will say, we need to really start catching up with all of these. I guess we're always thinking ahead. By the time they are rising seniors, we would hope that we had not missed anybody, but we certainly have." With the increasing number of recruiting reports and exposure events, however, coaches now have less chance of overlooking suitable prospects.

To offset the expense of the printed scouting services, sometimes coaches would photocopy them and share the cost. However, the directors have caught on. "A lot of coaches are getting smart and they're networking — they're sharing the reports," says Stony Brook head coach Trish Roberts. "Some of the people who own the services have gotten smart in that they're printing the stuff on colored paper, so that you can't photocopy it. It's not on white paper any more."

Recruiting report directors do not fall under NCAA sanctions. They can talk to whomever — college coaches, high school and or club coaches, parents, student-athletes — whenever. While reports may provide a service to the girls' basketball community, they also make an increasingly complex recruiting process more complex. "There's a lot of good people doing a lot of good things who don't make a lot of money," states White, "helping girls' basketball grow." The question is, exactly what are they trying to grow it into?

As women's basketball continues its upward trend, more girls' basketball recruiting reports emerge. It seems that college coaches will keep subscribing to this ever-increasing offering in the ceaseless effort to keep up with the competition. Though they disagree with the price, methods, and ranking systems, many do include the reports in their recruiting arsenals.

Camps, Tourneys, and Shootouts

Girls' basketball players have many more off-season options than ever before. Their families also shell out much more money for them to stay close to the sport all year long. Not too long ago, the main offerings were camps at the local high school or at universities. Some might say that club basketball, with its playoffs and tourneys, has somewhat replaced these two.

However, there are still several other types of off-season opportunities. Student-athletes can attend shootouts, usually one-day events. Some players attend invite-only camps, and the top level may even compete at one of two elite girls' camps. Camp, tourney, and shootout directors claim that their purpose is to help girls improve skills and to give them college exposure. One could present a strong argument that the latter reason has overpowered the former.

Mesa State College head coach Steve Kirkham sees about 3500 players per summer at his eight weeks of camp, which provides individual and team sessions. He has a small recruiting budget, and the camps provide him a chance to evaluate area athletes. They also give him an edge on finding a talented prospect who has gone largely unnoticed. "There's a great player in western Colorado right now, and I'll bet I'm the only guy who knows about her," Kirkham smirks. "She comes to our team camp because it's the nearest team camp, and they only get together for one week because they're all farm kids. Coach has to promise Mom and Dad that they'll be back by Thursday noon so they can help milk the cows. She's not going to the AAU stuff because she doesn't have the money. She's never been to the state tournament. She's going to end up coming to Mesa State College and probably average about 25 a game. Nobody else even knows about her." Not only does Kirkham get some extra cash through the camps (attendees pay anywhere from just under $100 for day camp to just over $200 for overnight individual camp), he might also get an extra step on the recruiting competition.

At his camps, Kirkham also educates campers and parents about the recruiting process. He gives his talk each summer, and at high schools other times during the year, about the actualities of recruiting. "When I speak to parents," Kirkham says, "I go 'Hey, do you want money for your kids to go to college?' Of course they all go yeah. I go, 'Then you'd better make sure they get straight A's.' And they all look at me like I'm on drugs. Then I go, "Well if they don't have straight A's, I hope you started a fund for them a long time ago. How many of you have a fund?' They don't raise their hands. I say, 'Well, the odds of your kids getting an athletic scholarship are this' — then I talk about the numbers and how many kids there are and how many scholarships there are, and how many full rides there are not. That only the top 150 Division I's give fulls and everybody else is down to partials. Boy, by the time they walk out of there they're just slack-jawed. I try to give them a little dose of reality."

Although high school and college camps are still popular, girls can also attend camps run by camp companies. Whoever runs the camp, though, some offer individual as well as team sessions, where athletes can play with their prep teammates as a squad for the week. Individual camps might also offer All-Star weeks, where participants must be varsity-level players or meet other requirements. Some companies also feature shootouts, day-long individual events where athletes essentially scrimmage all day in front of college coaches.

One such company, Pennsylvania-based Blue Chip Basketball, runs individual and team events, largely for girls. Blue Chip Basketball's primary focus is spring and fall shootouts, although it also features a tourney or two. "This is a vehicle in the recruiting package," says Blue Chip president Bill McDonough, who also coaches a girls' club team. "Another way for the kids to be seen and the coaches to see them." Teens who hope to play in college participate for this very reason. McDonough has been a boys' high school and college coach and a Division I assistant athletic director. He also worked for a scouting service affiliated with the NBA.

Technically, anyone can attend Blue Chip shootouts and tourneys. However, McDonough, who has been running camps for 35 years and shootouts for 15, tries to screen applicants through high school coaches. While he does not require a recommendation, he sends a letter to every high school coach in the country, indicating that the events exist for players with college potential. "But, that being said, if her application comes in, we put her on a team," McDonough says. "That's because of state federation rules that we have to be open to everyone."

At the shootouts, athletes pay around $100 to play three games in one day, with the guarantee that they will play at least half of every game. Teams cap off at 10 players. Since Blue Chip does not turn anyone away, what does McDonough do with an athlete who plays a reserve role on the junior varsity team? "The shootout does have, say 80 percent of the players can play Division III or II, maybe only 20 percent can play I, and there's some percentage that can't play at all in college," he states. "What happens is, if they're a guard they bring the ball up, they pass it to somebody else, and they stay out of the rest of the play. They kind of know themselves." In 2001, about 3300 players attended Blue Chip events, between the shootouts, team tourneys, and one invite-only week.

Partly to avoid direct competition with other girls' expo-sure events, McDonough focuses on the spring and fall. Dur-ing his busiest shootout month, September, college coaches are on the road doing home visits. Before or after the scheduled home visit, they can stop by a shootout on a Saturday or Sun-day and scope out talent. That way, coaches take care of two different recruiting tasks during one trip, and McDonough brings in more paying customers.

Blue Chip Basketball tries to prepare its charges in the morn-ing for the pressure-packed outing that lies ahead of them. While participants lace up and stretch, directors instruct them on how to have a successful day. "We try to tell them what the coaches are looking for and to forget them and just play," McDonough explains, "and make sure that they pass the ball because a lot of these kids go crazy and would shoot it every time. We try to tell them that they don't look at that . . . They watch their demeanor, their attitude, how they walk on and off the court." With girls knowing that they have a game and a half, perhaps two, to impress college coaches, it's no wonder that they need reassurance. "So we tell them that, but basi-cally we're one of the processes kids have to go through," McDonough states. "You should play on your high school team, you should probably play on [a club] team, you should try to go to camps for both education and exposure, and you can also go to perhaps what we call our shootouts."

Directors of exposure events often collect money from more than one source. Not only do girls pay to participate, college coaches pay for a booklet containing details on players and teams, "the stuff that really helps the recruiter to do what they gotta do," according to McDonough. This information may somewhat resemble that contained in a recruiting report, al-though it probably does not rank prospects. At Blue Chip shootouts, each of which features anywhere between 80-250 players, McDonough usually charges college coaches $35-$50 for their packets, depending on the number of competitors. At tourneys, he charges $100 for a booklet featuring 850 athletes and $125-$150 at his largest tournament, where coaches can see upward of 2000 athletes.

"We're sort of in the recruiting business as well," quips Hall-of-Famer and former winning Immaculata College head coach Cathy Rush, who started what is now Future Stars Basketball over 30 years ago. Although Future Stars Camps now offers field hockey and regular day camps, basketball has always been its staple. As far as events go, Future Stars Basketball does everything except shootouts — individual, team, and invite-only or All-Star weeks. The cost for campers runs anywhere from around $175 for team challenge commuters to $385 for overnighters who do not pay up well ahead of time. Future Stars tries to recruit players from all over the country and abroad for its All-Star camps, exposure events but with a different twist, its proponents say.

At the individual, non All-Star weeks, as with the typical skills camp, participants focus on fundamentals and play several games per day. College coaches do not sit in the stands evaluating campers, who are grouped by age and ability. Similarly, the Junior All-Star camp, geared toward sixth through ninth graders, is not billed as an exposure event. However, it's another story for Future Stars' two other different All-Star camps. Tenth through twelfth graders with college potential attend All-Star Camp, and NCAA Division I coaches select the invitees to the Senior All-Star Camp.

A major complaint about exposure camps in general is that they do no more than showcase players. Girls spend all of their time scrimmaging, when they should also work on fundamentals so that they can take something practical away from the session other than a phone call from a college coach. Both Rush and Mountain MacGillivray, Future Stars' director of basketball, insist that skill-building comprises an important part of all of their camps. "I think it is cheating kids to have them at camp and not teach them something," says Rush. "We have instructional sessions every segment, morning and afternoon, and we do two-man plays and all kinds of stuff. I watch these quote-unquote all-stars who don't have good footwork, who don't have good recognition skills, and it breaks my heart. I say to them all the time, if you're going to play in college, the college coaches are going to say that high school players coming into college don't have good skills, don't have good fundamentals. Don't kid yourself — if you want to play in college, you're going to be practicing every day for the next four years. Kids think that their skills are a lot better than they are."

Giving college coaches the opportunity to watch players' behavior outside of a game situation can be an important piece of the recruiting puzzle, according to MacGillivray. "When you come to a camp, a camp where you get an opportunity to be taught and learn skills, coaches can come to those practice sessions and see how you learn and how you work," he says. When you're at a shootout or at a tournament, all they get to see is you playing. So the kid who might not be quite as polished, you can get to see that she picks things up really quickly, and she might be a player who can learn a lot faster in your program. Or you might find kids who are maxed out potential-wise by seeing how they work in the drill segments . . . The player is getting instruction, where at most other events she's just getting exposure." The chance to exhibit positive attitudes, perseverance and work ethic proves especially important for those a tier below the elite. The setup also gives Rush and MacGillivray the opportunity to emphasize that their All-Star camps are more than just recruiting meat markets.

However, camp counselors and directors must also battle the reality that the higher the level of talent, the more resistant players might be to working on basics. Especially if they think a college opportunity is at stake, many athletes would much rather work on a sweet behind-the-back move than on setting a proper screen. Sometimes their parents share this belief. "I had a kid who was going into her junior year in high school, and we're doing all kinds of stuff," Rush recounts. "She came up to me and she said, 'I already know this stuff.' And I go, 'What's your point?' She said, 'Well, I can do this.' And I said, 'How many times do you think in the next six years, you're going to be practicing this play?' She said, 'Well, I don't think I'll practice it again.' I shook my head. Her father had called, and he was going to take her out of camp. I said look, whatever you want to do is fine, but every single person — you know, Michael Jordan practices his jump shot. We all do, in whatever sport we happen to play." Even for many parents and campers, then, the primary goal of camps is to be seen, not to improve their fundamentals. And perhaps club basketball engenders the idea that playing games, not going through drill stations, is what 'ballers do in the summer.

When asked how many coaches typically show up for the All-Star camps, the Future Star staff answered that attendance depends on the names in the packet. "The coaches are all very smart, so they're going to attend the event that's going to have the most kids that can go to their school," MacGillivray explains. "There have been some years where we had 25 Division I coaches and 40 Division II or 50 Divison III coaches because they realize that that's maybe how the camp was this year. Another year you have 150 Division I coaches and no Division II or III coaches because they don't think there are as many kids there for them. So it varies. For the most part, every year it's a mix of all of them. Obviously, we strive for the camp to be exposure for Division I recruitable athletes, and if you aim there you end up with a nice mix. If you open it up to anyone who might play in college, you won't get any Division I athletes. Every parent and every child thinks their kid's better than they are."

In addition to scouting services and other girls' basketball miscellania, Ohio Girls Basketball and Blue Star Basketball also operate shootouts and tournaments. Feasel runs fall and spring individual shootouts. His fall shootout features 64 players from each high school class. While he refuses to dub it invite-only, he does send out a mailing to a specific list of players. If those invitees do not fill the shootout roster, he sends another mailing out to his B list. "I won't turn a kid away and say, hey, no, you stink," Feasel states. "I won't do that. I let them come and get their ass kicked, and then they'll learn."

In addition, Feasel holds what he calls team shootouts for high school teams (no club teams allowed), which are for all practical purposes summer tourneys. For one of those summer shootouts, teams are guaranteed five games in two days. For the other, four games in one day. In 2000, Feasel ran a summer league, but he discontinued it in 2001 for lack of profit. Subscribers to Feasel's scouting service get a discount on the packet sold at each shootout or tournament. At the spring shootout, for example, while nonsubscribers shell out $75, subscribers pay $35. "We try to make it worth the college's while to join our service," explains Feasel. The last part of Feasel's girls' basketball cartel involves Asics. Feasel and Jenkins sell Asics kicks to Ohio high school girls' programs, and Asics supplies gear for Feasel's shootouts and tourneys.

Flynn is perhaps better known for the events he runs than for his recruiting report. His Blue Star Basketball also operates a series of spring, summer, and fall events, some of which are invitational, all of which Nike sponsors. Events open to all until enrollment fills are the position camps, Summer Showcase, Invitational, and fall shootouts. The elite camp is invite-only. The Blue Star web site clearly advertises all offerings except for the position camps as the best way for high school student-athletes to get college exposure.

Blue Star packages its September shootouts as high school seniors' last chance to be seen by and to interact with college coaches. In fact, the web site spells out the fact that attendees will be provided the unique opportunity to talk to college coaches at the event, all within NCAA regulations: "Blue Star will also have special 'senior contact sessions' where attending senior athletes and attending college coaches will be encouraged to meet during the shootout hours. Parents and high school coaches of participating senior athletes are encouraged to attend the shootout since, according to NCAA regulations, college coaches who wish to speak and meet seniors can make contact during the shootout. This 'contact' counts as one of the three NCAA-approved home visits. A complete list of all contacts will be forwarded to the NCAA at the completion of the shootouts. This special feature enables college coaches to watch the student athlete in action and then have the ability to contact senior student athletes during this shootout period." In this way, Blue Star bundles a full-blown, ready-made recruiting opportunity for college coaches and prospective student-athletes.

About 50 invited underclass athletes attend Blue Star Elite camp in Indiana. Flynn selects invitees from among those who have attended Blue Star camps or competed in the U.S. Junior Nationals or national AAU championship the previous year. Before the inception of the Nike Girls All-America Camp in 1996, the Blue Star Elite camp was regarded as the highest-level girls' camp, attracting every major college coach. However, the Nike Girls All-America Camp, and perhaps the Adidas Top Ten Camp, has since surpassed it.

Many consider Nike Camp the number one girls' elite camp. Its 80-plus attendees, primarily upperclass players, typically get full rides to top NCAA Division I schools. The gymnasium bleachers house a who's who of college basketball coaches, some of whom attend mainly to babysit. Flynn, in his Nike consultant capacity, often helps create the invite list and usually makes an appearance. Although a girl's recruiting worth can rise or fall at the camp, there are no sleepers. The camp schedule includes skillwork, game competition, and seminars designed with the future DI star in mind.

In 2000, White started the Adidas Top Ten camp, another invite-only elite camp that draws nationally. Top Ten, which caters more to underclass athletes, has about 150 campers. While the college coaches' packet at the Nike camp is free, White charges coaches. Like Feasel, he gives subscribers a discount. White says he charges because "I put the money back into the camp to help the camp run." He created Top Ten after the demise of the invitational WBCA camp, which he consulted on for a year. "I wanted to make sure we kept at least two great camps going," White states. "Especially with Nike and Adidas as a shoe war, it worked out really good, especially with my connections to Adidas that helped out with the sponsorship of the camp." The sponsorships differ, though, in that the Adidas side includes only gear and permission to use the brand name, not cash.

At this point, White's biggest claim to fame could the Deep South Classic, which he first held in spring 1997. The North Carolina tourney hosts 100 club teams and attracts many college coaches. Teams play five games in four different gyms over a three-day period in April.

However, a high school coach runs another of the largest and most successful girls' summer tourneys. Carl Tinsley, co-head coach at Oregon City High School, operates the End of the Oregon Trail tournament in July, which serves over 120 teams. "It's kind of a unique situation because I'm a high school varsity coach, and the major tournaments in the country are not run by high school coaches," Tinsley comments. "They're run by businessmen."

Since the End of the Oregon Trail debuted in the late 1970's, Tinsley has seen a change in its purpose. In the beginning, he just wanted to offer girls a fun summer basketball experience, something to compete with softball. "The real purpose of the tournament now I think is twofold," Tinsley begins. "One is exposure for kids, to give them an opportunity to play in a competitive atmosphere with a large number of college coaches in to watch them. I think that's what we would like to see happen, and hopefully that some of the kids that are playing in the tournament wherever they are around the country would get some kind of exposure from it." However, Tinsley downplays the role of tourney directors and other coaches in recruiting. "I don't believe that we get kids scholarships. I don't believe that AAU coaches get kids scholarships. I believe kids get scholarships for themselves." He sees the other purpose as providing a high-level tournament atmosphere in which girls compete against the best and improve their skills.

With the compactness of the current summer recruiting period for women, the End of the Oregon Trail spans four days as opposed to a full week. Though club teams dominate attendance, straight high school teams are welcome. There are also weeks for high school teams only, junior varsity-level players, and younger players. With Tinsley's reputation and connections in the college and high school realms, End of the Oregon Trail rosters fill quickly.

Contact with College Coaches

Those in the business of scouting services, camps, tournaments, or shootouts have different levels of interaction with college coaches. "Anywhere from being my good friends to trying to help kids get noticed to trying to help programs that help us get a good jump on players, getting a chance to see them first," says

MacGillivray of his relationships with college coaches. Many camp, tourney, and shootout staffers spend a good portion of their actual events working the college coaches' crowd. Directors talk up athletes they believe well-suited for particular college programs. It definitely behooves college coaches' recruiting to make friends with shootout, camp, tourney, and scouting service directors. It behooves high school and club coaches, student-athletes and their parents to do so as well.

"One thing we do, and I know no other service does this, I can guarantee it, if Sue Semrau from Florida State calls me, and she says 'Hey Feas, I'm coming up to watch a girl play in the middle of nowhere in Ohio,'" says Feasel. "They got our service, they found this girl, they want to go watch her play. There are schools that call us, and Troy State does it all the time, they'll call us. They'll fly up to Columbus, and they can't drive me, but I can pick them up. I pick them up at their hotel or whatever, I'll drive them out to the game, watch the game with them . . . We're going to go to the game anyway, so why not just go with them?"

Scouting service, camp, tourney, and shootout directors and staffers — and those who are a combination of the preceding — definitely affect the recruiting process. Chances are that some college coaches value their opinions of the players that they see. While they undoubtedly aid certain prospective student-athletes in the exposure realm, some also help college coaches. Not bound by any recruiting regulations, they can have infinite contact with everyone involved in the process.

A Unique Perspective on Recruiting

The groups featured in this chapter have an interesting look at the recruiting process. Unlike club or high school coaches, unless they happen to serve that role as well, they are not connected to a single team or player. They watch a lot of basketball, and many either just love to gab or have learned how to. Because of their conversations with the parties directly involved in recruiting, as well as personal observations, they offer enlightening commentary on the current state of affairs, the rules and regulations, and the future of women's basketball recruiting.

"Basketball is a business — it's a corporation," White remarks. "Head coaches and recruiting coordinators, they've got to recruit players. Just because player number five likes you doesn't mean that she is necessarily going to come there, so they're telling recruit number eight something different. You have to play that game. That's part of the deal. But you know what — these players know what's going on because they're doing the same thing. They're getting a feel by saying, 'Hey, how many minutes am I going to get?' Don't think that these 16-, 17-, 18-year-old kids don't know what time it is. Honestly, I've known programs that have said, recruits want to know if they're going to start, and they'll go, 'Yeah, you're going to start.' Yeah, she'll start. Play her the first three minutes of the game and then sit her because she's not ready. You're gonna to do what you've gotta do."

Not only has the perception of women's basketball recruiting shifted, the steps taken by coaches during the process have changed as well. These folks have seen a huge increase in the amount of time and energy coaches spend recruiting. "There are more college coaches working harder now," says MacGillivray. "I've seen programs go from coaches who really didn't go out that much and who didn't compete to get players, to programs that are really working hard now to find student-athletes to better their programs. I don't necessarily think it was as much the individual coaches as it was the athletic philosophy of the schools has all changed. They want to win and they want their programs to do well, and I don't know that before it was that important to the schools to have the women's basketball programs be successful. Because of the notoriety that some of the big schools have gotten, everybody wants to get a piece of that." Due to the improved reputation of women's college hoops, administrations place more onus on coaches to bring in talent. Coaches have more budgetary and personnel support in recruiting, but they also have more responsibility to produce results.

With this responsibility comes added duress, perhaps forcing coaches to say or do things they may not formerly have done to gain the competitive edge. "There's a whole carload of coaches out there that are known as negative recruiters," Smith asserts. "You know, you don't want to go there . . . or the coach is a bum, or stuff like that. That certainly has increased in the sense that there's so much on the line."

As recruiting rules and calendars have changed, so too have the relationships of high school and club coaches with recruiting, and with each other in recruiting. Overall, camp, tourney, shootout, and scouting service directors now have more contact with non-scholastic than with high school coaches. They have seen the club coach's emergence as a prominent figure. "There are certainly a lot of people involved in AAU basketball who are truly committed to doing something for the kids," Rush states. "And there are a number of people in AAU basketball whose only consideration is what's being done for themselves and what power base they're assembling. I keep telling people, we're talking about women's basketball. This isn't like U.S. senator. We're talking about basketball. People have grandiose expectations of who they are and what they're doing and what they're accomplishing. Rather than turning it around and saying, what am I doing for these kids — am I providing them a positive experience? Am I being a good role model? There are people who have changed dates on kids' birth certificates, and my question is, what are you teaching these kids?"

On the other hand, some believe that for all of the complication that club basketball has thrown into recruiting, it has equally or more benefited the process. "If it wasn't for girls' traveling teams, basketball recruiting would be horrible," White says. "A lot of towns, these high school programs are not any good. They play out of position. I know several girls who are point guards playing the five [center], and you would never know if you just went and watched the high school program what they could do. In turn, a lot of the high school coaches just don't really care. You have a handful of high school coaches in America that probably are very well-known and probably do a good job of promoting their players and helping them. Outside of that, it's AAU." According to White, who somewhat relies on club basketball for his livelihood, summer ball contributes to the current high level of women's college basketball. "If AAU is the root of all evil, it sure is keeping women's basketball going for the college Division I coaches making six figures," he adds. "And they're probably the ones saying this. Sometimes people need to take a step back and wonder how they're making a good living."

The experts interviewed for this chapter see firsthand interactions between college and high school or club coaches. Depending on their relationships, they may be privy to comments about the recruiting process. "I know a lot of college coaches won't deal with the AAU coach," MacGillivray remarks. "They feel that when you look at most kids, they've played on three or four different AAU teams. They've played for five or six different AAU coaches, and they don't really have a handle on the kid. They've enticed the kid because here you're going to get exposure with this team, we're going to be better than that team, and kids go from team to team. Typically, the kids stay with one high school team, so the coach gets to know them a little bit better and they feel that there's a little more character in a lot of the high school programs. However, AAU coaches are more directly involved than high school coaches in the summer." Despite the fact that college coaches may prefer to deal with high school coaches, they also realize the necessity of involving club coaches during the heart of recruiting.

According to Feasel, both high school and summer coaches need roles. At the same time, he believes that high school coaches can take a more objective overall stand. "I think the kid should have most of the say because they're going to go to the school, but I think the high school coach should be the one the college coaches go to and help out," Feasel comments. "The AAU coaches, now they can get slanted. I know there's a couple coaches here that push girls to Ohio State. That's just the way they are. They're big fans and you see them at every game.

"I know this one coach who just pushes girls toward Miami University," Feasel continues. "Every Miami game I go to, there she is sitting there watching. That's fine, but the high school coach is not like that most of the time. I think the AAU coach has got to be in it — there's no way you can get around them being in the recruiting process. They're going to have to see them during the summer and everything so the AAU coach is going to have to be in there, but I think the high school coach is a little more important. The high school coach has got to worry about the grades, whether they'll be eligible, getting them to the tests." Hopefully, both parties concern themselves with players' academic preparation and basketball welfare. And while most of us probably have favorite college teams, there is a distinction between enthusiasm for a school and shepherding athletes there, especially when we have not considered an individual's skills, needs, and desires.

Although the prospect ultimately makes the decision, college coaches often control the process. Only with elite athletes does the power base shift. "I've always thought that except for the very top players, the coaches have the upper hand in the recruiting process," McDonough states. "They know they need a two guard, and they're talking to say, number seven. In their minds, they know who's number one, two, three, et cetera. The player doesn't know where she is unless she's really, really good. Then she knows. So she doesn't know whether she's first or fifth. And the coach is probably going to tell her, 'Oh, we think you're the best, Mary Lou.' Well, is that the best that afternoon while they're talking?"

Compared to men's, women's basketball has not seen the same major recruiting violations. "Has there actually been the overt type of money cheating in women's basketball?" Smith ponders. "It hasn't happened that much. I think what has happened is there's grade cheating. In other words, people taking SATs for kids who don't have SATs. Certainly there's too many contacts, but that's always gone on. I would say the only thing that's actually changed is the aggressiveness." In considering these statements, one need not wonder why the NCAA has firmed up its grip on women's basketball recruiting.

Speculation is great among women's college coaches and experts alike regarding what future changes the NCAA will make in recruiting. Perhaps the NCAA will regulate club coaches. Perhaps academic requirements for prospective student-athletes will change. Maybe the July window will be further shortened from its present three weeks or will be eliminated altogether. Each party bases its reflections on its level of expertise and loyalties.

"If they shut down July," muses Feasel, who also thinks that college coaches should have more regular-season evaluations, "I would be doing cartwheels. I tell you why. I'd still have my shootouts. Bring them in, I evaluate them, I put them in the service. That way the college coaches have got to rely on me more. So it doesn't bother me if they shut them down or not. Shut them down, that means nobody else is going to have them. Then I'd still have team shootouts with my high school coaches, and I'm still going to see players . . . The kids and college coaches would rely on us recruiting people 10 times more because we'd be the ones seeing them. They wouldn't be the ones seeing them, and they'd have to find out from us who to see. It'd be a big burden for us, but it would make us more important."

In their relationships with students and parents, recruiting report and exposure event folks are often asked for specific recruiting help. On the general topic of college selection, families should consider the overall atmosphere, not just team dynamics. "Find a school where you really want to be that meets you academically and socially, and the fact that they have a great team is a nice topper to that," Rush says. "I've seen an awful lot of kids going someplace where they don't really offer their major, and they're going to end up another year at someplace else to get exactly what they want . . . Also, the school's not going anywhere, and the coach may. So you want to be with a group of people that you like in an academic setting that you will feel good in and will lead you in the direction that you want to go. Let's start with that premise as opposed to who's the best team." This sounds tough to do, but then again, so does the entire recruiting process.

MacGillivray emphasizes the practicality of making two lists; one contains colleges the student would like to attend if she did not play basketball, and the other features programs she thinks she can play for. Then she should see which schools show up on both lists. "Too many kids set their sights on playing Division I because that's what everyone talks about, and they go to a lesser school than they could have for the wrong reasons. There are Division II schools and Division III schools that as far as basketball is concerned, are much better than a lot of the Division I schools. St. Rose [Division II], they've got eight Division I players. And kids, I don't know if it happens as much in other areas, because obviously St. Rose has convinced the kids that playing Division II is OK. Around here, it's just, if you don't go Division I, you didn't succeed."

These directors see the truth of that last statement embodied in parents' mindsets. Furthermore, proportionately speaking, few college athletes participate in NCAA Division I athletics. "Is it such a secret how you get to be a better player?" asks Corwin. "It just really seems to me to be that. For example, if you're 5'8" and you want to play college basketball at the Division I or DII level, chances are you'd better be more than a back-to-the-basket low-post player. You understand that. But no, I've got one parent here who, I think the young lady will be a nice DIII, and Daddy feels absolutely confident that the phone's going to ring in June for the DI's. The AAU coach thinks so, too." Corwin drives home the point that while talent evaluation may be subjective, height is not.

On the academic front, taking tests early on can be almost important as the scores themselves. "The prospective student-athlete should take the SAT as early as humanly possible," Smith asserts. "Kids have told me this. You don't have to take it until the spring of your junior year. Well, that's not true if you're going to go to an NCAA school. You need to take it at the end of your sophomore year and see where you stand and see what you have to do." That way, recruits will have enough time to retest if necessary, with a better chance of meeting the academic regulations for college ball. Smith adds that the NCAA could also set up a direct phone line or email address where students can ask and get solid answers to questions. If their current coaches do not know much about recruiting, they should more easily be able to get direct help from the NCAA.

With the setup of the current women's basketball recruiting calendar, it is very possible for July-November following a player's junior year of high school to be her entire recruiting period. Those not noticed by college coaches until July must get to know coaches, research schools, and often make a decision within those four-plus months. If athletes are not noticed until that summer, they might feel forced to make the college choice too quickly. "Some of these kids going to these programs, they don't fit the system, they don't fit the style," says White. "Maybe that's not the coach they want to play for. People change. They transfer. It's just different. I think some people make the wrong decision because they're not well-informed." A few months just may not be enough time for athlete and coach to get to know each other, no matter how much research they cram into that period.

As a high school player in the early 1980s, Suzie McConnell-Serio "got seen" by playing in the national AAU tournament and attending a Blue Star camp. While those two events still play a role in the girls' summer basketball circuit, many other tourneys, camps, and shootouts abound to give prospective student-athletes college exposure. In addition, more girls' basketball scouting services, national and regional, have emerged to help college coaches make sure they have not missed any stars in their travels. Now more than ever, the venture of college basketball exposure for teenage girls is a business. Aside from promoting players, helping college coaches, and generating revenue, these events provide the opportunity for additional parties to witness, be involved with and reflect on the recruiting process.

9

The Others: Recruiting at the NAIA and Junior College Levels

Imagine having some scholarship money, recruiting a player and having as much contact with her and her family as you want, as early as you want. You have no contact, evaluation, quiet, or dead periods to deal with. Those coaching in the National Intercollegiate Athletic Association (NAIA) or at a junior college, live that dream. However, in return, they must often wait until late spring to fully assemble their teams for the following season. Though they may have athletic scholarship money, it may not be much. They must often take a back seat to the NCAA. Junior college coaches must completely replenish their squad every two years. And whether in the NAIA or junior college ranks, coaches wait, and they wait, and they wait for prospects to make up their mind. Even then, coaches can't be sure until they move onto campus.

What's more, the collegiate paths of NAIA and junior college student-athletes often have many bumps, turns, and stops. For Cloud County Community College (Kansas) coach Brett Erkenbrack, whose squad captured the 2001 National Junior College Athletic Association (NJCAA) Division I title, what began as a naïve recruiting venture resulted in the catch of a lifetime, if only for one season. In 1989-90, Erkenbrack's rookie year, he had recruited Tawana Jackson, the 1989 *USA Today* National Preseason High School Player of the Year. Jackson averaged 39 points her senior year at South Bend, Indiana's La

Salle High School. "I'd talked to her all year long, not knowing any better, thinking that I could get her," Erkenbrack recalls. He even went so far as to offer Jackson a campus visit. "She said, 'Yeah, I'll come visit.' So I actually bought two plane tickets for her and she never showed up." Jackson signed with NCAA Division I University of Kansas. However, her standardized test scores were not up to par, and she did not bring them up by the time fall rolled around.

"So 1990-91," Erkenbrack says, "Tawana Jackson enrolls at the University of Kansas, is ineligible to play, still didn't make her test scores, and is paying her own way to go to school. I didn't notice at the time. She ended up leaving the University of Kansas in October of 1990 and went to Palm Beach Community College in Florida. She played at Palm Beach Community College in the spring semester of 1991, and they ended up getting third in the national tournament."

At this point, Erkenbrack had long since moved on from hoping to land Jackson. However, he would hear from her again. "Tawana Jackson now calls me in the spring of 1991," he continues, "and wants to know if she can transfer back to Cloud County, if she can come here. I'm saying, 'Well yeah, yeah that's great. Come on. I'll get you a plane ticket, and let's do it.' And her mom is calling me, saying, 'Tawana really wants to come out there to Kansas and play for you and everything, and you've helped her.' I've never laid eyes on the girl — I just talked to her over the phone. OK, so I'm thinking I'm going to get her, and I'm going to have her and Shanele Stires." After Cloud County, Stires proceeded to Kansas State and then to the WNBA's Minnesota Lynx.

However, Jackson eluded Erkenbrack another time. He lost touch with her in 1991, once again believing that it was over and done with. But his phone rang on the first day of classes in 1992. The caller introduced herself as Sandra Crockett and said she was calling from a downtown Chicago phone booth. Crockett had played the previous year at a junior college but was not going back. She told Erkenbrack that one of her friends had told her to call him. "I said, 'Well now, who is it exactly that told you to call me?' She said, 'Tawana Jackson.' At this point in time, I've still never ever seen Tawana Jackson. I have about a 20-minute conversation with Sandra Crockett, and I say, 'Where is Tawana? What's she doing?' She said, 'Well, she's standing right here. Do you want to talk to her?'" Crockett ended up signing with Cloud County but never made it to campus.

Jackson had left Florida and enrolled at another junior college in the fall of 1991. However, that school could not gather all of her different school transcripts together and could not give her a scholarship. She told Erkenbrack that she was working at a candy factory in South Bend and getting ready to join the Army. "I said, 'Now are you sure that you're done with basketball? You don't want to play anymore?' She said, 'Well, I want to play, but I've been too many places, too messed up. Don't have my grades and transcripts and stuff.' I said, 'Tawana, if you want to play, this is what you do. You send me the transcripts immediately of all the schools that you've ever attended. You send me a deposit for a dorm room. You do this in the next week, and I'll have a plane ticket for you in December to come out here, get in school for the spring semester, get yourself eligible, and you have one year to play here.'"

Within a week, Erkenbrack had all of Jackson's transcripts and her dorm deposit. The third time he offered her a plane ticket, she took him up on it. During the spring of 1993, she focused on her classes at Cloud County and posted a 3.7 GPA. She stayed on campus during the summer, working at the public library and working out with Erkenbrack. The next season, she was ready. "She led the nation in scoring for us here in 1993," Erkenbrack remarks. "She averaged over 29 points a game, scored over 30 seventeen times, and five games in a row over 40 . . . We were 29-4 that year, won 24 games in a row, and then she signed at [NCAA Division I] St. John's University. She only had one year of Division I eligibility left because of all of this time that she had spent bouncing around, and she led the Big East in scoring in 1994-95." Sadly, says Erkenbrack, the ABL and WNBA came along a year too late for Jackson. After a year away from the game, she went to a pro tryout but failed to impress.

Jackson then retired from basketball and returned to South Bend, where she has a family and a career in social work. According to Erkenbrack, she could be an impact player in the WNBA right now had she not been out of shape at the tryout. In any case, Tawana Jackson's basketball journey may have ended quite differently had she not made pit stops at five collegiate institutions, three of them junior colleges, along the way.

More on Juco Recruiting

Junior college (juco) basketball has attracted some negative publicity. To the uninformed, all junior colleges might seem like NCAA Division I assembly lines. If a prospective student-athlete is talented but does not make the grades for NCAA Division I, she'll go the juco route for a year or two until she becomes an academic qualifier. Here's the other stereotypical scenario: a high school athlete is a fine student, but she might not yet feel mature enough to handle NCAA life, or perhaps she did not get recruited out of high school at a level that meets her goals. If she has a strong year or two in junior college, her dream school may then recruit her. And if she transfers from a junior college to an NCAA school, she does not have to sit out a year.

Truth be told, junior colleges are indeed a stepping-stone for some women's basketball players but an end point for others. Of those who do go on to four-year opportunities, they proceed to all types of colleges and programs — NCAA II and III, NAIA I and II, in addition to NCAA Division I. Some may try to follow in the wake of Sheryl Swoopes, Betty Lennox or Amanda Lassiter, for whom junior college was the first rung on the WNBA ladder. More girls may opt for top junior colleges in hopes of signing with an elite NCAA Division I college that might lead to a pro opportunity. However, for most juco athletes, junior college is a smaller-atmosphere experience in and of itself, one that may or may not lead to an additional chance to play college ball.

The fact that junior college is a two-year affair puts an interesting twist on recruiting. For the coaches, some of whom see recruiting from two different angles, getting talent truly becomes an exhaustive endeavor. NJCAA Division I colleges overall have more to offer prospects in terms of dollars than NJCAA Division II colleges, but they also have higher-level recruiting competition. NJCAA Division III, however, offers no athletic aid whatsoever. At any level, though, junior college coaches deal in higher volume on a more frequent basis.

"A lot of people tell you you shouldn't go juco," quips Teresa Atkinson, head coach at Florida's Tallahassee Community College, an NJCAA Division I school with a student enrollment of about 10,000. "Well, I would rather see you go juco if you are a Division I player than to go to a Division II or NAIA school. If you have that talent, what is wrong with going and bettering your game?" Atkinson's crew placed third at the national tourney in 2001.

Even though junior college coaches could recruit high school freshmen, they do not usually contact prospective student-athletes until their senior years. They may send out letters beforehand, but they will usually have to wait and see which athletes remain unspoken for after NCAA signings and commitments, as well as which athletes do not qualify academically for NCAA competition.

As far as scholarships go, NJCAA Division I basketball teams cannot have more than 16 athletic scholarships per academic year. These scholarships may cover the cost of tuition, books, room and board, and one trip home per year. However, those are just the upper limits instituted by the overall governing body. Many junior colleges do not have the budget to carry the 16 scholarships. In that aspect, Atkinson considers herself lucky. "We're blessed, and some other schools in south Florida are not, where we have 12 full scholarships and four partials," she says. "Some of the schools don't even have full scholarships. We're able to give the kid all of her financial aid. We don't touch any of that money. That helps because a lot of these kids' parents don't have money. All of the kids on [the 2000-2001] roster were on some athletic scholarship." This certainly helps when recruiting against NCAA institutions.

While many junior college coaches stay local for their recruiting efforts, Atkinson often pursues out-of-state and even international players. In a typical season, out-of-state athletes fill most of her roster slots. She says that she does this partly because of the belief that recruiting against coaches in her conference "becomes animosity. I don't have time for that ... Everybody kind of goes out because you don't want that ill feeling." Unlike many peers, she does travel a lot in recruiting, attending everything from AAU national tourneys to regular-season games in Maryland and Massachusetts. Tallahassee also an international department, through which Atkinson has brought in players from London, Germany, Jamaica, and Canada. Through her days of coaching at Florida Atlantic, an NCAA Division I university, she has personal connections in Jamaica. NJCAA rules limit foreign athletic scholarships to four per year.

Since her team went 12-18 her first year on the Tallahassee campus in 1997, Atkinson has turned the program around. Although she needs to constantly replenish her stable, the national spotlight has definitely aided her recruiting efforts. It has also meant more attention from NCAA Division I and II schools interested in her players. And she is not shy about touting the possibilities in her own recruiting schpiels. In the mail she sends to prospective student-athletes, Atkinson emphasizes the fact that Tallahassee Community College players can transfer any subject major into almost any university. "Any degree that they come out with," she comments, "they know if they leave Tallahassee, they can go right into that school and not have to look at, well I was short this and I didn't have this and they don't accept this. What we sell is our catalog and our degrees that we have. We have medicine, dental hygenist, math — you name it, TCC has it."

When she finds herself on the other end of the recruiting process, Atkinson tries to keep four-year college coaches at arm's length during her players' rookie years. Even during their sophomore seasons, she makes strict guidelines for both college coaches and athletes. In the beginning, she tells coaches to hold off. "I don't let the coaches call those players as freshmen," she says. "They shouldn't be calling anyway, but even the letters, I just tell them to wait. It's OK to send me a letter or something, and the kids can see, OK now, I've got something to work for, if they're interested."

Just as high school coaches want prospective student-athletes to stay focused on their senior outings, junior college coaches want their sophomores to concentrate on their final seasons as well. "I don't want a kid thinking, because I can go to Old Dominion or another school, I'm not going to give TCC anything, and they're footing your bill," Atkinson adds. "I explain that to the coaches, and they highly respect that. I say, if it was your program, I wouldn't step in and disrespect like that. I want the kids to finish well, and I'm not going to tell them not to be interested in your school, but I am telling them this — TCC is footing your bill right now, and what you need to do is focus on performing here in the classroom and on the court. I tell you what if you do those two things, those same coaches that I told to just step off and call you once a month, or call you while you're in the office, I guarantee they're going to continue to look at you." Atkinson keeps these beliefs in mind when recruiting players out of high school because she knows what it's like on the other end and she has seen the pressure of NCAA Division I recruiting. Although she could technically call prospects every single day, she does not phone them more than twice a month.

In addition, Atkinson insists that her athletes sign late with four-year schools. In fact, her players cannot sign early and continue playing for her. "If that coach really wants you, you don't have to sign early," she states. "To me, if you're still performing and doing the things that you did that made them take the interest in you. I tell the NCAA coaches that our girls will not be signing early, and I haven't had any problem with them . . . I've seen kids lose so much focus because they signed early. They thought, I don't have to perform. Well, I want the performance here, and our girls have that understanding, and most of the girls don't want to sign early . . . Don't let anybody tell you you're going to miss the boat. The boat won't go anywhere."

Erkenbrack, whose school is less than one-tenth the size of Tallahassee at about 850 students, takes quite a different tack in pursuing high school athletes. Conference rules on athletic scholarships dictate his recruiting. However, he has still transformed Cloud County women's basketball from slightly better than a .500 team in 1989 to 2001 national champ.

The Kansas Jayhawk Community College Conference, or KJCCC, allows a maximum of six out-of-state players on a squad's roster. Programs cannot carry more than 15 players, and there is no such thing as a full ride. Per the KJCCC, athletic scholarships cannot exceed the cost of tuition and books. "Here, I'm basically fully-funded in that I can give 15 tuition-and-book scholarships," says Erkenbrack. "So how we have to supplement that is that we can provide academic scholarships." Per conference rules, an athlete who posts a 3.5 GPA can receive a maximum of $500 academic scholarship each semester. Thus, books and tuition plus $1000 academic aid is the maximum amount awarded to any of Erkenbrack's players. Any sort of federal aid would supplement this sum. When Erkenbrack finds a high school player that he likes, he says right up front, "This is what I can do. Anything that you can qualify for in terms of federal financial aid, that's good for you."

Erkenbrack employs many of the same tactics that NCAA coaches do in recruiting — mass mailings of 400-500, watching games, talking on the phone. However, he does not go out in the summer to get a jump on the next recruiting class. "Pretty much, because with the NCAA's early signing period and the fact that a lot of these girls, the people that we are recruiting, they're getting recruited by a lot of Division II's and a lot of Division I's," he explains, "we make contact with the juniors and sophomores and send them letters and things, but we are not spending a great deal of time and effort on it. To a large extent, we really are picking up the leftovers in a lot of ways." An assistant watches a few summer and fall tourneys. During the winter, Erkenbrack, his assistant, and his father, a former Cloud County athletic director and men's coach, watch high school games three to four nights a week. Between the three of them, they scour Kansas, Nebraska, and Oklahoma looking for talent, often venturing into rural areas. Erkenbrack also spends time on the phone and in front of the VCR.

In preparation for the 2001-2002 season, Erkenbrack signed 10 players during the NJCAA Letter of Intent signing period in April. To arrive at this number, he actively recruited 35-40 athletes, calling them at least once a week. He estimates doing home visits for about half of his recruits, depending on geography and rank. "It has to do with the value that we place on that person," he says. "It has to do with how much of a battle we're in with other schools." The staff brings out-of-state recruits in for paid, overnight campus visits, while in-state recruits come for the day.

Cloud County has plenty of in-state recruiting competition, and according to Erkenbrack, Kansas players are overrecruited. The state has 360 high schools and close to 50 colleges and universities; it also has 19 public community colleges, all of which must carry at least nine in-state players on their rosters. "The Kansas players that we are recruiting," he explains, "we're usually up against eight to ten other junior colleges, let alone four-years." He uses the chance to play for a national title as his weapon in these recruiting duels.

In general, Erkenbrack does not see a need for more restrictions on recruiting at the junior college level. In any case, he thinks that it would be a near impossibility for the NJCAA to enforce additional recruiting rules. However, he does predict that the NJCAA will limit international recruiting sometime in the future. "With six being the number of non-Kansas players you can have [in the conference]," he says, "we've got schools here in Kansas that have six international students." Cloud County, on the other hand, may have one or two international players on its roster, who Erkenbrack will have heard about from other college coaches.

Most of Erkenbrack's recruits have NCAA Division I as their goal, and many of them do attain that goal. "In the recruiting deal, we try to specialize in young ladies who either were overlooked by Division I schools or were just not quite good enough to go Division I out of high school but have that burning desire to play at the Division I level," he remarks. Although each year he signs one or two that could not go NCAA Division I for academic reasons, most of his players have achieved passing marks.

Erkenbeck does pursue NCAA Division I talent, but he does not consider himself in competition with NCAA Division I colleges. He makes this point clear in early recruiting conversations with student-athletes. "If they are offered [a scholarship] by that Division I school and they feel like they have an opportunity to go in and play and they feel comfortable with that, I tell them not to hesitate," he states. "I tell them, if you came to Cloud County, my ultimate objective for you would be trying to get you into a Division I school. If you have that Division I opportunity now, go. And I'm dealing with the recruiting on both ends — trying to recruit players and trying to get my players on somewhere else."

However, Erkenbrack does not encourage NCAA Divison I in every single situation. "The Division I deal is not the end-all, be-all for everybody," he explains. "Even for some of my players, I discourage them from going Division I. But no, for a high school young lady that has a good opportunity at a good Division I, it's not too far away from home, and if they're going because they like it and they think that's the right thing for them instead of just signing Division I because it's Division I, then I'm all for it."

Every single day, Erkenbrack receives phone calls from four-year college coaches. The calls pick up after the NCAA's National Letter of Intent early signing period in November. Before early signing, the coaches all chase the same players. Afterward, some realize that they are not going to get athletes that they thought would commit. In other words, they need help.

Sometimes these inquiries do not concern specific players on Erkenbrack's squad. "I have a lot of people calling me saying, 'I am looking for post players. Do you know of any?'" he says. He sees his role in the other end of recruiting as giving honest evaluations both to his athletes and the coaches who come calling. "I want each of my players to have an opportunity to continue their education and their basketball at a level which they can be happy and successful," he insists. "I shouldn't oversell my players. I shouldn't preach to my players, you've got to go Division I, you've got to go Division I, you've got to go Division I, when they are not a Division I-

215

caliber player. The big deal here with me is that that I want all of my players to have an opportunity to go on and play, but more importantly, I want them to be able to go on and get their four-year college degree and have it basically paid for." Like Atkinson, he discourages his charges from signing early, having found that junior college athletes will have more opportunities, and better opportunities, if they wait.

Does junior college factor into NCAA coaches' recruiting plans? According to Erkenbrack, it depends entirely on the level of the program. "Louisiana Tech — now that's a top program that takes some junior college players and traditionally has and will continue to, I suppose," he comments. "But there is such a pecking order in Division I women's basketball. There are the definite haves and the have-nots. The further you move away from the Connecticuts and the Tennessees, the more interest there is in junior college. And then when you talk coaching turnover, I think if you have a program that brings in a new staff or changes coaches, then the interest in junior college recruiting picks up significantly because it is an opportunity for a so-called quick fix. You can bring in a couple of really talented, very experienced junior college players and be competitive right away." As an example, he mentions Baylor University. With the transition to new head coach Kim Mulkey-Robertson in 2000, Baylor signed a few junior college players over several years and has moved from the "bottom to the upper tier" of the Big Twelve Conference.

However, four-year schools that recruit junior college players do take a bit of a gamble. For schools that rely on the junior college level, it's even more of a gamble. "I think for a lot of programs, it can be a really good mix," says Erkenbrack. "It's a way of evening out some recruiting classes. I have a lot of coaches call me and say, we really need to sign one or two junior college players because our upcoming junior class consists of one person."

In all of his recruiting efforts, Erkenbrack stresses the merits of junior college, from better opportunities down the road to teacher-student ratio. "I think that junior college programs, junior colleges, community colleges in general get a bad rap academically, and that's unfounded," he states. "There are some bad places out there, there's no question about that, and there are some academically poor schools out there. But a place like ours, or for that matter basically anywhere in the state of Kansas, these schools are geared toward four-year transfer programs. Approximately 70 percent of all of our students here ultimately transfer on to a four-year college or university . . . You can get individualized attention. You are a person, and if you're a women's basketball player here at Cloud County, not only are you a person, you're more of a celebrity." Like many other college coaches, Erkenbrack uses his current players as his top recruiters. He might even have his athletes' parents call prospects' homes to discuss real life as a member of the team.

"Recruiting is a lot different at a two-year school," states Jack Mehl, head coach at Maryland's Frederick Community College, an NJCAA Division II institution of about 12,000 students. "I need to get seven kids every year to come in. You never know from one year to the next what's going to happen, so that's a huge difference with us. It's a neverending process. We recruit for two years, not for four years. We turn over our team 100 percent in two years." Mehl, who coached high school ball for 10 years, took over the helm at Frederick in 1990. Since then, he has led teams to the NJCAA national tourney three times, including 2001. He has managed to accomplish all of this while also teaching high school math full-time.

When Mehl first started at Frederick, the program had seen some successes but had problems, such as usually carrying only about six players on the roster. Almost every county in Maryland has a junior college, and Mehl was told to recruit from within the county. As his very first recruiting task, he wrote to every single senior girl who attended high school in his county, which included a grand total of seven high schools. "I wrote them a letter telling them that they had a tremendous opportunity in front of them, that I was starting a program, that they had a chance to be there at the beginning and be on board," he remembers. "I worked pretty hard with the kids. I had an advantage because I had just come from the high school, so I knew all the kids, and I knew all the coaches. That was a huge part of it for me, that I had some credibility with people initially." His first squad went 16-8, his second 17-10. Then he signed some top-rate County All-Stars, and every team since then has won 20-plus games.

Mehl's athletes are anything but homogeneous in terms of basketball and other career goals. "I'll get kids that only want to play for two years, and then graduate from FCC, and then get a job," he says. "I'll get kids that'll want to play for two years and go on to a four-year school, but they don't want to play at a four-year school. They just want to play two years with us. I'll get the kids that were the non-predictors that are going to be the DI kids. So it's a really interesting mix of kids that I end up with, which is different than a lot of the other junior colleges." Trying to determine whether a player interested in a four-year college is best suited for the NCAA or NAIA, and which division, has proven a constant challenge.

"There's other schools that are Division I factories," Mehl states. "We're not that way. I don't have the resources." Each year, Mehl has a few thousand dollars total to give in athletic scholarship money for his entire team. All schools in his conference face the same scholarship issue. However, when he travels outside his conference for state or national-level competition, it's a different situation. Furthermore, attending Frederick costs twice as much for out-of-county students and about two and a half times as much for out-of-state students as it does for in-county students. Mehl has had recent success recruiting players out of Washington D.C., though, due to a government law passed in 2000 that allows D.C. students to attend colleges in Maryland for the cost of in-county tuition.

Mehl's recruiting methods seem as unorthodox as the makeup of his teams. Much of his recruiting is word-of-mouth, and he completely trusts others' evaluations, so much so that he does not feel the need to see a prospect play, either in person or on videotape. During the winter, he and two part-time assistants try to watch every high school team in the county. He also fields calls from high school coaches. "I've had coaches call me and say, 'Coach, I've got somebody who can play for you, this and that,'" he says. "'Do you want me to send you a tape?' And I say 'No, if you're calling me, and you're telling me that the kid can play, then that's fine with me. You don't need to send me a tape, because of the fact that I have all sorts of different kids.' I have kids that'll play and not play ever again, I have kids that'll go to Division III, Division II, Division I. We'll just take everybody." So Mehl will sign a recruit without ever having seen her in action on the court. He says that he has had to draw a clear line on his recruiting efforts due to the fact that he essentially has two full-time jobs. "We'll take what we've got, and we'll adjust our offense or defense to fit the kids that we have each year and go from there." He only occasionally watches summer ball, not necessarily to find recruits but to see a student-athlete who will be on his team the next season who he has not yet seen play. In addition, he does not often send out letters or use e-mail, preferring phone calls and in-person meetings.

Another crucial component of Mehl's recruiting is having prospects watch his games. "I like to have the kid and her parents come and watch us play," says Mehl, "because I think that it's very important that they have an opportunity to see me and to see my kids and to see how we play and what style we play. I think that's really important, that they need to be able to feel comfortable with me. We spend a lot of time looking at them, but I think they need to look at us, too." Because of the proximity of the recruiting area, prospective student-athletes do not ordinarily stay overnight. However, many end up visiting the campus several times before they sign the Letter of Intent that Mehl instituted upon his arrival.

Another of Mehl's interesting recruiting practices is that one of his best recruiters is not an assistant but Frederick admissions officer Sandy Smith. Since Mehl cannot be found on campus during the day, Smith serves as the "team mother," starting almost the day a high school student-athlete expresses interest in the college. He calls her "a tremendous recruiting tool."

"She advises my kids, and my first step is to get the parents and the kid on campus," Mehl states. "I sit down with them, and I have them meet Sandy first. I do not talk to them about

219

anything about school. Sandy does all that because I'm not there. I've told them that I don't want to give them wrong information. There have been other coaches and schools that you hear about that the kid goes there and says, the coach promised me this and promised me that. I don't ever do any of that. So Sandy sits down and goes over all of the academics with them, talks to them about what they have to do to get financial aid and all that stuff.

"Then they meet with me and we talk about basketball," Mehl continues. "I tell them, 'Look, I have $4000. I do not have enough money to give everybody a full scholarship.' I don't have enough money to give two kids a full scholarship. But what we do, what Sandy and I do, is we figure out how best to use our money. We just try to give it to the kids that need it. What we'll say to them is, I'll say to the parents, 'You need to be honest with me. If you need money, you need to let me know.' Sandy will call and we'll sit down and talk and we'll get some general ideas, and then Sandy will say, 'Hey Jack, so-and-so, have you got $500 for her? She's going to be a little bit short in this semester.' I'll say fine, and that's how we do things." This creative way of conducting business seems to work for Mehl, who continues to assemble tournament-quality teams.

The limited recruiting and athletic scholarship money available to Mehl also affects the way he and his staff run the program. In his mind, the money his student-athletes receive to attend school and his expectations of them are intertwined. "I always had told my assistant coaches, if I was paying every kid to come to school, I think I could have a little bit more say over what they're doing," he says. "If I'm paying every kid to go, I think I would have a little bit different expectations. But my kids are all paying their own way, for the most part."

Mehl says that he can never tell what specific four-year chances will await his players. In 2001, he thought he had two or three legitimate NCAA Division I athletes, but only one went that route. More frequently, team members progress on to NCAA Division II or III colleges, or to none at all. However, Mehl compiles every year's game schedule with exposure in mind, supplementing conference matchups with traveling to play tough out-of-conference opponents in key locations such as Florida or North Carolina. In addition, he says that these contests get his student-athletes exposure with two-year as well as four-year schools, which can lead to valuable networking opportunities.

"There have been times when a coach will call me up and say, 'I was talking to so-and-so at Lewisburg, and he said you guys have a nice point guard,'" Mehl states. "Lewisburg is one of the teams that we play — it's a junior college. So we do a lot of recruiting that way, where we try to help each other out. A four-year school will call and say, 'I'm looking for a point guard,' and he'll say, 'Have you looked at the kid at Frederick?' That's one of the reasons why I like to try to play a good schedule and get outside the area as much as possible, to get more exposure for our kids. Then having an opportunity to compete at the national tournament, that gets a lot of exposure for us." One advantage of recruiting at the smaller levels is that coaches may be more willing to trade information.

Mehl experienced word-of-mouth, networking-based recruiting at its best with one of his starters. Patrick Knapp, head coach at NCAA Division I Georgetown, was interested in another of Mehl's players, but the feeling was not mutual. "He said, 'Do you have any other post players?'" Mehl remembers. "'I said, I've got a 6'2" kid, but I tell you what, she's a great kid, good student, works hard — I don't think she can play for you.' He said to me, 'I'll be the judge of that.' He came up and watched us play, came over to me afterwards and was glowing in his recommendation of her." Knapp said that if he did not sign a 6'5" international player that he was recruiting, that he wanted Mehl's athlete. Unfortunately for Mehl's player, Knapp got his international player.

"About four days after that, we got a call from [NCAA Division I] Charleston Southern," Mehl continues. "The coach at Southern called me because Pat Knapp had called him. He never saw her play, flew her down for a visit, offered her a three-year full ride. He said, 'Look, you started on this team.' We were something like 54-6 in two years. He said, 'If you started for two years on a team that was 54-6, you've got to be a player.' That's another type of thing that happens in terms of the networking thing. I think the four-year schools do a lot of that. It's a cutthroat thing for them, but at the same time, they are not beyond trying to help a kid. If they see a kid that I've got, and they know that they can't use her but maybe there's another school that can use a kid like her, I've gotten a lot of calls that way."

Junior college recruiting differs from NCAA recruiting in a number of ways. As mentioned previously, coaches operate on a two-year, or sometimes a one-year, rather than a four-year mindset. Also, the club circuit, the NCAA's recruiting staple, does not play an important role at the juco level. Whether they coach in the NJCAA Division I, II, or III, most junior college coaches do much of their recruiting in the spring, for the following year. Some rely on others' assessments or videos more than on watching games in person. Finally, many see the process from the perspective of both recruiter and recruitee, helping their players secure suitable four-year opportunities. From all angles, recruiting is completely different at two-year colleges. And as more high school girls dream of four-year scholarships at top schools, the junior college option seems a viable progression to that end.

NAIA Recruiting

At the approximately 300 women's basketball programs of the NAIA, recruiting can also be challenging. NAIA Division I and II coaches compete against the prestige and popularity of the NCAA and against junior colleges as a path to the NCAA. Some NAIA coaches recruit junior college players as well as high school prospects. Like the NJCAA, the NAIA is free of strict recruiting rules and regulations. It provides another generally smaller-environment alternative for those seeking to play at a four-year school.

Top NAIA colleges frequently recruit against NCAA Division I institutions. Janell Jones, head coach at NAIA Division I Oklahoma City University, which has about 4500 students, has found this to be the case with in-state schools. Jones served as an assistant coach at Oklahoma City in 1998-99 and 1999-2000, and she took over the head slot for 2000-01; the squad won the national crown all three seasons. Jones names in-state NAIA Division I and NCAA Division I schools, even top-ranked NCAA Division I University of Oklahoma, as recruiting competition. Although she may sometimes lose out to the NCAA, she definitely uses the laxity of NAIA recruiting regulations to her advantage.

"I think one thing that we have, because of [the lack of] all the rules and regulations, we can treat people like human beings," Jones says. "You can talk to them. If they need a ride to the airport, we can give them a ride to the airport. Our hands aren't tied to where you can't treat them as normal human beings and things like that. You can have them over for dinner and not worry about, we've got to find a rule to match that out there. I like that, being able to have that relationship." In addition, Jones scopes out the Oklahoma club basketball scene as much as possible to try to get an edge over NCAA coaches. Since NCAA Division I coaches cannot do home visits until September, she does some home visits in August. That way, she can establish a relationship with recruits before "they are so bombarded and they have to narrow it down and things like that."

Unlike many of her conference foes, and many other NAIA schools, Jones has a full-time assistant. Aside from covering non-scholastic events in Oklahoma, the pair also attends fall shootouts. During the regular season, they watch high school games twice a week. Armed with 11 full scholarships, a few of which they usually split into partials, they do their best to entice athletes away from NCAA ball. During talks with prospects, Jones discusses impact and playing time. "With [NCAA] Division I having 15 scholarships," she explains, "a lot of kids don't realize that . . . coach isn't going to tell them, 'I'm recruiting you just to be a role player. I'm recruiting you to potentially maybe develop.' But I'm also, because I have all of these scholarships, they can be an average player sitting on the bench in Division I, and they could be a great player getting lots of playing time for us. I don't think kids really understand that, but they are really being recruited to be a great practice player. If they accept that role and are fine with that, then that's great. But a lot of them have to find that out themselves after they get there. I wasn't recruited really to play. I was recruited because I'm a great kid and I work hard, and I'll make their team better. That's OK, because I've recruited some kids that way, too. But I try to make sure that they know what the potential is."

Competing against NCAA Division I in recruiting has also prompted Jones to go international. Five of the 12 athletes on Oklahoma City University's 2001-2002 roster hail from foreign countries, and the other seven are from Oklahoma. According to Jones, this reflects the entire school population, as the college's administration focuses on attracting international students. Indeed, its web site has a special section for prospective international students and boasts that attendees come from 48 U.S. states and 70 foreign countries. Jones believes that recruiting internationally is an important contributor to her team's success. "Being able to get the international students separates us into why we're at the level we are," she says. "A 6'4" post for us, in the state of Oklahoma — I don't care how good she is, if she is horrible or if she is great, she is going Division I. We have to get our post players from international. The worst post player in Oklahoma, a 6'4", will go Division I." Her five 2001-2002 international players are listed at 6'4", 6'3", and 5'11".

Recruiting international student-athletes often begins with one and proceeds from there. At Oklahoma City University, one player from Colombia came and had a good experience, and Jones kept the lines of communication open. "I make contact with the Colombia coach," she says, adding that international recruiting is difficult. "He knows to send his players because the players have had success here and they have liked OCU, and they have been taken care of. They encourage more of the players to come." Three of Jones' 2001-2002 international contingent came from Colombia. She and her assistant depend on email and videotape, as well as examining the levels of prospects' current programs, to recruit internationally.

In addition, Jones also relies on junior college players. In fact, she uses much of her recruiting budget for paid campus visits for junior college athletes. "I try to get a balance in of freshmen from Oklahoma, some jucos, and internationals," she says. The jucos bring experience. They want to play. They haven't made the grades or whatever. For whatever reason, they aren't going DI. They just bring experience and a lot of times strength. You bring in a freshman versus someone who has been in a gym for two years on a weight program, that's extra speed and quickness."

However, even with her winning record, Jones battles against the superior reputation of the NCAA. "You know, we have won three national championships here," she states. "We have all that. I recruited our top players, and it was like every single one of them, 'It's between you and some other [NCAA] Division I, Coach Jones.' We really like you, and we really want to come, but it's the public and the social image of Division I. You can't fight it out there. What I hope to do in recruiting them is, if they go to Division I and they don't like it, then they'll come back to you." When she does win one of those battles, she considers a signee "a great steal," as with her current superstar, Kesha Watson. Watson, who came on board in 2000, could have gone junior college and NCAA Division I but opted for Oklahoma City; after her freshman year, she already had a national championship.

"The hardest part of recruiting is convincing a kid that . . . Division I is not for everyone," Jones says. "On our national championship team of [1999], we had five All-Staters who were all up for Division I scholarships, but they didn't want that. They just didn't want the pressure. They wanted to be a student-athlete. They wanted to get their degree, and they were rare kids."

While getting her master's degree, Jones completed a research project on recruiting. She interviewed players on her team and across the state, dividing them into "unhappy versus happy," and she says that many of the NCAA Division I athletes she spoke with fell into the first category. She explains that this reflects the pressure on prospective student-athletes to attend the highest level possible as opposed to what may be the best fit. "My hypothesis on that was that in the NAIA, we don't have rules and regulations on how much time we can spend with them, so they really get to know who we are," she says. "We are who we are. We spend more time with them, either on the phone or whatever. In the NCAA, because there have been so many rules broken, they have so many limits, so whatever time they get, they're going to give them their best show. They don't get to see them on a daily basis or get to talk to them and really get a feel for who they are. The longer you're with someone, obviously, the more you get to know them. What they have is three days with them and then a couple of visits, and then the home visit, and then they've got to make the decision." Of the students Jones interviewed who left NCAA Division I universities, she says that most of them left after realizing that the college coaches were not as they described themselves during recruiting visits.

The belief that NCAA Division I is the only trail to the WNBA has affected recruiting for some NAIA schools. "First of all, it's the same thing with the guys," Jones states. "You know how many players are actually going to go? And that's not even true either. I've got players, and I've got one playing in Korea, and one in Ecuador, and they're looking at Kesha [Watson] and Jhudy [Gonzalez] for the WNBA . . . That's created a false sense of, I have to go DI to make the WNBA. First of all, the chances of you making it are so slim, and you don't have to go. If you're that good, the WNBA will find you. I think that's been the biggest difference because we used to be able to get DI's a lot easier if it was between us and a DI. Still, I love the fact that we have the WNBA, but it's just the misconception out there that the men have to face, too, that you're not all going to be NBA players." Now, prep players have not only NCAA Division I in their minds as the only way to the pros, it must be top-level NCAA Division I. Accordingly, for girls who may not qualify academically or may not have the skill for NCAA Division I out of high school, the juco-NCAA route may seem more enticing.

Primarily in-state talent, but also junior college recruits, make up Coach Kevin Engellant's roster. Engellant assumed head coaching duties at University of Montana-Western, an

NAIA Division I university with about 1100 in its student body, in 1996. Since his arrival, Western has made two national tourney appearances. Technically, his full-time job consists of half women's basketball coach and half microcomputer center director. He has two student assistants, one of whom coaches the women's junior varsity team. His recruiting consists of no full rides but a constant juggling of in-state tuition, out-of-state tuition, and room waivers.

Engellant's explanation of doling out athletic scholarship money can give even the most clearheaded listener a headache. He has 10 in-state tuition waivers and two out-of-state tuition waivers; out-of-state tuition is an extra charge on top of in-state. He also has seven room scholarships. However, while the price of a room has gone up every year, the scholarship amount has not. "So in essense, we are saying we have seven rooms and seven boards, but in our budget, we've actually only got five rooms, but you can offer more," Engellant explains. When he says "you can offer more," Engellant means that he fundraises to make sure he can offer prospects a somewhat worthwhile deal. In addition, board functions only as a work-study opportunity, not as a grant. In order to receive the full board amount, players need to work close to three hours every day, which is tough for any college student.

During the recruiting process, Engellant must take all of these details into account. "If I am recruiting a kid, let's say my out-of-state kids, I'll offer them a full out-of-state and a full in-state and a full board," he explains. "It's as full as we can actually get. I could give a booster club scholarship to supplement for fees and books and what-not, but it still doesn't cover everything like a Division I scholarship where you say, here's your scholarship and everything is covered — books and fees and everything."

However, he does use some discretion with his funds, depending on a prospect's recruiting status and financial situation. "I try to get a little bit of a background in terms of where they're at financially," he adds, "if they've got some money, and it depends on who else is recruiting them. But if it's a top kid, I'd for sure go full tuition and then the room and the board.

The tuition is a little more important to the kids. I might go full tuition, full room, maybe half board. If I think it is a really poor kid, I would just say full, full, full, and if I really, really wanted them, I would even say I'll cover your fees, and I'll take that out of a booster club. So we have some flexibility there, but it's a little bit misleading when you say, I'll give you a full. Well, just on the face value, it doesn't cover everything."

Typically, Engellant's top prospects are his out-of-staters. He takes this into consideration when dealing with his finances. "My out-of-state kids are hopefully some of my better players or impact players," he says. "To get them, usually you have to offer them a little more money, so I try to give them as good a scholarship as we can. So they're all 1.0 room, 1.0 board, 1.0 in [state], 1.0 out [of state]."

Engellant leads another venture of which NCAA coaches would be terribly jealous. It serves as an additional example of the huge disparity in strictness between NCAA and other recruiting rules. Every year since 1996, he has brought a group of 30 quality Montana high school girls' basketball players to the U.S. Junior Nationals in Las Vegas. Assembling the team and attending the Vegas tourney give him a chance to see and connect with some top prospective student-athletes. People are often surprised to hear that Engellant is allowed to organize and coach his Montana Hoops, and he admits that it helps his recruiting. In addition, he runs a high school tournament at Western with the dual purpose of fundraising and giving him a chance to watch prep players.

Even though he may have to wait until late spring of recruits' senior years to sign them, Engellant still follows younger players. "I guess the big thing is trying to identify kids as early as I can," he states. He also has a big Rolodex of high school coaching contacts made through Western and three years of coaching high school basketball. "Obviously, the toughest thing is that Montana is a huge state," he says. "My top kids, I try to watch them play as much as I can and meet the parents right away and keep in contact through phone calls and emails . . . Then when our season gets over, we try to get them on campus as soon as they can for campus visits. They get a chance to come in and meet the team and practice with us and kind of get a feel for what we do." In addition, Montana high school girls played basketball in the fall through the 2001 season. This provided Engellant ample opportunity to watch games in September before his own season picked up. However, as of 2002-03, the season changes to winter. Not only does this alter Engellant's recruiting schedule, it will result in fewer prospect evaluations overall.

In general, however, Engellant focuses on one recruiting class at a time, the seniors. When he makes contact with juniors, he can run up against NCAA Division I competition. "You hate to spend all of your time and energy and then all of a sudden, a Division I school comes in," he comments. He observes freshmen and sophomores but will not contact them. If he thinks an underclass athlete shows promise, chances are that NCAA I coaches do, too, and he has rarely lured away a recruit from one of them.

In addition, the existence of a junior varsity team means more recruiting effort and twice as many players. "We recruit a lot of kids, and some kids are just borderline, but you just don't have the room or the money for them," Engellant says. Western JV athletes receive $500 in athletic aid. "You offer them a little bit of money, and if nobody else is recruiting them, then they might come here, but otherwise if there's anybody else recruiting them, they're probably going to go where they get a little bit of a scholarship, better offer." Western did not have junior varsity basketball prior to 1999, and Engellant says that if he does not receive better funding for the team, he may discontinue it.

Engellant takes care never to tell prospective student-athletes that they will definitely be on either the varsity or JV squad. "I guess some kids the past couple of years, they pretty much, or we pretty much know that they're OK, but they're not going to be a varsity player," he explains. We have to be a little bit careful, but any of those kids that may think they have a chance, we don't want to not have them come here because we have them labeled a JV kid. For the most part, there are a few kids where I have pretty much just mentioned the junior varsity, but for all of those kids, especially the borderline kids, the bubble kids who you think, well gosh, she's a big kid, or she's pretty athletic . . . I say, we have varsity and JV. If you're one of our top 10 or 12 players, you'll be on the varsity. If not, we can redshirt you, we can play you JV, we can play you both. We have lots of options here. If you're good enough, you'll be on the varsity." The university as a whole loves the junior varsity program, as it brings in mostly-paying customers who may not have otherwise chosen to enroll.

Whether recruiting against in-conference opponents, junior colleges, or NCAA schools, Engellant often sees the financial aspect as the deciding factor. "Unfortunately, I think a lot of kids, and this is what my big sell is, a lot of kids just go where the money is," he comments. "Maybe they come here and they think it's awesome. They like everything about the program. We are a smaller school, a smaller community, which scares some people away, but we think we have a great thing going here. That's one thing that I can sell on my players. I tell every one of them, 'I went to school here, and I had a blast.'"

As a high school standout, Carla Sterk definitely felt like she wanted to play NCAA Division I ball. She did just that at Central Michigan University, where she holds the school record for blocked shots and falls in the top five of several other categories. Sterk spent a few months as a replacement player for the ABL's New England Blizzard, followed by a year of pro ball in Portugal. As of 1999, she has been head coach at Cornerstone University in Michigan, an NAIA Division II institution. In 2001, Cornerstone advanced to the national tourney for the first time in the program's history, making it all the way to the Sweet Sixteen. Sterk, who has one part-time assistant, also serves as the school's assistant sports information director.

Although NAIA Division II allows women's basketball teams to carry the equivalent of six full athletic scholarships, Sterk receives her scholarship budget from her athletic director in the amount of a lump sum. The money equals about four full scholarships, and the team roster usually features 14 players. Throughout their collegiate careers, players' scholarship money usually remains constant, with a few exceptions. "There are a couple of them, maybe their role on the team had changed quite a bit, or maybe their financial situation," Sterk states. "Our tuition did increase [in 2001]. Our athletic director was given by the school two full rides that he, with the request of the coach . . . I requested, saying that I wanted one of my players to get an increase of a thousand dollars with her scholarship. So then he approved that, and it came from his fund."

Athletes on the Cornerstone roster usually come from Michigan, and Sterk focuses her recruiting on the immediate local area, Grand Rapids. Although she does not have far to travel to scout high school talent, she finds it difficult to keep up with recruiting correspondence given that she has no full-time help. In the spring, she attends non-scholastic matchups in Michigan. Come summer, she runs camps, which she describes more as developmental than exposure opportunities. She and her assistant try to watch games twice a week in the fall. Once her own season starts, she invites recruits to a home game.

Although Sterk does not say that Cornerstone's being a Christian school has limited her in recruiting, she always mentions that characteristic in her first conversations with prospective student-athletes. "I'd say, what do you know about Cornerstone?" she explains. "Did you know that it's a private school, that it's a Christian college? It used to be Grand Rapids Baptist. Some people view it as being a little more strict than other schools. Is this something that you're interested in?" Some, but not all, of her players come from Christian high schools.

Again the topic of NAIA scholarship aid becomes more complex. Michigan natives who attend college in-state automatically receive $2700 in state funding. They may also receive college money based on their Michigan Educational Assessment Program test scores. In addition, the state determines the maximum amount that a prospect may receive in financial aid. Thus, the sum of state, institutional, and athletic aid cannot exceed that amount. "Sometimes I'm waiting on that until January, and meanwhile these other kids are like OK, I want to sign, and [NCAA] Division II and Division I schools are snatching them up," Sterk states. "But I can have an idea . . . If this is a player that is in high need, then she may be getting more athletic aid. I also weigh it as, is this a position that I really need or a player that is of a Division II or a Division I caliber that could really boost our program to take it to the next level? Then I think, well this is how much money I'm going to need." Twelve of 14 players on Cornerstone's 2001-02 roster received basketball scholarship money, and the other two also played volleyball, from which they received athletic aid. Sterk has never offered a full scholarship.

To get a first choice, Sterk might go over the limit set by the state. "I had a player [in 2000], this was a recruit that I really wanted, and it didn't really matter to me if we did lose out on the state aid," she remarks. "I said, 'We'll give you this amount of money,' and it exceeded the state cap. So we lost all the state money, but I was willing. I was fine with that because this was a player that I really wanted." After financial aid information comes out in January, Sterk will offer scholarship money first to girls atop her list, wait for them to respond, and move down her list from there.

As recruits debate their decisions in the spring of their senior years, Sterk often has them as well as other local prep athletes come by and compete with her team. "We always play pickup," she says. "I'm allowed to have kids come on campus, and they can practice with us and play with us. I think that's been great because it gets those kids connected to my current players."

Although she sometimes waits for prospects to hear from NCAA Division I and II institutions, Sterk's main recruiting adversaries are two NCAA Division III Christian colleges in Michigan. "When we come up in those battles, I always use the crutch as, we have athletic scholarships we can offer and they don't," she comments. "And Cornerstone is a little cheaper tuition-wise than those schools. If it ends up being a financial thing, they'll at least be getting some money for playing basketball. Then I would just say, too, just competing with those schools, we've got awesome facilities." Lately, though, as Cornerstone garners more of a national reputation, NCAA Division I and II have more often been her recruiting foes.

Sterk's recent success also means that she receives more calls from high school players, parents, and coaches. Often times, these calls do not lead to anything. "They figure, well, it's a Christian school, and I should be able to come there," she says. "You might be able to at a different school, but I feel like the majority of my kids on my team could probably play [NCAA] Division II. In order for us to win that national championship or be at a consistent place in nationals, this is a year-round commitment. I don't think some kids are ready to give that type of commitment."

Overall, Sterk believes that a scarcity of recruiting restrictions allows her to at least have a fighting chance against NCAA institutions. "We are competing against all of these other bigger schools with bigger budgets, and you end up still recruiting, I'm still recruiting for the seniors, whereas these other schools are looking at their juniors and sophomores already," she explains. "I think that if we are given a bunch of rules that we have to follow, then we're going to miss out on some opportunities for getting players to come here." She appreciates not having to worry about keeping track of recruiting rules and says that she does not even have an NAIA rulebook.

However, coaches with no limits also feel that they should always be recruiting. When they don't have much help, and when they themselves have other job responsibilities, this is difficult. "Sometimes it's got its pluses and minuses," Sterk says, "just because, how many times do I really have to go watch this player to make sure that she comes here? I can watch kids as many times as I want and as young as I want, so it seems insurmountable sometimes."

As advice to prospects and parents in recruiting, Sterk echoes the importance of determining athletes' most suitable collegiate level. Although she believes that girls' high school and/or club coaches are usually the best judges, she herself has been asked to fulfill that role. "Kids that come to my camp . . . There's one girl, she's home-schooled . . . and her aspirations, she wants to play in the WNBA," Sterk says. "There's no way that she's going to play in the WNBA. She said, 'Can you watch me, and tell me what you think and what I need to do?' I just had to tell her honestly, 'It's great to have goals like that, and there might be a place for you to play. There might even be a junior college or something. But I don't think, in order to be in the WNBA, you pretty much have to play Division I basketball, just about. You have to be one of the elite players.' From what I've seen, it's so hard to be honest with kids. It would have to come from me as opposed to one of my college players who are their counselors. I think for a kid that's not really sure where they fit in, they need to really have a sit-down talk with their high school or AAU coach to find out."

From being resourceful with athletic scholarship money to helping campers to finding the time to keep in touch with prospects, NAIA Division II recruiting can definitely be a challenge. Perhaps the biggest challenge, however, comes in waiting for girls to choose from among the NCAA, NAIA, and junior college levels. To stay competitive in NAIA II, Sterk must often convince recruits with options that the small college route is the way to go.

Student-Athlete Perspective

A growing number of athletes endure the college recruiting process more than once. Not only is the number of transfers increasing, many female athletes also see junior college as the first step in a longer basketball career. For some, having multiple colleges on the résumé leads to perhaps better athletic opportunities.

Vanika Dickerson has had the good fortune of going through the recruiting process twice. After graduating in 1999 from Thomas Jefferson High School in Auburn, Washington, she spent two years at Peninsula College. Peninsula is a junior college not affiliated with the NJCAA but with the Northwest Athletic Association of Community Colleges (NWAACC), a group of 36 schools in Oregon and Washington. During her sophomore year at Peninsula, several NAIA Division I coaches recruited her, including Engellant, and she began the next phase of her college competition at the University of Montana-Western in fall 2001.

Grades had nothing to do with Dickerson's decision to go juco. An honor student, she considered many community colleges in the state of Washington as well as several NCAA Division I and NAIA Division I schools. Before her senior year, she only considered four-year colleges. However, in the end she opted to wait to pursue that route. "I didn't think I was mature enough to go that far away from home," she says, "and I wasn't ready to play at that level."

Dickerson credits her high school coach with promoting her in the first recruiting process. "He's the one that mainly got my name out to a lot of colleges, just because of the school we went to," she states. "We didn't get a lot of attention from colleges. He started with people he knew, and then he just started calling people up." Although she got some college exposure from a few camps and tourneys, her coach's proactive measures were instrumental in getting her name out.

In addition, as with many recruiting situations, the college coach's personality proved significant. For Dickerson, the extra efforts made by the Peninsula coach also weighed heavily on her choice of college level. "The main reason why I went to a junior college, too, was because the Peninsula coach, Curt Bagby, went through a lot to get me there," she explains. "He came down to my house quite a few times and helped me fill out all of the papers because I didn't really know much about the application process. He filled out all of my financial aid stuff and all of my admissions stuff, helped me fill it all out, which was really helpful. That made a big difference."

Dickerson says that she started thinking about her next step "the day I walked into Peninsula." From day one, she considered the classes she would need to take and how she would need to play in order to move on. She kept her bargain on both ends, earning First Team All-Conference honors at the end of her freshman year. That season, Bagby had received calls from four-year coaches about Dickerson, but her second recruiting process did not begin until the end of her freshman year. While she was still playing games, he told her only that coaches were calling about her.

Although Bagby had good intentions, he was also close to retiring and did not go the distance to market Dickerson. "He wanted to help me out, but I don't think that he had the motivation to pursue it farther and push it harder," Dickerson says. "It made things a lot harder just because I wasn't sure what to tell coaches. I didn't understand the recruiting process very well either, so I didn't know who I needed to get in contact with, who I needed to talk to, what I needed to get out to people."

As a result, Dickerson turned to the Peninsula men's basketball assistant to help her through. "Pretty much, he took me under like one of the boys and he got my name out to colleges," she remembers. "He started calling people. He found out who had been calling me and who was interested in me, and he started arranging recruiting trips to go up and visit them." She had asked the boys' head coach, assistant coach, and her family for honest assessments about where they thought she could play. "Then it was just a matter of sending out the tapes and seeing who called me back." Engellant had begun calling her midway through her sophomore year and kept in touch through phone and mail.

When Dickerson's second recruiting process heated up toward the end of her sophomore season at Peninsula, six different colleges either came to watch her play or watched her on tape. Many of them called her about once a week, which she thinks was just the right amount of contact. "Mainly all of them were NAIA Division I's," she recalls, adding that one NCAA Division II also showed interest. "Other than that, it just came down to mainly who was trying to get in contact with me because it was so late in the recruiting process. This all started happening in April, once the season was over, because I was told by [Bagby] to wait until the season came to an end before we started talking to colleges. That way I could tell them where I went in the tournament and all that. Then he retired. He left at the beginning of April, and our season was over at the end of March."

Although Dickerson seems happy with her ultimate choice, she would do quite a few things differently if she could go back to Peninsula. First, she would not wait until her sophomore season there was almost finished to begin contacting four-year schools. "By that time, a lot of colleges have signed people," she states. "They have people in mind. And if your name is not out there, it's not saying that they don't want you — maybe they don't know about you. So you need to give them the opportunity to know who you are and know about you. And so waiting until April, most people sign most of their players. It's a couple last-minute players, who are maybe pretty good and are waiting for their grades to come through or waiting for their test scores to come through, who they're waiting for." Aside from the blue-chippers, athletes looking to be recruited cannot afford to wait to publicize themselves.

As overall counsel to any female student-athlete beginning the recruiting process, Dickerson firmly believes in targeting a level. She also does not see anything wrong with aiming high to begin with and letting coaches dictate the next move. "You need to go to coaches that are honest and ask them to be up front with you and say, 'Hey, where do you think I'm at? What level?'" she says. "And then send your tapes out. If you think that you're an NCAA Division I player, you send your tapes out, and if those coaches agree, they'll call you back. If not, then you need to start looking at different levels. But I think it all depends on where you play, city-wise, state-wise, because some places get bigger exposure from NCAA Division I's and Division II's than other places do." Small-town girls who aren't nationally-ranked can get good opportunities if they work a little bit harder on promoting themselves.

Above all, Dickerson learned from her own experiences the importance of an early start on researching schools, contacting coaches, and thinking about what it takes to succeed at a collegiate institution, athletically and academically. "It's never too early, whether you're a freshman in high school or a freshman at a junior college," she advises. "And just working hard, you've just got to work hard no matter what. Just because you're good in high school doesn't mean that you're going to have that same exposure if you go to a junior college, and vice versa. Just because you don't get a lot of exposure in high school doesn't mean there's not a school out there that you'd like to go to that wouldn't want you. They just maybe don't know about you."

Essence Perry, on the other hand, made sure that colleges knew about her when she decided to transfer from NCAA Division I Kansas State University after one year. Following her freshman season in 1999, she sent out highlight tapes to other NCAA Division I institutions that she was interested in and waited for college coaches to call. Once Louisiana Tech head coach Leon Barmore picked up the phone, her search was over.

While in high school in Lawton, Oklahoma, Perry had been recruited by several NCAA Division I and II institutions. However, she discovered during her freshman year at K-State that the program's style of play did not fit her. She had not watched the team in action before making her decision. "I didn't really look into their program that much," Perry says. "I was so into the players and the coaches that I didn't really go into detail about how their program was really run." Once she decided to leave, the staff posted that information on the team web site, which Perry believes helped in her second recruiting process.

Having grown up watching Louisiana Tech on TV, Perry jumped at the chance to be part of such a top-notch program. Although other NCAA Division I schools also pursued her, including Stanford and Texas Christian University, she immediately decided to go for the college that she had dreamed about. While Barmore did not recruit her out of high school, he was impressed with the tape she sent him following her freshman season at Kansas State.

However, Perry would add yet another school to her collegiate résumé before arriving at Louisiana Tech. Had she transferred directly from Kansas State to Louisiana Tech, she would have had to sit out a season of game competition, in accordance with NCAA regulations. Instead, Barmore presented his recruit with the option of playing junior college basketball for one season. "[Coach Barmore] said he wouldn't mind signing me early, but that he would want me to go to a junior college," Perry recalls. "He really didn't want me coming here sitting out a year and doing nothing. He wanted me to just keep getting that experience." Had Perry insisted on going straight to Tech, Barmore would have gladly signed her then. However, she decided to take his advice.

As soon as Perry told Barmore she would be willing to spend a year honing her game at a junior college, Barmore called Kurt Budke, then the head coach at Texas' Trinity Valley Community College. WNBA star Betty Lennox had followed that same route from Trinity Valley to Louisiana Tech. Budke contacted Perry, she liked what she heard, she visited the campus, and that was it. Trinity Valley won four national titles in the 1990s, so she knew that she would be competing at a high level.

Perry says she probably would not have spent a year at a junior college if Barmore had not made the suggestion. "I think I would have gone on and come here and then sat out a year," she explains. "But I knew [Coach Barmore] knew that that was a good program, and I had talked to Coach Budke. I liked what he was talking about. I decided that that would be the best fit for me."

During her year at Trinity Valley, Perry garnered All-Conference honors. Barmore saw her practice and then-assistant Kim Mulkey-Robertson watched a game. After her season finished, she signed with Louisiana Tech during the late period, not once having considered signing early. "I was trying to focus on my season and worry about signing later," she comments. She instantly became a starter at her third, final, and highest-level collegiate institution.

Looking back, Perry does not seem to regret any of the basketball decisions that she made. She did not find acclimating herself to each new team too difficult, and she does not wish that she had played out her NCAA eligibility differently. "I felt like the junior college I went to was a great program and was a great experience for me," she says. She also offers a retort to the naysayers of juco basketball: "Junior college can get you farther than you coming out of high school and going to a Division I college that you probably were better than. It helps you mature as a person and develop your game." For a select few, but not many, it may even help clear a path to the pros.

Postgame Summary

In the course of writing this book, I've come to realize that recruiting really is a courting process. In the beginning, excitement carries the participants, who all do their best to impress. As the process develops, the different parties size each other up and try to determine whether it's worth their time to work toward a serious relationship. The courtship ends as each side makes promises and commitments to the other. As the relationship begins, do recruiters, coaches, parents, and student-athletes know whether they have made the right choice? If a breakup ensues, it's never pleasant.

The rules of women's college basketball recruiting, both written and unwritten, further complicate the courtship. Indeed, most girls who continue with basketball past high school do not go on to top-level NCAA Division I. As a matter of fact, in 1999-2000, almost 14,000 student-athletes played NCAA women's basketball; only 720 of them competed at the top 50. The majority of high school girls' basketball players do not get recruited by the elite schools.

Where does this leave the masses? Wallowing in an assortment of equally confusing tasks. First, and early on, these players must learn the rules that regulate and direct the recruiting process. They also need help in determining their skill level and potential for specific college levels. In addition, they should take the time to evaluate programs and coaching staffs. They need to promote themselves, but not in ways that will diminish their stature. At the same time, they must also take care of academic requirements specific to their desired level(s) of competition. Furthermore, getting through recruiting is even more complex and stressful for those who draw interest from different divisions and/or levels. One college coach is allowed to do something that another is not, and it's up to families to keep track of these actions; however, it's also up to the families to make sure their children get the best opportunities that they can.

For all of the different sides, recruiting is a game. Parents and student-athletes want college coaches to be completely honest about their styles, their teams, and their recruiting lists. College coaches want families and prep-level coaches to be up front about the recruit's ability, academic background, and top choices. However, those who want others to be frank are not straightforward themselves. That's how it has to be, they say, in order to keep options open.

The money game of dispensing scholarships plays a part in recruiting as well. With the rising cost of a college education, often the amount of the college scholarship weighs more heavily than the association, be it NCAA, NAIA, or NJCAA. While many think only in terms of full rides, the full athletic scholarship only dominates at the top institutions and in the most heated recruiting battles. Fortunately, there is a lot of money finagling in many levels of women's college hoops — combinations of athletic, academic, and need-based aid as well as other slush funds. This sometimes permits college coaches to stretch their scholarships and allows students to receive more money than they might have originally thought. But because higher-touted recruits hear first about the creative financing, it further complicates the entire recruiting process.

If the best players always got the best opportunities recruiting-wise, women's basketball recruiting would be simple. However, the overrecruitment or underrecruitment of prospective student-athletes is another hitch in the process. If a girl plays for a certain level program or coach, or knows a certain expert, she already has an advantage regardless of her basketball ability. She could receive a chance where a more talented player with a different team and coach does not. Those without the connections or spotlight, though, can do things to sell themselves to college coaches.

Prospective student-athletes are college programs' lifelines. Competitiveness in women's basketball has forced coaches, athletes, and peripheral players to resort to recruiting practices they may not have otherwise undertaken. The short history of women's basketball has already seen many changes in the regulations that guide the process. Yet within a system many see as too restrictive, they find a way to sidestep the rules to their advantage. Women's basketball equals men's in number of reported NCAA recruiting violations. There are more than we know about as well, as women's coaches are reluctant to tattle on their peers in the name of growing the sport. While the abuses may not be as flagrant as on the men's side, they add up, and the women's basketball community should be concerned.

Above all, recruiting really never ends. Even after signees arrive on campus and progress through their collegiate tenures, the recruiting process still affects them. Not only are their coaches still recruiting, coaches always want to recruit up, over the current level of talent. Although this will help a program get better, it contributes to the transferring and cuts into athletes' confidence. Though some meet the challenge, others play out their college careers in fear of losing their roster slots.

In actuality, women's college basketball may be more popular than the pros right now. Even so, few women's college basketball teams make money. Since success generates revenue, hopefully the increased parity in women's college hoops will result in more programs turning a profit. Coaches thrive or flounder on their prospects' decisions. While collegiate administrators place increasing pressure on their women's basketball coaches to succeed, coaches compete harder than ever for their recruits. As a result, the recruiting process is constantly evolving. It's both an exciting and precarious time for women's college basketball recruiting and for women's basketball itself.

Appendix: Team Roster

Following are the basketball backgrounds of the 79 diverse college coaches, college players, high school and club coaches, parents, exposure event directors, and recruiting experts featured in the book. Many thanks to all of them for sharing their recruiting experiences and thoughts on the process.

James Anderson is head coach at Narbonne High School in Harbor City, California, where his nationally-ranked teams captured the state title in 2000 and 2001. He also coaches in the OGDL club organization. Anderson arrived at Narbonne in 1991.

Teresa Atkinson has been head coach at Florida's Tallahassee Community College, an NJCAA Division I institution, since 1996. She previously coached at NCAA Division I Florida Atlantic University and Florida International University, her alma mater.

David Belleau is the father of Ohio University student Hallie Belleau. He lives in Pickerington, Ohio.

Hallie Belleau graduated from top-ranked Pickerington High School in Pickerington, Ohio, in 2001. Although recruited by several NCAA Division III institutions, she decided to give up competitive basketball and enroll at NCAA Division I Ohio University in Athens, Ohio.

243

Stan Benge has been head coach at national powerhouse Ben Davis High School in Indianapolis, Indiana, since 1985. His squads won back-to-back state titles in 2000 and 2001. Benge, who graduated from Ben Davis, also coaches girls' club basketball.

Dorena Bingham is head coach at East High School in Anchorage, Alaska. Since taking over the helm at East in 1994, she has led her teams to state champion honors in 1999 and 2001. In addition, she has also organized and coached club teams since 1989.

Joanne Boyle spent nine years as an assistant coach at NCAA Division I Duke University in Durham, North Carolina, her alma mater. In 2002, she took the reins at NCAA Division I University of Richmond in Richmond Virginia. After completing her successful playing career at Duke, Boyle played and coached professionally in Europe.

Dave Butcher arrived at Pickerington, Ohio's Pickerington High School in 1982 and built the school's girls' basketball program into a national contender. His Tigers have captured six state championships.

Vincent Cannizzaro led the charge at Christ the King Regional High School in Middle Village, New York, for 19 years. He compiled a 410-56 record, winning three national championships, 12 state titles and two National Coach of the Year awards. In 2000, he joined the college ranks as an assistant at NCAA Division I Stony Brook University in Stony Brook, New York.

Eddie Clinton is senior sport manager for the AAU, where he deals with girls' and women's basketball and golf. He serves as the liaison between the AAU's girls' basketball committee and its national headquarters in Orlando, Florida. Clinton used to coach girls' club basketball.

Steve Cochran has been assistant coach at NCAA Division III Washington University of St. Louis in St. Louis, Missouri, a four-time national champion, since 1997. He also has experience coaching at both the high school and NCAA Division I levels.

John Coffee has been coaching in Ohio's Dayton Lady Hoopstars club organization since 1989. He has also coached girls' high school basketball.

Jill Cook has been assistant coach at Christ the King High School, her alma mater, since 1992. In 1993, she also took over duties as president of the New York Liberty Belles club organization. Cook played college ball at NCAA Division I Georgetown University.

Bob Corwin is the founder and director of The Corwin Index scouting service, which focuses on the Southeast. A former high school teacher, Corwin, who lives in Florida, founded the service in 1987, around which time he also organized girls' club teams.

Chris Dailey has been associate head coach at NCAA Division I University of Connecticut in Storrs, Connecticut, since 1985, when she arrived on campus along with head coach Geno Auriemma. Since then, she has helped the program win two national crowns. One of the most visible assistant coaches in women's basketball, she spent her collegiate years at NCAA Division I Rutgers University. She coached at Ivy League Cornell and at Rutgers before joining the Huskies' staff.

Jenni Dant, a 2001 *Parade Magazine* High School All-American, graduated that same year from Lincolnshire, Illinois' Stevenson High School. She plays for NCAA Division I DePaul University in Chicago, Illinois.

Michael Deady is head coach at Attleboro High School in Attleboro, Massachusetts.

Mickie DeMoss, NCAA Division I University of Tennessee associate head coach, is known as one of the top recruiters in women's college basketball. After playing at Louisiana Tech, she served as an assistant at Memphis State, head coach at Florida, and assistant coach at Auburn (also NCAA Division I schools) before arriving in Knoxville in 1985. She has helped the Tennessee program to six national championship titles. DeMoss has served on the NCAA Division I Women's Basketball Rules Committee.

Vanika Dickerson graduated from Washington State's Auburn High School in 1999. After playing for two years at Peninsula College, a junior college in Washington, she continued her collegiate career at the University of Montana-Western, an NAIA Division I institution.

Lori Elgin is head coach at Hoover High School in Hoover, Alabama. Her team won the state championship in 2001, her second season with the program. She has also coached in NCAA Division III and at another high school program.

Jean Ely is the mother of University of Tennessee player Shyra Ely. She lives in Indianapolis, Indiana.

Shyra Ely, the 2001 Naismith and Gatorade National High School Player of the Year, graduated that year from Indianapolis' Ben Davis High School. She signed with NCAA Division I University of Tennessee.

Kevin Engellant is head coach at NAIA Division I University of Montana-Western in Dillon, Montana, where he also teaches business and heads up the school's microcomputer center. Before arriving at Western in 1996, he coached at the high school level.

Brett Erkenbrack, the 2000-2001 NJCAA National Coach of the Year, is head coach at Cloud County Community College in Concordia, Kansas. Erkenbrack, who assumed his role in 1989, led his team to the national title in 2001.

Abby Everitt graduated from Middlebury, Vermont's Middlebury Union High School in 2001. She now plays for NCAA Division II Bentley College.

Sandi Everitt is the mother of Bentley College player Abby Everitt. She lives in Middlebury, Vermont.

Nancy Fahey is head coach at NCAA Division III Washington University of St. Louis. Since arriving on campus in 1986, she has captured four consecutive national titles (1997-2001) as well as several Coach of the Year honors. She previously coached at the high school level. Fahey played at NCAA Division I University of Wisconsin-Madison.

John Feasel is the director of Ohio Girls Basketball, which operates a magazine, scouting service, shootouts, and exhibition team. He founded Ohio Girls basketball in 1994 and is a former club team coach.

Myra Fishback, former assistant coach at NCAA Division I Stony Brook University, is now assistant director of compliance at the school. She also assisted at NCAA Division I Tennessee Tech and Southern Illinois.

Don Flanagan, head coach at NCAA Division I University of New Mexico in Albuquerque, New Mexico, arrived on campus in 1995. He previously coached both boys' and girls' high school basketball.

Gail Goestenkors has been head coach at NCAA Division I Duke University since 1992. She began her coaching career at Iowa State and continued on to Purdue University (both NCAA Division I institutions), where she served as an assistant under WNBA Seattle Storm head coach Lin Dunn. She has built the Duke team into a nationally-ranked program.

Julie Goodenough spent nine years as head coach at NCAA Division III Hardin-Simmons University in Abilene, Texas. She moved to the Division I ranks in 2002, taking over the program at Oklahoma State University in Stillwater, Oklahoma. Before arriving at Hardin-Simmons in 1993, she served as an assistant at the NCAA Division I and NAIA Division I levels.

Cisti Greenwalt, who graduated from Clovis High School in Clovis, New Mexico, was the 2001 Gatorade New Mexico Player of the Year and a 2001 *Parade Magazine* All-American. She plays for NCAA Division I Texas Tech University.

Terri Greenwalt is the mother of Texas Tech player Cisti Greenwalt. She lives in Clovis, New Mexico.

Zareth Gray coached at Ball State and was an assistant at Eastern Illinois University in Charleston, Illinois from, 1999-2001. Gray, who also played at Michigan State and overseas for a season, now coaches at NCAA Division I Wichita State University.

Carol Harrison has been assistant coach at NCAA Division II Humboldt State University in Arcata, California, since 1988. She served as interim head coach during the 2001-02 season. Her previous coaching experience includes stints at Division I UC Berkeley, Division III Cal State Hayward, and the high school level. Harrison played volleyball and basketball at Division II UC Davis.

Janell Jones has been at Oklahoma City University, an NAIA Division I institution, since 1998. After serving as an assistant coach, she took over head coaching duties in 2000. She has also coached at the junior high, high school, and NCAA Division I levels.

Steve Kirkham is head coach at Mesa State College, an NCAA Division II institution in Grand Junction, Colorado. Since his arrival on campus in 1988, his teams have captured three conference and five division championships. He has also coached basketbll and football at the high school and junior college levels.

Kelli Layman has been assistant coach at NCAA Division II North Dakota State University in Fargo, North Dakota since 1986. She also played and served as a student assistant at NCAA Division I Purdue University.

Kara Leary has been coaching in the New England Crusaders club organization since 1995. She was also the head coach of New Hampshire's Nashua High School, her alma mater, from 1999-2001. Nashua captured the state title in 2001. Leary played at NCAA Division I Notre Dame, and she also played professionally overseas for a year.

Joe Lombard has been head coach at Canyon High School in Canyon, Texas since 1985 and has almost 25 years of head coaching experience. His Canyon teams have won three state titles, and he has seen a total of nine state championships in his coaching career.

Mountain MacGillivray is director of basketball at Future Stars Camps in Southeastern, Pennsylvania. He has been involved with Future Stars since 1991 and assumed his current position in 2001. He also coaches at the club and high school levels and has experience as an NCAA Division I assistant.

Pam Martin has been head coach at NCAA Division II Humboldt State University since 1987. She had previously been an assistant at NCAA Division I University of San Francisco, and she also played at Division II UC Davis.

Dennis Masi has been head coach at NCAA Division II Southern New Hampshire University in Manchester, New Hampshire, since 1999. For the five seasons previous, he was an assistant men's and women's coach at NCAA Division II University of New Haven. He has also coached at the high school level.

Bernadette Mattox is head coach at NCAA Division I University of Kentucky in Lexington, Kentucky. Mattox also played and coached at NCAA Division I University of Georgia. She gained national attention after being hired by Kentucky head men's basketball coach Rick Pitino in 1990 as the first female assistant bench coach in NCAA Division I men's basketball. After four seasons with the men's team, Mattox became assistant athletics director at Kentucky. The next year, 1995, she took the reins of the women's team.

Frank Mattucci is head coach at Linconshire, Illinois' Stevenson High School, where he has seen two state titles and surpassed the 300-win mark. Mattucci, who has over 20 years of high school coaching experience, took over the Stevenson program in 1991.

Suzie McConnell-Serio, former star floor general for NCAA Division I Penn State University and the WNBA's Cleveland Rockers, has been head coach at Pittsburgh, Pennsylvania's Oakland Catholic High School since 1990. In 1993 and 2001, her Oakland Catholic team brought home the state championship. McConnell-Serio is also a former Olympian.

Bill McDonough is founder and president of Blue Chip Basketball in Pennsylvania, which operates camps, tournaments, and shootouts, mostly for girls. He also coaches a girls' club team. In 1966, he began running camps, turning to Blue Chip full-time in 1991. His experience includes stints in boys' high school basketball, men's NCAA Division I athletics administration and basketball, and NBA scouting.

Jack Mehl is head coach at Frederick Community College, an NJCAA Division II institution in Frederick, Maryland. Since taking over the helm in 1989, he has led his squads to three national titles. Mehl, who got his start coaching high school ball, is also a full-time high school math teacher.

Tammy Metcalf-Filzen has been head coach at Carleton College, an NCAA Division III institution in Northfield, Minnesota, since 1997, during which time she also served as head soccer coach. She served as an assistant in the program for the five previous seasons. Her coaching résumé also includes head coaching experience at NCAA Division III St. Olaf College, her alma mater, as well as assistant coaching duties at NCAA Division I Temple University and University of Minnesota.

Leslie Nichols, who played for NCAA Division I University of Kentucky, has been an assistant coach at Kentucky since 1996.

Tony Pappas became head coach at Waterloo, Iowa's West High School in 1980. Aside from building a strong high school program, he serves as floor director at the Nike Girls All-America Camp. In addition, Dr. Pappas is a camp director for Blue Star Basketball and gives group clinics and individual instruction to professional, collegiate, and high school players.

Essence Perry, a native of Lawton, Oklahoma, played out her collegiate career beginning in 1998 with one year at NCAA Division I Kansas State University and one year at Trinity Valley Community College. She finished up with two seasons as the starting point guard at NCAA Division I Louisiana Tech University in Ruston, Louisiana.

Azella Perryman, a two-time *USA Today* Alaska Player of the Year, graduated from Anchorage, Alaska's East High School in 2001. She plays for NCAA Division I Stanford University in Stanford, California.

Christine Powers is a former assistant coach at NCAA Division I Eastern Illinois University. Her coaching résumé also includes a stint in NCAA Division II. She currently teaches elementary school.

Trish Roberts, head coach at NCAA Division I Stony Brook in New York, has years of experience in the collegiate and professional women's basketball ranks. Before arriving at Stony Brook in 1999 as the program made its transition from Division II to Division I, Roberts coached at the University of Maine,

University of Michigan, and in the ABL. She also had a distinguished playing career, capped off by being named the University of Tennessee's first-ever women's basketball Kodak All-American and competing in the 1976 Olympic Games.

Scott Rueck has been head coach at George Fox University, an NCAA Division III institution in Newberg, Oregon, since 1996, after first serving as an assistant on the team. He got his start coaching at the high school level.

Amy Ruley is head coach at NCAA Division II North Dakota State University. Since assuming the head coaching job at the school in 1979, she has led the Bison to five national crowns and has notched several coaching awards. She has also served on the NCAA Division II Women's Basketball Rules Committee.

Cathy Rush, a women's basketball icon, founded what is now Future Stars Camps over 25 years ago. Rush made a name for herself, and for the sport, by leading Pennsylvania's Immaculata College to three consecutive NAIAW championships in 1972-74. In addition to serving as Future Stars' president, she has also done women's basketball color commentary for the major sports networks.

Yvonne Sanchez is an assistant coach at NCAA Division I University of New Mexico. Prior to arriving on campus in 2001, she assisted at several other NCAA Division I institutions. Sanchez spent four years coaching in the high school ranks.

Anne Schwieger graduated from Waterloo, Iowa's West High School in 2001. She plays at NCAA Division I Cornell University in Ithaca, New York, a member of the Ivy League.

Dale Severson was the head girls' basketball coach at state champ Clovis High School in Clovis, New Mexico for 22 seasons. He also coached girls' club basketball for nine years. In 2001, he began the next phase of his career as the boys' assistant coach at Texas' Weatherford High School.

Brad Smith is co-head coach at Oregon City High School, along with Carl Tinsley. In the 1990's, the program captured six state championships. Smith has been at Oregon City since 1979, aside from a one-year hiatus in 1998-99 when he was an assistant coach at NCAA Division I Vanderbilt University. Smith, who runs a series of summer camps at Oregon City, also teaches at the high school.

Joe Smith of Long Island founded the Women's Basketball News Service in the mid-1970's. He produces a high school scouting service and also names high school and college All-America teams.

Carla Sterk has been head coach at Grand Rapids, Michigan's Cornerstone University, an NAIA Division II institution, since 1999. She played and served as assistant coach at NCAA Division I Central Michigan University. She also competed in the ABL, overseas, and with Athletes in Action.

Barbara Stevens is head coach at NCAA Division II Bentley College in Waltham, Massachusetts. Since assuming that post in 1986, she has led her team to 13 Sweet Sixteen appearances and five Division II Fab Four appearances. Stevens, a two-time Coach of the Year, began her coaching career at NCAA Division III Clark University, moving on to NCAA Division I University of Massachusetts before arriving on the Bentley campus.

Naomi Stohlman served as assistant coach and recruiting co-ordinator at NCAA Division II North Dakota State University from 1999-2001. She had previously coached high school and club basketball and currently coaches at the high school level.

Carl Tinsley is co-head coach at Oregon City High School, along with Brad Smith. Tinsley, who has been at Oregon City since 1979, is also the director of the summertime End of the Oregon Trail tournament, which attracts over 120 club teams. He teaches at the high school as well.

Mark Traversi is the father of University of Maine athlete Missy Traversi. He lives in Attleboro, Massachusetts.

Missy Traversi graduated from Attleboro, Massachusetts' Bishop Feehan High School in 2001. She plays for NCAA Division I University of Maine in Orono, Maine.

Sue Traversi is the mother of University of Maine athlete Missy Traversi. She lives in Attleboro, Massachusetts.

Gale Valley is an assistant coach at NCAA Division I Duke University. She arrived on campus in 1989, following coaching stints at San Jose State, Delaware, and Vermont — all NCAA Division I colleges. Valley played for NCAA Division I Michigan State University.

Chelsea Wagner, the 2001 *USA Today* Oregon Player of the Year, graduated from Oregon's Springfield High School that same year. After spending her freshman season at NCAA Division I University of Hawaii in Honolulu, Hawaii, she transferred to the University of Oregon in Eugene, Oregon, another NCAA Division I school.

Mike White, a Floridian, is the founder of the All-Star Girls Report, which operates a scouting service, tournaments and camps, and exhibition team. Before creating All-Star Girls Report in 1995, he worked on the men's side as a club and junior college coach as well as an adidas consultant.

Norma Whitley is the mother of NCAA Division I Duke University player Wynter Whitley. She lives in Kennesaw, Georgia.

Wynter Whitley, a 2001 *Parade Magazine* High School All-America and 2001 Gatorade Georgia Player of the Year, graduated from Holy Innocents Episcopal School in Atlanta, Georgia that year. Whitley is now a member of the NCAA Division I Duke University program.

Chris Wood served as assistant coach at NCAA Division II Southern New Hampshire University from 1999-2001. He was previously a high school coach, during which time he served a four-year stint as president of the New Hampshire Basketball Coaches Association.

Linda Wunder, head coach at NCAA Division I Eastern Illinois University arrived on campus in spring 1999. Her experience includes head coaching slots at NCAA Division I Fresno State University, NCAA Division I Miami of Ohio, and NCAA Division III University of Wisconsin-Stevens Point; she led Stevens Point to the national championships.

Ed Wyant became head coach at NCAA Division I Wofford College in Spartanburg, South Carolina in 2002. He had previously served as an assistant coach at NCAA Division I University of New Mexico for seven years. Wyant began his coaching career with eleven seasons in the high school ranks.

About the Author

Lisa Liberty Becker is a senior writer for *Women's Basketball* magazine and a contributor for *Sports Illustrated for Women* and *SportsFan* magazine. She covers high school, collegiate, international, and professional women's sports. She earned a bachelor's degree while playing basketball and soccer at Tufts University and a master's degree from Boston University.  A former high school English teacher, she has also coached high school and college basketball. She is a Maine native and lives in Waltham, Mass. *Net Prospect* is her first book.

Index

End of the Trail summer tournament, 153, 197

Engellant, Kevin, 226–30, 234, 236

Erkenbrack, Brett, 206–9, 212–17

evaluation periods, definition of, 4–5, 17

Everitt, Abby, 100–101, 106, 111, 116, 119, 129, 133–34, 138, 140

Everitt, Sandi, 129, 133, 137, 140

exposure camp, 176, 180

Fahey, Nancy, 82, 85, 90–91, 93

fax, 15–16

Feasel, John, 144, John, 182–84, 194–95, 196, 198, 201–2, 203

Fischer, Alia, 83

Fishback, Myra, 50, 51

Flanagan, Don, 25, 27, 28–29, 30, 32, 36, 39–40, 187

Flecky, Katy, 121

Florida State, 198

Florida, University of, 11

Flynn, Mike, 177–78, 180–81, 195–96

foreign athletic scholarships, NJCAA, 211

Frederick Community College, 217

Future Stars Basketball, 192

George Fox University (Oregon), 82, 84

Georgetown, 221

Georgia, University of, 47

Gibbons, Bob, 179

Goestenkors, Gail, 3, 31, 37, 41–42, 50, 52, 55

Gonzalez, Jhudy, 226

Goodenough, Julie, 82, 85, 89, 90, 92, 94, 95

GPA (grade point average), 13–14, 18

Gray, Zareth, 24

Greenwalt, Cisti, 100, 102, 105, 107, 108, 111, 112, 115, 121, 129, 132, 137, 138

Greenwalt, Terri, 129, 130–31, 132, 137, 138, 142

Hardin-Simmons College (Texas), 82, 90

hardship waiver from NJCAA, 19

Harrison, Carol, 64, 65, 67, 68, 70, 71, 73–74, 77

Hawaii, University of, 114

High School All-America game, xii

high school coach, xi, 10, 39, 69–73, 77, 102, 119, 123, 124, 127, 132, 200

    role of, 144–75

    Division II recruitment and, 69–73

    perspective of recruiting by, 163–65

    versus club coaches, 157–60, 169

high school game, 89

high school sports for girls, statistics, 38

Holdsclaw, Chamique, 1

home visits, 10–11, 30–31, 123, 127, 195

Hoover High School (Alabama), 148

Humboldt State University, 58, 61–62, 64–65, 67, 74

Immaculata College, 192

instant messaging, 15–16

international players, 211, 214, 224

Ivy League institutions, 6, 103

Jackson, Brittany, 121

Jackson, Tawana, 206–9

Jenkins, Tom, 182, 183, 195